Gorsebrook Studies in the Political Economy of the Atlantic Region

General Editors: Ian McKay and L. Anders Sandberg

The Gorsebrook Research Institute for Atlantic Canada Studies was formed in 1982 to encourage and support interdisciplinary research concerned with a variety of socio-economic, political, environmental and policy issues specific to Canada's Atlantic Region. Closely allied to the Atlantic Canada Studies programme at Saint Mary's University, Halifax, the Gorsebrook Research Institute encourages interdisciplinary co-operation across the Atlantic Region.

Trouble in the Woods:
Forest Policy and Social Conflict
in Nova Scotia and New Brunswick

Edited by

L. Anders Sandberg

Published for the Gorsebrook Research Institute for
Atlantic Canada Studies
by
Acadiensis Press,
Fredericton, New Brunswick
1992

© Acadiensis Press 1992

Canadian Cataloguing in Publication Data

Main entry under title:

Trouble in the Woods

(Gorsebrook studies in the political economy of the Atlantic region ; 3)
Includes some text in French.
Includes bibliographical references.

ISBN 0-919107-37-0

1. Forest products industry — Social aspects — New Brunswick — History.
2. Forest products industry — Social aspects — Nova Scotia — History.
3. Forest policy — New Brunswick — History.
4. Forest policy — Nova Scotia — History.
I. Sandberg, L. Anders   II. Gorsebrook Research Institute for
Atlantic Canada Studies. III. Series.

HD9764.C32T76 1992   333.75'09715   C92-098592-0

Printed in the Maritimes by union labour.   ® 36

Acadiensis Press is pleased to acknowledge the support of the New Brunswick
Department of Municipalities, Culture and Housing and of the Writing and Publish-
ing Section of the Canada Council.

Cover Design: Cardinal Communications

The paper used in this publication meets the minimum requirements of the
American National Standard for Information Sciences — Permanence of Paper for
Printed Library Materials, ANSI Z39,48-1984.

Trouble in the Woods: Forest Policy and Social Conflict in Nova Scotia and New Brunswick

Edited by L. Anders Sandberg

Table of Contents

Acknowledgements

All people associated with the Gorsebrook Research Institute deserve credit for their encouragement and help during all phases of work on this volume. I would also like to thank the contributors, and the editors of *Acadiensis*, Phil Buckner, Gail Campbell and David Frank. I am indebted to Ian McKay, the driving force behind the book series of which this book is a part, and to Peter Clancy, my present research partner, for their solid support and constructive criticisms. I am grateful to the Social Sciences and Humanities Research Council whose financial assistance has allowed me to conduct research on forest-related issues in the Maritimes for the last four years. Fraser Ross of Cardinal Communications skilfully designed the cover. Finally, I would like to acknowledge the contribution by the cartographers, secretaries and fellow faculty at York University. The book I dedicate to those who work in the forest, and who labour collectively for a more humane and healthier forest environment. I hope they will benefit from reading this book.

L.A.S.

Introduction:
Dependent Development and Client States:
Forest Policy and Social Conflict
in Nova Scotia and New Brunswick

L. Anders Sandberg

"Them mills is ruining everything and you know it as well as I!" David Adams Richards, *The Coming of Winter*, 1974.

"It is interesting to read the financial reports of the big pulpmills and to then know what they want to pay for pulpwood. The lot owner, and the labourer is getting a raw deal, and sometimes I find it hard to sit tight". J. Leonard O'Brien, MP for Northumberland, New Brunswick, 1940.

"One winter we worked for seven solid months sawing and cording wood for $1.50 a cord...After paying all his expenses, the best man pocketed only $120.00...." Fred Cormier, retired woods worker, commenting on woods work in northern New Brunswick in the 1930s.

"You know, I've lived to see long rafts on this river — I've lived to see long logs on this river — I've lived to see pulp drives on this river — and now I've lived to see nothin on this river". David Adams Richards, *Blood Ties*, 1976.

Large foreign transnational pulp and paper corporations dominate the life and politics of many resource towns in New Brunswick and Nova Scotia. Pulp and paper is the very lifeblood of such towns, where the acrid stench of sulphur represents the sweet smell of money. The surrounding rural areas also feel the corporate presence. The pulp and paper companies maintain a firm grip on the pulpwood market by controlling large freeholds and Crown land leases. In spite of the relatively large portion of forest land held by small woodlot owners (33 per cent in New Brunswick and 52 per cent in Nova Scotia), Maritime pulpwood receives the lowest price in Canada.

Conventional thinking has it that this development is an inevitable result of changing resource and market conditions, as well as the pressure on governments to create and maintain jobs and revenue in a poor region.[1] Few accounts deal with the historical and contemporary consolidation of power by the pulp and paper com-

---

1   A.R.M. Lower, *The North American Assault on the Canadian Forest* (Toronto, 1938), Wilfrid Creighton, *Forestkeeping* (Halifax, 1988), p. 110.

panies, their support from and sometimes collusion with government, and the challenges and options posed by dissenters both inside and outside the government and corporate sectors. The intent of this book is to document the process of consolidation of power by the forest industry and the provincial government, and to record the struggles of the men and women challenging that power structure. In the essays that follow, the authors attempt to disentangle and put into context some of the complex interactions, social forces and conflicts in the forest sector of New Brunswick and Nova Scotia.

This introductory essay will first sketch the broad outlines of the political economy of the Maritime region, in particular the legacy of merchant capital during the colonial period and its importance in the formation of provincial governments, here referred to as client states, and government's subsequent quest for pulp and paper industry development during the era of monopoly capital. This will be followed by a brief look at the impact of client state policies on working people, woods workers, mill workers and small woodlot owners as well as on the forest environment. Here, one cannot avoid being impressed by the persistent biases of government forest policy in favour of the pulp and paper companies.

During the colonial period, both New Brunswick and Nova Scotia were dependent upon merchant capital in the development of various resource sectors. Merchant capital sought to monopolize resource production for export and quick profit.[2] Pockets of enclave development funnelled raw materials to foreign markets, local markets were supressed and few industrial linkages developed to the local resource base. Merchant capital even lobbied against tariffs promoting import substitution, preferring to buy supplies from foreign sources.[3] Under merchant capital, the colonial state became a client state, highly dependent on resource rent for overall revenue. A client state is here defined as a state whose revenues are over-dependent on a few key, often externally based companies. The ideological and institutional support for such companies is co-ordinated in an "active" process, where the state has considerable room to manoeuvre. A client state has been, and continues to be, presented with opportunities to move in a variety of directions, but remains financially dependent on, and ideologically committed to a few large monopoly capitalist firms.[4]

---

2   Many of the following comments were inspired by Ian McKay, "The Crisis of Dependent Development: Class Conflict in the Nova Scotia Coalfields, 1872-76", *Canadian Journal of Sociology,* 13 (1988), pp. 9-48.

3   T.W. Acheson, "The Great Merchant and Economic Development in Saint John, 1820-1850", in Phil Buckner and David Frank, eds., *Atlantic Canada Before Confederation* (Fredericton, 1985), pp. 165-89.

4   The client state thus did not constitute a mere passive instrument in the hands of capital. Nor was it a neutral actor or arbiter in a pluralist society, where everybody had a fair chance at influencing government policy. Rather, client state policy was

In the same way that the state became a client to large mercantile ventures, so too did individual households. Merchant capital employed debt bondage when engaging workers in seasonal spells of work.[5] Even "wage work" was affected by the merchant capital stamp. The coal mined under merchant capital in Nova Scotia was extracted from easily exploited coastal seams, and then transported in local schooners to United States markets.[6]

The merchant capital legacy of the colonial period made a distinct imprint on the formation of New Brunswick and Nova Scotia in the post-Confederation period. Client states were consolidated and pursued large foreign capital for resource extraction and export in return for rent, jobs and electoral support. It was a strategy that Tom Naylor has named "industrialization by invitation".[7] The strategy did not engender balanced industrial development.[8] Many locally owned secondary manufacturing plants were established in the region after the National Policy Tariffs of 1879, but many had closed by the turn of the century. The branch plant economies of Ontario and Quebec emerged as the leading industrial centre in the Canadian economy. The Maritime strategy of industrialization by invitation, meanwhile, had a resource bias which tied the regional economy closer to the large capital and consumer markets of Central Canada.

Maritime development followed two trajectories in the post-Confederation period. In the traditional resource sectors such as fishing and lumbering there was business as usual. Resource revenue flowed through patron-client networks that remained mercantile in nature. By contrast, in the booming foreign-controlled and

---

shaped by the social history of the Maritime Region, its social composition and relationships with other regions, and various external and internal contingencies. For an excellent discussion of the role of the state in a comparative historical perspective, see Theda Skocpol, "Bringing the State Back In: Strategies of Analysis in Current Research", in Peter Evans, Dietrich Rueschmeyer and Theda Skocpol, eds., *Bringing the State Back In* (Cambridge, 1985), pp. 3-43.

5   Richard Apostle and Gene Barrett, *Emptying Their Nets: Small Capital and Rural Industrialization in the Nova Scotia Fishing Industry* (Toronto, 1992); Judith Fingard, *Jack in Port: Sailortowns of Eastern Canada* (Toronto, 1982); Rosemary Ommer, "'All the Fish of the Post': Resource, Property Rights and Development in a Nineteenth-Century Inshore Fishery", *Acadiensis*, X, 2 (Spring 1981), pp. 107-23; and Roch Samson, *Fishermen and Merchants in 19th Century Gaspé: The Fishermen-Dealers of William Hyman and Sons* (Ottawa, 1984).

6   McKay, "The Crisis of Dependent Development".

7   R.T. Naylor, *The History of Canadian Business, 1867-1914* (Toronto, 1975), 2 vols.

8   Glen Williams, *Not For Export: Towards a Political Economy of Canada's Arrested Industrialization* (Toronto, 1983) and Gordon Laxer, *Open For Business: The Roots of Foreign Ownership in Canada* (Toronto, 1989).

capital-intensive resource sector, where one found the extensive employment of wage labour, the client state used fiscal and legislative powers to respond to and appease militant coal miners and industrial workers. In the Nova Scotia coal mining industry, for example, relatively strict safety standards ruled work, training programmes were introduced and collective bargaining rights were implemented at an early stage. At the same time, debt bondage and paternalism continued to prevail in the other resource sectors.[9]

While resource extraction can yield generous state revenue and electoral support during periods of boom, the prospects for long-term stable development are tenuous. Resource development goes through periods of boom and bust. The 1920s were a period of absolute and relative bust in the region, with the lumber market crashing in 1921 and the steel and coal industries beginning their long-term decline. It was at this stage that the pulp and paper industry became one of the new prospective candidates for economic prosperity.

In the early-19th-century New Brunswick timber trade, the colonial state pursued a policy of administration and revenue maximization in support of large merchant capital.[10] Sawmills with rudimentary technology produced square timber and crude lumber for export. Industrial capital, applying more capital-intensive sawmill technology, dominated in the second half of the 19th and beginning decades of the 20th centuries. But the transition was by no means clean. The legacies of merchant capital continued. The export of crude lumber persisted, and the client state continued to rely on timber revenues from large foreign sawmilling interests. Merchants dominated woods workers, small woodlot owners and smaller sawmillers through patron-client relations based on credit. These relations were often coloured by politics, when access to Crown wood was dependent on the right political connections in Fredericton, the provincial capital. From the 1870s on, extensive Crown land leases and a free market in forest lands were the chief incentives in maintaining and boosting such a system.[11]

In late-19th-century New Brunswick, forest lands were increasingly concentrated in the hands of large sawmilling interests, either through the purchase of

---

9   For the contrast in working conditions and state intervention in the coal mining and fishing industries of Nova Scotia, see Michael Earle, ed., *Workers and the State in Twentieth Century Nova Scotia* (Fredericton, 1988).

10   Graeme Wynn, *Timber Colony: A Historical Geography of Early Nineteenth Century New Brunswick* (Toronto, 1980).

11   For comparative studies in Newfoundland, see James Hiller, "The Origins of the Pulp and Paper Industry in Newfoundland", *Acadiensis*, XI, 2 (Spring 1982), pp. 42-68, "The Politics of Newprint: The Newfoundland Pulp and Paper Industry, 1915-1939", *Acadiensis*, XIX, 2 (Spring 1990), pp. 3-39; and John Gray, *The Trees Behind the Shores: The Forests and Forest Industries in Newfoundland and Labrador* (Hull, 1981).

freeholds or the acquisition of Crown land leases. In this volume, Raymond Léger describes the relationship between the client state and four powerful sawmilling concerns on the Acadian Peninsula, Gloucester County, New Brunswick, from 1875 to 1900. Here, in the northern half of the province, where the state owned most forest lands, well-favoured absentee capitalists and sawmillers were granted large areas of virgin forest lands and/or exclusive cutting rights on Crown lands. By 1893 the sawmillers held 25-year leases, at a cost of $8 per square mile (3 cents per ha) for the first year and $4 (1.5 cents per ha) for each subsequent year.

These liberal concessions to the large sawmillers were aimed at boosting provincial revenue. Paradoxically, however, the close connection between the sawmillers and the client state at times impeded the collection of revenue. Stumpage payments — payments made for the volume of wood harvested — were never paid in full. Sawmillers concealed the amount of wood harvested; government scalers, appointed on a patronage basis, could do very little given the collusion beween the industry and government. Even serious scalers were hampered by overwork and cheating by the leaseholders.[12]

The concentration of forest lands in the hands of large sawmillers preceded the emergence of the pulp and paper industry in New Brunswick. By the turn of the century, forest companies (holding more than 1,000 acres or 405 ha) possessed 20 per cent of all freehold forest lands. Two hundred large companies held on lease most of the Crown forests, which constituted 50 per cent of all forest lands. Twelve companies controlled cutting rights on 65 per cent of all Crown lands. By 1913, such leases, invariably purchased for the minimum fee of $8 per square mile (3 cents per ha), extended for 50 years for pulp and paper industry operators and 30 years for sawmillers. As documented by Serge Côté in this volume, Bathurst Lumber, one of the large sawmilling establishments, typified the transition. The control of forest lands was the key. Before the company built the first large pulp and paper mill in New Brunswick in 1915, it consolidated several sawmills and extensive forest holdings. By 1915 the company possessed 2,600 square miles (673,920 ha) of Crown leases in New Brunswick and 15 square miles (3,888 ha) of freehold lands on the Gaspé Peninsula in Quebec.[13] The promoters were Americans and Upper Canadians with good local political connections, who were part of a continental network of financiers and industrial promoters.

---

12 For the problems of an earlier period, see Graeme Wynn, "Administration in Adversity: The Deputy Surveyors and Control of the New Brunswick Crown Forest Before 1844", *Acadiensis*, VII, 1 (Autumn 1977), pp. 49-65.

13 Serge Côté, "Naissance de l'industrie papetière et mainmise sur la forêt: Le cas de Bathurst", in this volume; "New Brunswick Rough on Pulp and Paper Interests", *Pulp and Paper Magazine of Canada*, 1 May 1913, pp. 289-90; Catherine Johnson, "The Search for Industry in Newcastle, New Brunswick, 1899-1914", *Acadiensis*, XIII, 1 (Autumn 1983), pp. 93-111.

Following Bathurst Lumber, the New Brunswick pulp and paper industry slowly expanded, but not without resistance. Some sawmillers still in possession of large Crown land leases and freeholds saw the pulp and paper industry not only as a political threat, but also as a competitor in the wood market. But the depression in the lumber market in the 1920s eroded the political clout of the sawmillers and accelerated the transition from lumber to pulp.[14] The client state was also intent on restructuring the forest industry in favour of pulp, thereby filling the vacuum left by the lost revenues from sawmilling. The revenue from the forest industry as a percentage of total provincial revenue dropped from a high of 46 per cent in 1920 to a low of 22 per cent in 1922.[15] In the years that followed, the pulp and paper industry filled the gap left by the sawmilling industry.[16] From 1942 on, the production of roundwood for pulp exceeded that of sawlogs.[17]

With the rise to hegemony of the pulp and paper industry, warmly supported by the client state, the sawmilling industry suffered a serious setback. Sawmillers had problems gaining access to sawlogs on the freeholds and Crown leases of the large pulp and paper companies. In this volume, Nancy Colpitts investigates the political and economic adversity faced by sawmillers in Alma, Albert County, New Brunswick, from 1921 to the 1947. Most forest land fell into the hands of an absentee landlord, the Hollingsworth and Whitney Paper Company of Boston, which restricted sawmillers' access to sawlogs. The local branches of the large Central Canadian banks discriminated against the sawmillers in favour of the pulp and paper industry. A marketing structure dominated by powerful middlemen — a legacy of the era of merchant capital — was ultimately an obstacle to adequate returns and investments in the industry.

Dependence on political and economic patron-client relations was used by the local sawmillers to pry stumpage from the absentee landholders, to obtain capital from the local branch banks, and to find markets and sometimes finance capital from the large export firms. Recovery was tenuous and sometimes dependent on the right political connections in Fredericton. It was therefore understandable that the local sawmillers would put up little resistance to the promotion of a local tourism industry with the establishment of the federal Fundy National Park in 1947.

Since the Second World War, the political and economic position of the pulp and paper industry has grown stronger. At one point in 1992, six large transnational cor-

---

14 L.D. McCann, "Table 24", in Donald Kerr and Deryck Holdsworth, eds., *Historical Atlas of Canada, Volume III: Addressing the Twentieth Century* (Toronto, 1990).

15 Bill Parenteau, "The Woods Transformed: The Emergence of the Pulp and Paper Industry in New Brunswick, 1918-1931", *Acadiensis*, XXII, 1 (Autumn 1992), forthcoming.

16 Parenteau, "The Woods Transformed".

17 Statistics Canada, *Historical Statistics of New Brunswick*, 1984, Table J-2, p. 145.

porations dominated the forest industry in New Brunswick: Fraser Inc. in Atholville and Edmunston; Irving Pulp and Paper Limited in Saint John; NBIP Forest Products Inc. in Dalhousie; Miramichi Pulp and Paper in Nelson-Miramichi and Newcastle; Ste. Anne Nackawic Pulp Co. in Nackawic; and Stone Consolidated in Bathurst. Some of these pulp and paper companies operated the largest sawmills in the province (Figure 1).[18] These corporations also dominated the independent saw-millers, who relied on the pulp and paper companies for a supply of sawlogs as well as for the sale of woodchips, a relatively new source of input in the pulp process. In the 1980s, pulpwood exceeded sawlog production by a ratio of three to two.[19] Large private owners held 18 per cent of all forests lands in the province. The province held 47 per cent but most of these lands were leased to the large pulp and paper companies.[20]

In Nova Scotia, the forest did not constitute as important an export staple and source of revenue as in New Brunswick. Crown lands were rapidly and hap-hazardly transferred to private interests as political favours or to settlers for revenue into the 1920s.[21] Provincial revenue from the forests was meagre, exploitation was crude, the products were exported and the Crown lands were pillaged on a regular basis. Coal, not the forest, was the engine of growth for the client state in Nova Scotia. Its production was until 1857 monopolized by the British merchant capital of the General Mining Association. After the monopoly was abrogated, client state policies provided an attractive investment climate for foreign industrial capital in the coal sector, as well as in primary and secondary steel manufacturing.[22] In the last two decades of the 19th century, Montreal capital dominated the coal industry, and redirected the flow of coal from the United States to Montreal and other settlements along the St. Lawrence River. The objective, as before, was to secure revenue, jobs and development from coal leases let to foreign capital. By 1894,

---

18 A number of these operations were closed or had their operations scaled down later in the year. See Peter Clancy and L. Anders Sandberg, "Maritime Forest Sector Development: A Question of Hard Choices", in this volume.

19 Statistics Canada, *Historical Statistics of New Brunswick*, 1984, Table J-2, p. 145.

20 M.S. Jamnick and S.E. Clements, *Modelling NIPF Wood Supply in the Maritimes: Description and Analysis* (Fredericton, 1988), p. 18.

21 For the development of Nova Scotia Forestry, see Ralph Johnston, *Forests of Nova Scotia* (Halifax, 1986); Creighton, *Forestkeeping*; L. Anders Sandberg, "Swedish Forestry Legislation in Nova Scotia: The Rise and Fall of the Forest Improvement Act, 1965-1986", in D. Day, ed., *Geographical Perspectives on the Maritime Provinces* (Halifax, 1988), pp. 179-96.

22 See McKay, "The Crisis of Dependent Development", L. Anders Sandberg, "Dependent Development and the Trenton Steel Works, Nova Scotia, c. 1900-1943", *Labour/Le Travail*, 27 (Spring 1991), pp. 127-62.

Figure 1

PRINCIPAL PULP AND PAPER MILLS IN NEW BRUNSWICK AND NOVA SCOTIA

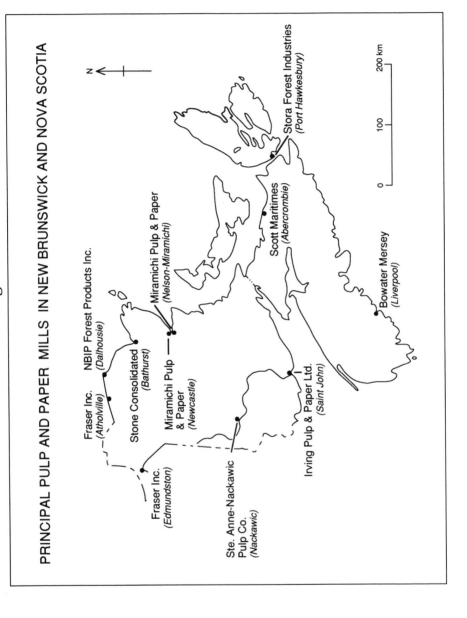

provincial revenues were estimated at $821,000, the highest since Confederation, and $250,000 (30 per cent) came from coal royalties.[23] The short-term success of the client state is evidenced in the 44-year rule of the provincial Liberals during the era of boom in the economy of coal, steel and rails. Its long-term failure, by contrast, was expressed in the decline of the steel and coal industries in the 1920s.

In the Nova Scotia forest sector, the New Brunswick lease system was not introduced until the end of the 19th century, but it was ineffectual and continued the pattern of bestowal followed in the case of granted forest land.[24] Anders Sandberg documents the history of the "Big Lease" on Cape Breton Island, the only large contiguous piece of Crown land left in Nova Scotia, which in 1899 was let to a Gilded Age entrepreneur for sale to a large foreign pulp and paper company. The Big Lease set the stage for subsequent Crown land and forest industry development policies in the province. The initial terms were generous and stipulated that two pulp mills be built and an annual fee of $6,000 paid, with no stumpage payments, in exchange for the use of 640,000 acres (259,200 ha) of forest lands for 33 years. The terms of the lease were soon relaxed, extending the term to 99 years and allowing the export of pulpwood, as long as it was de-barked. The lease was sold in 1920 to the Oxford Paper Company of Rumford, Maine. A short exploitative phase in the 1920s was followed by a new speculative phase in the 1930s, leading to the expropriation of parts of the lease in 1936 to make room for the Cape Breton National Highlands Park, one feature in the province's new strategy to promote a tourism industry. The remainder of the lease was bought back in 1957, and then re-leased on new, and liberal, terms to the Swedish pulp and paper company giant, Stora Kopparberg, in 1960.

The pulp and paper industry thus emerged even more slowly in Nova Scotia than New Brunswick. The Mersey Paper Company's newsprint mill in Liverpool (established in 1928 and until the 1960s the major pulp and paper mill in the province) was almost totally reliant on wood from its own freeholds and wood purchased from contractors and small woodlot owners. The company nevertheless wrested a generous deal from the provincial government, consisting of a cheap source of hydro-electric power and a supply of one million cords of pulpwood from Crown lands over a 30-year period.

In the 1920s, the most attractive and accessible forest lands in Nova Scotia were acquired by local pulpwood exporters, small groundwood pulp mills operating on a cut and run basis, and absentee pulp and paper companies holding land on a speculative basis or as pulpwood reserves. The client state joined the speculative

---

23 J. Murray Beck, *Politics of Nova Scotia, Volume One, 1710-1896* (Tantallon, 1985), p. 260.

24 For the early differences in the development of forestry in New Brunswick and Nova Scotia, see Barbara Robertson, "Trees, Treaties and the Timing of Settlement: A Comparison of the Lumber Industry in Nova Scotia and New Brunswick, 1784-1867", *Nova Scotia Historical Review*, 4, 1 (1984), pp. 37-55.

frenzy in the 1930s. At that point, the state instituted a programme to reclaim its Crown lands for forest management, and to use them as locational incentives for foreign corporations, a policy that heralded the repurchase of the Big Lease in 1960.

The development of the pulp and paper industry in Nova Scotia was slow because of the scarcity of Crown lands and the presence of a politically strong (although economically weak and divided) sawmill industry, organized as the Nova Scotia Forest Products Association in the 1930s. The pulp and paper segment also faced opposition from local communities that had taxing powers over forest lands, and were accustomed to certain common property rights (such as the taking of firewood) on private as well as Crown lands. In Nova Scotia, Mersey (taken over by the British Bowater Corporation in 1955) was joined by two other large pulp and paper mills in the 1960s: the Stora Kopparberg (Stora) mill at Port Hawkesbury in 1962 and the Scott Maritimes mill at Abercrombie in Pictou County in 1965. The former mill was the result of the province's land acquisitions over a 30-year period, while the latter was the outcome of the accumulation of forest lands over a 40-year period by the Hollingsworth and Whitney Paper Company, which merged with the Scott Paper Company in 1954. It was at this stage that the pulp and paper segment first rose to industrial hegemony in the Nova Scotia forest economy. By 1965 pulpwood had become more important than sawlog production.[25]

In 1992, three transnational corporations dominated the wood market in Nova Scotia: the British Bowater Mersey in Liverpool, the Swedish Stora in Port Hawkesbury, and the American Scott Maritimes in Abercrombie (Figure 1). Pulp and paper has come to dominate the forest economy to an even greater extent than in New Brunswick. Pulpwood exceeded sawlog production by a ratio of more than three to one in the 1980s.[26] Large private landowners held 24 per cent of all forest lands. The three major pulp and paper companies held Crown leases on most provincial forest lands, which amounted to 21 per cent of the total forest.[27]

The consolidation of the pulp and paper industry in New Brunswick in the 1940s and Nova Scotia in the 1960s, coupled with state policies in support of such consolidation, has led to increased domination of local economies and forests by the pulp and paper industry. Workers in the corporate pulp and paper enclaves include both the relatively well-paid beneficiaries of consolidation and its alienated insecure victims. Like the coal miners before them, pulp and paper mill workers have struggled successfully to obtain union recognition and relatively high wages. At the

---

25 Nova Scotia, Voluntary Economic Planning Board, *Plan for the Forestry Sector* (Halifax, 1966), p. 5. For the general dominance of the pulp and paper industry in the two provinces, see Atlantic Development Board, *Forestry in the Atlantic Provinces* (Ottawa, 1968).

26 Nova Scotia, Department of Lands and Forests, *Forest Production by Year, and Ownership, 1935-1989* (Truro, 1989).

27 Jamnick and Clements, *Modelling NIPF Wood Supply in the Maritimes*, p. 35.

same time, however, the novels of David Adams Richards provide an eloquent voice for these workers as victims.[28] In Richards' Miramichi region in northern New Brunswick, the routine and monotony in the work at the pulp mill is transferred to the life of the community: "a moral vacuum prevails where pointless violence and thoughtless cruelty are common-place and where the characters are victims of foreign capitalist forces that they do not understand and cannot control".[29] The pulp and paper mills hold incredible power in communities such as Atholville, Bathurst, Dalhousie, Edmundston and Newcastle in New Brunswick, and Abercrombie, Liverpool and Port Hawkesbury in Nova Scotia.[30] This is perhaps to be expected given the lack of alternatives and local high unemployment. For the same reason, the large, mostly foreign, pulp and paper mills are political capital instrumental in the electoral success and survival of the provincial governments.[31]

Small woodlot owners, invariably farmers, were distinctly disadvantaged during the growth of the sawmilling industry and the emerging pulp and paper industry. Low prices and insecure markets are usual for Maritime small woodlot owners. In many cases, as on the Acadian Peninsula examined by Léger, farmers were granted land, but the wood cutting rights were often retained by the Crown and assigned to the large sawmillers. In other cases, the sawmillers cut wood illegally on granted land before, or even after, the settlers arrived. Many settlers, through lack of forest and/or agricultural land, were thus forced into wage work in sawmills and forests; others supplied the mills with wood on unfavourable terms. Some large farmers and subcontractors may have profited from this system, but, as Léger points out, the resource control and dominance of the sawmilling industry on the Acadian Peninsula contributed to a state of general poverty among settlers.[32]

---

28 See also L. Anders Sandberg, "The Forest Landscape in Maritime Canadian and Swedish Literature: A Comparative Analysis", in Paul Simpson-Housley and Glen Norcliffe, eds., *A Few Acres of Snow: Literary and Artistic Images of Canada* (Toronto, 1992), pp. 109-21.

29 French referred to in Sandberg, "The Forest Landscape in Maritime Canadian and Swedish Literature", p. 116.

30 Nicole Lang, "L'impact d'une industrie: Les effets sociaux de l'arrivée de la Compagnie Fraser Limited à Edmundston, N.-B., 1900-1950", *Revue de la Société Historique du Madawaska*, 15, 1-2 (janvier-juin 1987).

31 Della Stanley, *Louis Robichaud: A Decade of Power* (Halifax, 1984). For accounts of the New Brunswick pulp and paper industry in the modern period, see Senopi Consultants Limited, *A Report on Noranda Mines Limited for Conseil Régional d'Aménagement du Nord* (Petit Rocher, 1979). See also, Russell Hunt and Robert Campbell, *K.C. Irving: The Art of the Industrialist* (Toronto, 1973).

32 The state and process of social stratification is only beginning to be documented in the Maritime provinces. For an excellent case study, see Rusty Bittermann, "The Hierarchy of the Soil: Land and Labour in a 19th Century Cape Breton Community", *Acadiensis*, XVIII, 1 (Autumn 1988), pp. 33-55. See also Richard MacKinnon and

The perennial complaints of settlers who encroached on lands of the large leaseholders, and of bogus settlers who harvested the forest on their lands and then moved on, so well covered in the writings of Arthur Lower, can be seen in a completely different light in this context.[33] As Côté suggests, the settlers were squeezed by the monopolization of land and merely reproduced the behaviour of the large leaseholders: they pursued immediate profits without regard for the long-term well-being of the forest.

In the local wood markets, the pulp and paper companies held a monopsonistic position through control of extensive Crown leases and freeholds: they virtually dictated the price of pulpwood to small woodlot owners. Company freeholds and Crown leases were a key to the monopsony. If the price was not right, the company-controlled lands served as an alternative source of pulpwood as well as an acute reminder to the small woodlot owners that their pulpwood was dispensable.

Small woodlot owners were the subject of repeated exploitation by the pulp and paper industry and the client states.[34] Pulp and paper companies recognized early that small woodlot owners could provide pulpwood to the pulp mills more cheaply than the companies themselves. As mentioned, one means to guarantee such a system was for the pulp companies to hold freeholds and Crown leases in reserve. Another means was for the client state to ensure that organizational efforts of small woodlot owners were either thwarted completely or contained to "minimize damage" to the industry. As early as 1924, the report of the federal Royal Commission on Pulpwood recognized the exploited position of small woodlot owners, and recommended that "the only apparent way in which such difficulties [can] be overcome [is] through organization of the settlers of a district to demand their just

Graeme Wynn, "Nova Scotia Agriculture in the 'Golden Age': A New Look", in Day, *Geographical Perspectives on the Maritime Provinces*, pp. 47-60. For an analysis of the large disparities in the production of wood by individual households in various townships of Nova Scotia, using the 1861 census returns, see Alan MacNeil, "Household Wood Production in Nineteenth Century Nova Scotia: Some Evidence from a Sample of 1861 Census Returns", mimeo, 1989.

33 See especially A.R.M. Lower, *Settlement and the Forest Frontier in Eastern Canada* (Toronto, 1936).

34 David Curtis, *Woodlot Owner Organizations in Eastern Canada: Historic Development, Legislation, Structure, Financing and Services* (Fredericton, 1987); Bill Parenteau, "Pulp, Paper, and Poverty", *New Maritimes*, VII, 4 (March/April 1989), pp. 20-6; Kevin Whelton, "The Bathurst Blockade", *New Maritimes*, VI, 2 (October 1987), pp. 3-5, and "Down the Long Road Ahead", *New Maritimes* VI, 9 (May 1988), pp. 10-12; Peter deMarsh, "Pulpwood Producer Marketing Organizations in New Brunswick", in Bryant Fairley, Colin Leys and James Sacouman, eds., *Restructuring and Resistance: Perspectives from Atlantic Canada* (Toronto, 1990), pp. 227-33; James Cannon, "Comment on deMarsh", in Fairley, Leys and Sacouman, *Restructuring and Resistance*, pp. 235-38; Peter Clancy, "Crossroads in the Forest: Change is in the Air for Nova Scotia Woodlot Owners", *New Maritimes*, IX, 5 (May/June 1991), pp. 5-8.

right".[35] Yet no provisions were made to accommodate the small woodlot owners. In Nova Scotia, farmers' pulpwood was excluded from marketing legislation in the 1930s, and pulpwood marketing was assigned to an indifferent Department of Lands and Forests whose main duties were fire protection and the accumulation of Crown lands.

In spite of repeated agitation, it was not until the 1960s that formal small woodlot owner organizations were formed in the region. Their powers, however, were seriously circumscribed by the client states. Bill Parenteau, in his essay, notes the rise of woodlot owners' associations and their calls for marketing structures to counter the decline of the rural economy and the low pulpwood prices in New Brunswick in the early 1960s. At that point, the previously diversified market for raw wood had narrowed to a pulpwood market. Woodlot owners called on government to introduce marketing legislation with binding arbitration, and to request that pulp and paper companies buy wood from private lands before harvesting Crown lands, the latter to encourage the companies to bargain in "good faith". The organizational drive was spearheaded by an emerging Acadian nationalism promoted by fishermen, woods workers and farmers in the northern half of the province, who challenged the old company order and the compliant Acadian elite.[36]

The government paid little heed to the aspirations of the woodlot owners. The establishment of a diluted and weak marketing legislation was the result of two serious recessions in the pulp and paper industry (the early 1960s and 1970s), the technological neglect of the province's pulp and paper mills, and the government's desire to use the marketing boards to promote forest management on small woodlots. The protests of the independent producers was only one weak influence on government action. As in the past, the favoured position of the pulp and paper industry prevailed, based on the arguments that the industry provided jobs and revenue and, as one government spokesperson had been told, "is quite prepared to negotiate in good faith"[37] without legal rules and regulations.

After 1975, independent producers achieved their demand that pulpwood from Crown lands be a secondary source of wood. It was a qualified victory, however, which allowed for a continued, and invisible, corporate dominance of the small woodlot owner sector. The marketing boards that regulate the sale of pulpwood to the companies were forced into the pulpwood trade almost exclusively, with few possibilities to diversify the wood market or find new markets.[38] In many ways,

---

35   Canada, *Report of the Royal Commission on Pulpwood* (Ottawa, 1924), p. 234.

36   For the new Acadian nationalism, see Michel Roy, *L'Acadie perdue* (Montréal, 1978). For the comparative challenge in the fishing industry, see Sue Calhoun, *A Word To Say: The Story of the Maritime Fishermen's Union* (Halifax, 1992).

37   George Horton, Minister of Agriculture and Rural Development, in Bill Parenteau, "'In Good Faith': The Development of Pulpwood Marketing for Independent Producers in New Brunswick, 1960-1975", in this volume.

38   DeMarsh, "Pulpwood Producer Marketing Organizations in New Brunswick", and Cannon, "Comment on deMarsh".

they were dominated by contractors rather than woodlot owners. Contractors are dependent on the pulp mills through contracts and pressured by heavy debts incurred through the acquisition of expensive harvesting machinery.[39] In spite of this, the marketing boards are now under attack from both the pulp and paper industry and the government.[40]

The struggle of Nova Scotia woodlot owners has yielded even less success. Peter Clancy investigates the impact of provincial policy on the economic viability of small woodlot owners in Nova Scotia. He shows how the very strength of, and direct ties between, the pulp and paper sector and the province, and the restructuring of the woodlot sector itself, set up barriers to the organization of small woodlot owners in Nova Scotia from 1960 to 1985. The Pulpwood Marketing Board was created in 1972. It was late in coming, legally tenuous, and challenged repeatedly and successfully in the courts by the corporate sector. As these battles raged, the small woodlot sector was being transformed. In the early years, it was dominated by small woodlot owners, often farmers, who also harvested their own woodlots. With the decline of farming and the growth of the pulp and paper industry, however, the farmer-operator gave way to the full-time contractor, operating expensive machinery and working on contract for the pulp mills. As in New Brunswick, it is this segment of the forest industry that has split the original woodlot owners and operators' association and now dominates the producer divisions for Stora and Scott. The client state clearly favoured the provision of cheap pulpwood for the pulp companies over the organizational efforts of the Nova Scotia woodlot owners.

The monopsony in pulpwood held by the pulp and paper companies engendered cheap and exploited labour in the forest, a situation reinforced by the client states and the divisions among contractors, forest workers and small woodlot owners.[41]

---

39 Whelton, "The Bathurst Blockade", and deMarsh, "Pulpwood Producer Marketing Organizations in New Brunswick".

40 Clancy and Sandberg, "Maritime Forest Sector Development", in this volume.

41 L. Anders Sandberg, "The Forest Worker in Nova Scotia", *Gorsebrook Research Institute Occasional Paper Series*, no. 2 (September 1990); Eric Mullen and Millie Evans, *In the Mersey Woods* (Liverpool, 1989); Narcisse Doiron, "1930: Working in the Woods", *New Maritimes*, IV, 6 (February 1986), pp. 8-9; Parenteau, "Pulp, Paper, and Poverty"; Whelton, "The Bathurst Blockade", and "Down the Long Road Ahead". For some studies on forest workers elsewhere in Canada, see Ian Radforth, *Bush Workers and Bosses: Logging in Northern Ontario, 1900-1980* (Toronto, 1987); Peter Neary, "The Bradley Report on Logging Operations in Newfoundland, 1934", *Labour/Le Travail*, 16 (Fall 1985), pp. 193-232; H. Landon Ladd, "The Newfoundland Loggers' Strike of 1959", in W.J.C. Cherwinski and G. Kealey, eds., *Lectures in Canadian Labour and Working Class History* (St. John's, Newfoundland, 1985), pp. 149-64; Jerry Lemcke and William M. Tattam, *One Union in Wood: A Political History of the International Woodworkers of America* (Madeira Park, B.C., 1984); and Gordon Hak, "British Columbia Loggers and the Lumber Workers' Industrial Union, 1919-1922", *Labour/Le Travail*, 23 (Spring 1989), pp. 67-90.

Farm-forest workers laboured with relatively crude technology for the pulp companies on a seasonal basis before and even after the Second World War. The mechanization of forest harvesting had to await the 1960s.

Radforth has outlined the change in the labour process in woods work for northern Ontario.[42] His description provides an apt comparison for the Maritime region. Prior to 1950, pulp and paper companies employed labour-intensive, seasonal methods, combined with piece work, to employ woods workers. Woods workers enjoyed considerable independence and possessed remarkable skills under this system, employing the axe and the bucksaw, and working individual and isolated strips of trees in the bush. Once trees were cut, they were piled manually, and then skidded by horses to road-sides, rail-sides or lake-sides for further transportation to the mill.

Different forms of worker protest transformed the labour process in the latter half of the 20th century. Worker militancy and unionization was one factor, more pronounced in northern Ontario than in the Maritimes, but not completely absent in the latter region. Pulp and paper mill workers were organized relatively early in the Maritimes. By the late 1930s, the Canadian Paper Workers' Union had made serious inroads, and this constituted a dangerous example for company-employed forest workers. Another, more important form of protest, was the practice of "jumping" from one lumber camp to another in search of better working conditions and wages. After the Second World War, woods workers often "jumped" into other forms of wage work, resulting in severe labour shortages.

The labour militancy (real and potential) and labour shortages of the 1950s prompted two responses from the forest companies. One was the development and adoption of mechanized pulpwood-logging methods. The powersaw and the "articulated wheeled skidder" were pioneer inventions which in northern Ontario increased by 48 per cent the amount of wood cut by production workers per work hour from the mid-1950s to the mid-1960s.[43] Mechanized harvesters, which cut, delimbed and transported logs to roadside, followed in the 1960s. Most of the woods workers employed directly by the pulp companies embraced these new technologies. They meant higher wages and year-round employment. And while the old skills of woods work were now irrelevant, new mechanical and operating skills were needed to keep the expensive machinery functioning properly. The regions with the most militant workers and highest wages became the leaders in the new technologies. Northern Ontario led the way, while the Maritimes lagged behind.

The contract system provided a second strategy to cope with labour militancy and labour scarcities, by allowing the pulp and paper companies to transfer the capital and labour costs of harvesting wood to other parties. Under this system, con-

---

42 Ian Radforth, "Logging Pulpwood in Northern Ontario", in Craig Heron and Robert Storey, eds., *On the Job: Confronting the Labour Process in Canada* (Montréal, 1986), pp. 245-80.

43 Radforth, "Logging Pulpwood in Northern Ontario", p. 261.

tractors own logging equipment, employ workers and work on contract for the pulp and paper companies. Contractors cut wood throughout the year, compete for pulpwood contracts and are often desperate to meet monthly debt payments on increasingly expensive and elaborate harvesting machines. With few exceptions, they employ non-unionized workers at low wages with minimal job security. Periodic layoffs, dependence on unemployment insurance and high labour turnover are very common.[44]

In northern Ontario, woods workers gained union recognition and collective bargaining rights during the Second World War, and have since fought battles against the contract system. In New Brunswick and Nova Scotia, forest workers have not enjoyed the same degree of unionization and union recognition. In New Brunswick, some contractors and forest workers have obtained blanket certification for unionization under specific companies. In Nova Scotia, there are approximately 100 unionized forest workers employed by Stora.

Most forest workers in New Brunswick and Nova Scotia labour under the harsh conditions of the contract system.[45] There are several reasons for the predominance of the contract system in the region. The regional economy has been depressed since the 1920s, unemployment being high and alternative jobs scarce. Forest workers have traditionally come from diverse rural backgrounds with firm local roots, for instance, farmers and fishermen, who have worked only seasonally in the forest. Woods work paid poorly, and the woodsman's wages had to be complemented by household activities. Most of the woodsmen who worked for the Mersey Paper Company in Nova Scotia lived in rural areas where their wives lived on small farms or in farmhouses. The women "were mother and father to their children and effectively raised them alone", and it was tradition that women were not allowed to visit the company camps.[46] Much of the pulpwood in the region has come from farmers, who have cut their own wood and hauled it to delivery points. These conditions have provided ready labour for contract work, in spite of poor wages and working conditions. Finally, and perhaps most important, the contract system has roots that lie deep in history, in the colonial mercantile economy. Lumber dealers during the era of sawmilling became pulpwood dealers in the era of pulp; in both cases they bought wood from small woodlot owners. This system evolved into the contract system, once new harvesting technology and rural wage labour were available. It is not surprising, given the dependence of contractors on the pulp mills and the wage disparity between forest workers and pulp mill workers, that there is often

---

44 Sandberg, "The Forest Worker in Nova Scotia"; Whelton, "The Bathurst Blockade", and "Down the Long Road Ahead"; Richard Corey, *An Atlantic Forestry Vocational Training Program, Final Report* (Maritime Ranger School, 1989).

45 Sandberg, "The Forest Worker in Nova Scotia".

46 Mullen and Evans, *In the Mersey Woods*, pp. 82, 87.

an uneasy relationship between workers in the primary and secondary forest sectors — a condition exploited by capital.[47]

The hegemony of the pulp and paper industry has also shaped the agenda for forest management in New Brunswick and Nova Scotia. The Maritime forest is unique in the Canadian forest flora: it is classified as a mixed deciduous-coniferous forest and called the Acadian forest region. The Acadian forest region has undergone the longest spell of exploitation in Canada. Many areas have been harvested several times, and there are only patches of virgin forest left. During these phases of exploitation, the forest has been transformed and degraded. In the past, the sawmill industry practised high-grading in harvesting the forest — removing the best, leaving the rest — and took no part in facilitating new forest growth. The vast and majestic pine trees were the first to go, initially reserved for the colonial state as ship's timber, and later harvested and exported as square lumber. Spruce lumber, exported as deals (lumber sawn further once it reached distant markets), was the next export commodity. High-grading continued, and trees of smaller and smaller dimensions were cut. The pulp and paper industry practised an equally wasteful method of forest harvesting: large-scale clearcutting of forest stands with no concern for future quality in species or balance in age structure. These forms of "forest mining" took place in spite of urgent appeals for an alternative approach. Forest management was limited to fire protection, some limited chemical spraying and restrictions on the exploitation and export of pulpwood from certain Crown lands.[48]

It is indeed paradoxical that the large Crown leases were let on the basis of promoting forest management, for they did the exact opposite. By the 1920s, many of the most accessible Maritime forests were mere pulpwood propositions. Local forest management theorists promoted the preservation of resources through fire protection, and argued against European "sustained yield forestry", a programme which entailed selective cuts and left seed trees for natural regeneration.[49] The industry blamed settlers for forest fires and recommended the setting aside of forest reserves for exclusive industry use. Paradoxically, this reserves policy contributed to the degradation of the forest. Fire protection of existing stands deflected attention from the regeneration of forest lands on cutovers; indeed, pine tree regeneration is induced by fire. Cutovers remained bare or were restocked by non-commercial

47   Sheri King, "The Scott Paper Strike, 1982", in C.H.J. Gilson, ed., *Strikes in Nova Scotia, 1970-1985* (Hantsport, 1986), pp. 114-128; Whelton, "The Bathurst Blockade", and "Down the Long Road Ahead".

48   For an early critical account, see Peter Caverhill, *Forest Policy in New Brunswick* (Fredericton, 1937). See also Paul Webster, "Pining for Trees: The History of Dissent Against Forest Destruction in Nova Scotia, 1749-1991", M.A. thesis, Dalhousie University, 1991, and "Pining for the Forest", *New Maritimes*, X, 1 (September/October 1991), pp. 14-18.

49   Peter Gillis and Thomas Roach, "Early European and North American Forestry in Canada: The Ontario Example, 1890-1941", in H.K. Steen, ed., *History of Sustained Yield Forestry* (Santa Cruz, California, 1984), pp. 211-19.

species, because no attention was paid to cutting techniques or to the tending of growing stands. The preservation of existing stands promoted in turn the spread of over-mature forests, prone to disease and insect infestations.

Contemporary sources make it clear that small woodlot owners in the Maritimes practised sustained yield forestry in the period up to 1930.[50] They employed a method referred to as "cropping", cutting only trees that were defective or of a certain size. It was only with the introduction of the pulp and paper industry that small woodlot owners began to "mismanage" their woodlots. But this "mismanagement" was prompted by economic necessity. The financial returns from agriculture were declining, pulpwood prices were rock bottom and economics dictated clearcutting. Contractors, working for the companies, often bought farmers' trees on the stump, then stripped the lots without care for the soil or the remaining seedlings and trees.

The pulp and paper industry only promoted "intensive forest management" when faced with future wood scarcities in the 1960s. A new view of forest management emerged, promoting the mechanization of forest harvesting and transportation, using machines and trucks, practising clearcutting, planting desirable species in monocultural plantations, and tending the stands using herbicides and pesticides.[51] Suddenly, funds were available for small woodlot owners through federal and provincial assistance, and in the mid-1970s the first federal-provincial agreements were signed, providing almost 100 per cent funding for the promotion of forest management in the region. The assistance, however, was tied to intensive forest management, and therefore benefited the pulpwood economy. To this day, the subsidies for forest management have not been matched by similar support for pulpwood marketing and alternative forest management practices.

In this volume, Glyn Bissix and Anders Sandberg explore forest legislation promoting mandatory forest management in Nova Scotia, through Swedish-inspired forest practices improvement boards in the 1960s. The Forest Improvement Act (FIA) was conceived and supported by the province's professional foresters and pulp and paper industry when first enacted in 1965. At the time, the major source of pulpwood came from small woodlot owners, and the act was aimed at boosting production in this sector. The act was also aimed at replacing the Small Tree Act, which promoted forest management through the enforcement of diameter limits on lumbering operations producing more than 50,000 board feet measure or its equivalent per year.

The forest practices improvement boards of the FIA, however, soon challenged the pulp and paper industry. Sawmill owners, small woodlot owners, and environmental and wildlife interests, disconcerted with the Crown lease arrangements and

---

50   Thomas Roach, "From Woodlots and Pulpwood Exports from Eastern Canada, 1900-1930", in Steen, *History of Sustained Yield Forestry*, pp. 202-10.

51   A good description is provided in Gary Burrill and Ian McKay, eds., *People, Resources, and Power* (Halifax, 1987).

forest practices of the pulp and paper companies, gained control of the boards.[52] Bissix and Sandberg explore the history of the FIA by focusing on the pulp and paper industry's influence on the Department of Lands and Forests, the provincial forest trade and foresters' organizations, and their collective assault on and eventual defeat of the FIA.

The defeat of the Forest Improvement Act must be seen in the context of the federal and provincial intervention and generous subsidization of Canadian forest management since the mid-1970s. In spite of the first federal-provincial agreement being conditional on the full proclamation of the FIA in 1976, no funds were provided for its implementation. Instead, the monies of the federal-provincal agreement were used to set up a private lands directorate with the Department of Lands and Forests, staffed with professional foresters and forest technicians. This new administrative unit, with substantial funds to distribute for forest management, provided a powerful weapon against the forest practices improvement boards and the mandatory forest legislation of the FIA. The provincial foresters' association, the Department of Lands and Forests, the provincial trade association and the pulp and paper companies soon joined forces, using arguments in favour of professionalism, the public's lack of education on forestry matters and the "inviolability" of private property rights, to defeat the FIA.

One aspect of this new forestry professionalism was the doctrine of "multiple use". This concept is often applied to the forest resource in Nova Scotia and New Brunswick. It states, simply, that the forest is not merely an industrial input, but should also be considered a recreational ground, a repository for a diverse flora and fauna, and a scenic tourist attraction. But here too the forest has increasingly become an exclusive commodity for the few rather than the many. In the late 19th and early 20th centuries, several writers, such as Charles G.D. Roberts, S.W. Mitchell, and Albert Bigelow Paine, portrayed the forest as "an escape for wealthy British and American fishermen, hunters, and nature-lovers who flee their starch collars for the freedom of the wilderness".[53] In later years, the client state promoted the establishment of national parks for the tourist trade, often expropriating bitter local residents. Some transnational corporations now restrict access, and charge

---

52 The environmentalists had no direct representation on the forest practices improvement boards but nevertheless had a strong indirect influence, through their own lobbying efforts and their shaping of local public opinion. For the environmental position, see Elizabeth May, *Budworm Battles: The Fight to Stop the Aerial Insecticide Spraying of the Forests of Eastern Canada* (Tantallon, 1982); the contributions in Burrill and McKay, *People, Resources and Power;* Aaron Schneider, ed., *Deforestation and "Development" in Canada and the Tropics* (Sydney, 1989), chs. 11 and 12; Dietrich Soyez, "The Internationalization of Environmental Conflict: The Herbicide Issue in Nova Scotia's Forests and Its Links with Sweden", in Jørn Carlsen and Bengt Streijffert, eds., *Canada and the Nordic Countries* (Lund, 1988), pp. 309-20

53 Sandberg, "The Forest Landscape in Maritime Canadian and Swedish Literature", pp. 112-13.

recreationalists an entry fee to Crown leases and freeholds they supposedly — as taxpayers — already own. Wealthy non-residents can even buy their forest refuge (or any other form of recreational land) with sanctions from client states concerned with attracting and providing a safe climate for foreign investments.[54] In this volume, Kell Antoft shows how the Land Holdings Disclosure Act (LHDA, enacted in 1969), which aimed at revealing the extent of non-resident ownership of land in Nova Scotia, was watered down and rendered ineffective in spite of widespread and strong public support. Little heed was paid to the majority of interest groups who were in favour of the act. This was done by insisting on the rights of landowners to manage and dispose of their land without state interference. Use rather than ownership was stressed, and non-residents were often considered better managers of their properties than local residents.

The LHDA and the Forest Improvement Act (FIA) illustrate some of the contradictions in the rhetoric over property rights in a client state economy where development policy is based on the attraction of large foreign corporate capital. The sanctity of corporate property rights is strong in a client state.[55] Provincial politics are dominated by the legal profession; lawyers and politicians are commonly engaged in land and real estate transactions; and, in the past, the agreements between the Nova Scotia government and the large foreign pulp and paper companies were formulated by the companies' legal counsels in the province.

The emphasis on corporate property rights has typically precluded provincial interference in individual private property rights, usually by employing populist rhetoric to label such interference socialistic and inimical to the cultural values of Maritimers. Such was the case with the LHDA and the FIA when they posed a threat to the pulp and paper companies and foreign buyers of recreational forest lands. Yet, at one point in the mid- and late 1960s, the acts were introduced in spite of such a supposed threat to property rights. The acts were only stalled and resisted actively when their provisions challenged (or were perceived to challenge) the pulp and paper industry development agenda and the more general development strategy of industrialization by invitation.

The domination of foreign corporations, the economic development agenda based on industrialization by invitation and the emphasis put on corporate property rights (and individual private property rights when it is politically convenient) have been persistent features of forest sector development and the emergence of the pulp and paper industry in both provinces. Business interests and client states set the stage for development. In the past, forest policies in Ontario and Quebec were admired and uncritically promoted in spite of the region's less extensive resources, the large areas held by small private woodlot owners and (in Nova Scotia in particular)

---

54 Land Research Group, "Whither Our Land: Who Owns Nova Scotia? And What Are They Doing With It?", *New Maritimes*, VIII, 6 (July/August 1990), p. 20.

55 For a useful discussion on property rights, see C.B. Macpherson, *Property: Mainstream and Critical Positions* (Toronto, 1978).

the virtual absence of Crown lands. Nelles' concept of the state in the development of the forest industry in Ontario fits the New Brunswick and Nova Scotia situations. Public ownership was aspired to as the legal basis of the forest industry, but the provinces did not use this ownership to assert any major claim upon the resource development process. In fact, the reverse was the case. Foreign corporate hegemony prevailed as extensive Crown leases were let (in New Brunswick) and repossessed and let (in Nova Scotia) to large pulp and paper companies on liberal terms while, contrary to corporate rhetoric, such leases were not subject to a more systematic pursuit of conservation.[56] More recently, federal and provincial forest management programmes have mirrored the corporate wishes of "intensive forest management", in spite of widespread and public support for alternative management regimes.

Corporations now dominate the forest. With the sanction and active enthusiasm of the client states, they determine the strategies for development, with all their immense implications for the environment and Maritime communities. Alternative approaches become almost "unthinkable". Critics are few and quickly marginalized. A large part of the electorate is dependent on this system or has been lulled into the belief that such developments are inevitable. The monopsony of the pulp and paper industry heightens the receptiveness of small woodlot owners to the political rhetoric in favour of the right of landowners to manage and dispose of their land as they see fit. Low prices and insecure markets for pulpwood are not conducive to government regulations in forest management and the sale and purchase of forest lands. Sawmillers' dependence on the pulp and paper mills for the sale of woodchips and the purchase of sawlogs tempers their hunger for change. The tight pulpwood market constrains the initiatives of small woodlot owners. Finally, the cost-price squeeze on contractors and truckers, their dependence on contracts from the pulp mills, their illusory independence and their traditional role as power brokers in rural communities make them powerful actors, who frequently intervene on behalf of the pulp and paper industry.[57] Such are the obstacles in the path of a more equitable and responsible strategy for the region's forests — the goal, pursued by movements of workers and producers, that for decades has been a vision beyond reach.

---

56 H.V. Nelles, *The Politics of Development: Forests, Mines and Hydro-Electric Power in Ontario, 1849-1941* (Toronto, 1974), p. 491. See also Peter Gillis and Thomas Roach, *Lost Initiatives: Canada's Forest Industries, Forest Policy and Forest Conservation* (Westport, Conn., 1986); chapter 7 is entitled "The Dimensions of a Client Province: Forestry in New Brunswick to 1939". The client status of the state applied equally to the Liberals and Conservatives.

57 Clancy, "Crossroads in the Forest".

L'impact de l'industrie du bois sur le territoire et la main-d'oeuvre de la Péninsule acadienne, Nouveau-Brunswick, 1875-1900

Raymond Léger

L'historiographie de l'histoire des Acadiens est vaste et très riche. Cependant pour ce qui est de l'histoire économique et en particulier de l'industrie du bois dans les régions acadiennes la récolte est très faible. Tous les ouvrages de synthèse se contentent d'éviter le sujet ou tout simplement de n'avoir pas de données précises sur le sujet.[1] Même ceux, qui, comme Aurèle Young et Raymond Mailhot traitent plus spécifiquement de l'économie tombent dans les généralités. Ils n'apportent aucune contribution significative dans leurs travaux au sujet de l'industrie du bois dans les régions acadiennes.[2]

Cet article vise donc à apporter une contribution nouvelle dans l'étude de l'économie des régions acadiennes. Il a pour but de mettre en lumière l'impact de l'industrie du bois sur le développement de la Péninsule acadienne, dans le comté de Gloucester au Nouveau-Brunswick. Dans un premier temps il analyse l'impact de la venue des scieries sur la forêt et le territoire de la Péninsule. Cette industrie naissante, dans la région, va à la fois utiliser et transgresser les politiques que le gouvernement provincial a mis sur pied pour l'utilisation des terres de la Couronne. Dans un deuxième temps il se concentre sur la main-d'oeuvre. Les habitants de la région vivent dans une économie agro-forestière dominée par les entrepreneurs de l'industrie du bois. Une main-d'oeuvre considérable est nécessaire pour couper le bois sur les terres de la Couronne. Les compagnies utilisent un système de sous-traitance pour recruter et contrôler la main-d'oeuvre. Au même moment, les entrepreneurs ne se contentent pas de la ressource sur les terres de la Couronne mais utilisent le bois sur les terres privées pour approvisionner les scieries. Plusieurs habitants deviennent donc très actifs en vendant aux compagnies le bois qu'ils coupent sur leurs terres.

---

1   À ce sujet, voir Michel Roy, *L'Acadie, des origines à nos jours, essai de synthèse historique* (Montréal, 1981), pp. 188-9; Régis Brun, *De Grand-Pré à Kouchibouguac, L'histoire d'un peuple exploité* (Moncton, 1982), p. 120; et Léon Thériault, "L'Acadie, 1763-1978, Synthèse historique", dans *Les Acadiens des Maritimes* (Moncton, 1980), p. 82.

2   Aurèle Young, "L'économie acadienne, histoire et développement" dans *Les Acadiens des Maritimes*, p. 214: et Raymond Mailhot, "Quelques éléments d'histoire économique de la prise de conscience acadienne, 1850-1891", *La Société historique Acadienne, les Cahiers*, 7, 2 (juin 1976), pp. 67-8.

A partir de 1875 une industrie du bois se développe dans la Péninsule acadienne. Le nombre de scieries passe de 10 en 1871 à 14 en 1881 alors que le nombre total d'employés passe de 67 en 1871 à 492 en 1881. Il est alors évident que les nouvelles scieries sont plus grosses avec plus d'employés. D'ailleurs cette situation n'est pas unique au comté de Gloucester. Dans l'ensemble du Nouveau-Brunswick, on s'aperçoit que ce phénomène est encore plus accentué; on y constate, entre 1871 et 1881, à la fois une baisse dans le nombre de moulins et une hausse dans la main-d'oeuvre. Pour ce qui est de la Péninsule acadienne le recensement de 1871 nous indique qu'il y a seulement un petit moulin qui emploie deux employés,[3] en fin de compte aucun signe d'une vraie industrie. Entre 1871 et 1881 la Péninsule acadienne accueille deux importantes scieries. Une autre vient s'ajouter entre 1880 et 1885 et une dernière s'établit en 1896.

La première scierie d'importance s'établit à Tracadie en 1875 sous l'initiative de Henry Hoste Swinny. Cette entreprise qui emploie environ 75 employés tombe rapidement sous le contrôle de la firme anglaise Guy, Stewart & Co. Cette firme change de nom pour devenir R.A. & J. Stewart et par la suite la N.B. Trading Co. avant de faire faillite et de fermer la scierie de Tracadie en 1889. En 1895, l'entreprise est achetée par J.B. Snowball qui possède une importante scierie à Chatham au N.-B.[4] Voici une description de cette scierie à ses débuts:

> ...still further down the road is the steam saw mill of Messrs. Guy, Stewart & Co. furnished with gang and rotary saws and in addition to deals etc., manufacturing palings, laths and clapboards. The cutting of the mill runs only in the summer and the lumber is sent to Miramichi by boat.[5]

Une deuxième scierie s'installe dans la Péninsule en 1875. Cette fois c'est un marchand de Bathurst, Kennedy Francis Burns[6] qui établit une scierie actionnée par le pouvoir de la rivière Caraquet dans un petit village qui portera éventuellement le nom de Burnsville. Burns implique tour à tour son frère Patrick et son beau-frère Samuel Adams dans les firmes qui sont connues sous les noms de K.F. Burns & Co., Burns & Adams & Co. et la St. Lawrence Lumber Co. Cette dernière a des actionnaires canadiens et des capitaux anglais en plus de ceux de la famille Burns. Lorsqu'elle fait faillite en 1894 et que Kennedy Burns meurt en 1895, ce sont Samuel Adams et Patrick Burns qui forment une compagnie sous le nom de Adams, Burns & Co. Cette nouvelle compagnie opare la scierie de

---

3   Recensement du Canada, 1871, Gloucester, Inkerman 2, Cédule #6, p. 1.

4   Raymond Léger, "L'industrie du bois dans la Péninsule acadienne (Nouveau-Brunswick), 1875-1900", thèse de maîtrise, dans *La Revue d'histoire de la Société historique Nicolas-Denys* [*RHSHND*], XVI, 2 (mai-août 1988), pp. 20-6.

5   *Miramichi Advance*, 18 octobre 1877, p. 3.

6   Raymond Léger, "Kennedy F. Burns", *RHSHND*, XIII, 3 (octobre-décembre 1985) pp. 12-15

Burnsville jusqu'en 1901 ou elle la vend à John Robertson.[7] Deux ans plus tard la scierie est détruite par le feu. Pour la période d'opération de la scierie, de mai à novembre, la production a été d'environ 4,5 millions de pieds.[8]

Aux alentours de 1883, Bennet Morton, un marchand de New Germany en Nouvelle-Écosse, établit une scierie à vapeur à Pokemouche. Après plusieurs transactions la scierie passe sous le contrôle de la compagnie W.S. Loggie Co. Ltd. de Chatham.[9] Cette compagnie ne s'occupe pas principalement de la transformation du bois d'oeuvre. Les domaines d'activités de W.S. Loggie Co. Ltd. sont les conserveries de poisson, les magasins et l'exploitation des bleuets. La scierie de Pokemouche brûle en 1911 et elle est reconstruite quelque temps plus tard dans le village voisin d'Inkerman.[10]

Finalement une dernière scierie sera établie à Sheila près de Tracadie en 1897 par la Tracadie Lumber Co. Voici une description de cette industrie:

> Le moulin sera une bâtisse de 150 pieds sur 80. La chambre de l'engin est
> de 70 pieds sur 50, avec fondation en pierre de granit. La capacité du moulin
> sera de 15 millions de pieds par saison.[11]

À présent, nous allons examiner l'impact que la venue de l'industrie du bois a eu sur la forêt de la Péninsule acadienne pendant ces quelques 25 ans d'exploitation. La première constatation que l'on peut faire sur la coupe de bois, est qu'il existe une région de la Péninsule acadienne particulièrement propice à l'exploitation forestière. C'est la partie ouest de la Péninsule, à l'exclusion du littoral et en particulier de l'Île Miscou et de l'Île Shippegan. L'emplacement des régions boisées au XIXe siècle est illustré par la Carte 1. Conçue par l'arpenteur-cartographe Thomas C. Loggie et imprimée en 1875, elle illustre les terres à bois appartenant au Département des Terres de la Couronne. La carte montre les limites des terres réservées à l'exploitation forestière par le gouvernement de la province. On peut aussi constater que ces forêts sont situées près du système hydrographique des rivières Caraquet, Pokemouche et Tracadie. Les terres à bois de la Couronne

---

7   Léger, "L'industrie du bois", pp. 11-20.

8   Tout au long du texte pied signifie; pieds mesure de planche qui équivaut à une pièce de bois d'un pouce d'épaisseur et mesurant un pied de long par un pied de large.

9   Greffe du comté de Gloucester, vol. 30, no. 42, pp. 80-4, vol. 31, no. 171, pp. 226-7, vol. 31, no. 370, vol. 31, no. 372, vol. 33, no. 86, p. 175.

10   "Lettre de W.S. Loggie à Allison Gray, le 12 juin 1911", MC1049, Fonds W.S. Loggie, boîte 29, no. 4, Archives provinciales du Nouveau-Brunswick [APNB].

11   *Le Courrier des Provinces Maritimes [CPM]*, 12 mai 1897, p. 3.

Carte 1

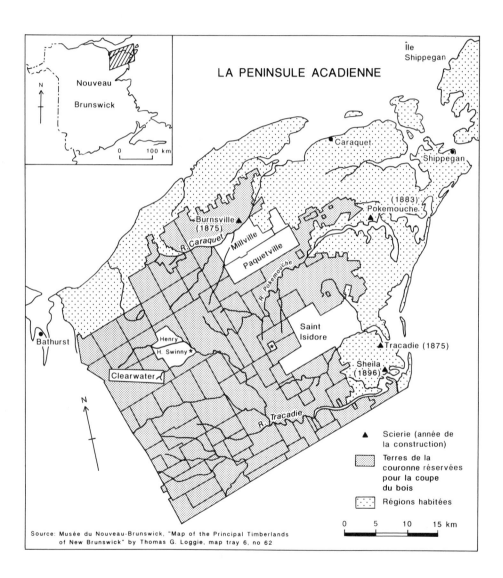

Source: Musée du Nouveau-Brunswick, "Map of the Principal Timberlands of New Brunswick" by Thomas G. Loggie, map tray 6, no 62

sont divisées en parcelles et certaines sont numérotées de A à Z. D'autres sont retenues pour les colonies de Millville, Paquetville, Saint-Isidore et Clearwater.[12]

Il ressort de l'infrastructure indiquée sur la carte que de grandes étendues de terres sont entre les mains du gouvernement et sont réservées aux entrepreneurs forestiers. Cependant, il y a des exceptions à cette règle. Il s'agit premièrement des propriétés appartenant à Henry Hoste Swinny. Ce dernier, comme nous l'avons vu précédemment, est impliqué dans l'industrie du bois. Sur la Carte 1 nous pouvons voir une de ses terres située dans la partie ouest entre les parcelles K, I et O. Cette énorme terre lui est accordée en 1873 et elle a une dimension de 7 750 acres (3 139 ha).[13] Ce domaine important est découpé par la grande rivière de Tracadie ainsi que ses branches sud et nord. Mais ce n'est pas tout. Swinny s'est vu accorder une autre concession de 1 730 acres (701 ha) la même journée. Celle-ci est située un peu plus à l'ouest le long de la rivière Tabusintac. L'année suivante, Swinny reçoit une autre terre d'une superficie de 520 (211 ha) acres située à l'est du village de Saint-Isidore.[14] En tout le gouvernement provincial accorde à un seul individu 10 000 acres (4 050 ha) de terres propices à l'exploitation forestière.[15] Il est impossible de connaître les motifs qui poussent le gouvernement à être aussi généreux envers Swinny alors que d'autres entrepreneurs forestiers n'ont pas eu ce privilège. Le prix payé pour ces terres n'est pas indiqué dans les documents que nous avons trouvé mais il est certain qu'elles ont été achetées par Swinny. Le journal *The Union Advocate* de Newcastle explique d'ailleurs qu'il y a eu de la spéculation pour obtenir ces terres.[16] De 1873 à 1891, Swinny n'est pas résidant de la Péninsule acadienne, il habite le comté de York au Nouveau-Brunswick et, par la suite, Londres en Angleterre. Finalement, en 1891, il vend ses grandes propriétés à des commerçants de Bangor au Maine qui font partie de la Tracadie Lumber Co.[17] Si Swinny a obtenu une vraie concession de terre pour effectuer la coupe de bois, la plupart des entrepreneurs doivent faire leur coupe sur les terres de la Couronne. Pour avoir accès à ces terres, ils font une pétition au Département des Terres de la Couronne. Une fois la pétition envoyée, une demande est faite pour faire arpenter la terre. Un arpenteur fixe les limites du permis pour la coupe de bois. Ce plan est remis au Département et constitue l'illustration du permis en question.

---

12 "Map of the Principal Timberlands of New Brunswick Showing the Boundaries of the Timber Berths as They Now Exist, and the Outline of the Granted and Located Lands" (New York, 1875), carte géographique, tiroir 6, no. 62, Musée du Nouveau-Brunswick [MNB].

13 RG10, RS107, RNA/C/6/8/21a, 1852-96, APNB.

14 RG10, RS107, RNA/C/6/8/21a, 1852-96, APNB.

15 "North Shore Lumber interests", 1889, p. 30, MNB.

16 *Union Advocate*, 13 octobre 1875, p. 1.

Entre 1875 et 1900, plusieurs changements se produisent dans la politique d'octroi de permis de coupe. En effet, ceux-ci sont octroyés pour des périodes de temps variant de 1, 3, 5, 10 et finalement 25 ans en 1893. Le prix payé par les compagnies pour le permis est de 8,00$ par mille carré (3 cents par ha) à la première demande et de 4,00$ par mille carré (1.5 cents par ha) pour le renouvellement.[18]

Pendant le dernier quart du XIXe siècle, il y a une extension continuelle des activités de coupe. Les permis sont donnés au début de l'automne afin de permettre aux compagnies de planifier les coupes de bois hivernales. Au niveau des sites et emplacements des permis il faut aussi remarquer le rôle important joué par les rivières et les ruisseaux, parce que les permis sont toujours situés près des cours d'eau afin que l'on puisse y faire flotter le bois coupé. En 1876-7 on s'aperçoit que les permis sont entre les mains de sept personnes et que, 14 permis sur 25 sont octroyés à K.F. Burns et John Stewart, opérateurs de scieries dans la région. De plus, John Young, qui obtient cinq permis en 1876-7, vend le bois qu'il coupe au moulin de Swinny, contrôlé par Stewart.[19] La mainmise des compagnies sur les permis pour la coupe de bois sur les terres de la Couronne caractérise l'ensemble de la période. C'est toujours le nom des compagnies qui possèdent les scieries qui ont les permis et les rares exceptions sont ceux qui ont des contrats de vente de bois aux compagnies.[20]

De 1875 à 1892, il est possible de voir, annuellement, la situation d'ensemble pour la Péninsule, parce que les permis doivent être renouvelés chaque année. Après 1893, les permis sont offerts pour une période de 25 ans et il n'existe plus de données annuelles. Le Tableau I montre le nombre total de permis accordés de 1875 à 1892 et le nombre total de milles carrés sur lesquels la coupe de bois est autorisée à chaque année. Nous avons aussi évalué le pourcentage des terres vendues en permis. Calculé sur la base que la Péninsule a une surface de 877 milles carrés (227 318 ha),[21] on constate que les entrepreneurs occupent entre 8,27 pour cent et 18,7 pour cent du territoire selon les années. Ce pourcentage est très élevé, si l'on considère que la région comprend un littoral sur lequel il n'y a pas de ressources forestières propres à l'exploitation. Les fluctuations sont dues à plusieurs facteurs. Un des éléments est le nombre de moulins en opération dans la région. En 1875, il y en a deux alors qu'en 1885 le nombre est de trois. De plus, les crises de surproduction dans l'industrie du bois liées aux cycles de crises mondiales, dans les années 1880 et 1890, affectent l'offre et la demande pour le bois d'oeuvre, ce qui a pour

---

17 Greffe du comté de Gloucester, vol. 26, no. 176, p. 368.

18 Murray B. Morison, *The Forests of New Brunswick* (Ottawa, 1938), p. 33.

19 RG10, RS107, RNA/C/11/1/20, 1872-82, APNB

20 RG10, RS107, RNA/C/11/1/20, 1872-82, RNA/C/11/1/21, 1883-92, APNB.

21 Morison, *The Forests of New Brunswick*, p. 75.

effet que les entrepreneurs peuvent ou ne sont pas capables d'avoir de grandes étendues de terres pour la coupe de bois.

Outre l'espace réservé pour l'exploitation forestière sur les terres de la Couronne, il y a les colonies de Paquetville, Millville et Saint-Isidore qui sont destinées aux colons qui veulent s'y installer. Ceux-ci peuvent recevoir 100 ou 200 acres (81 ha) de terres selon la grandeur de leur famille.[22] Toutefois, à maintes reprises les compagnies obtiennent des permis pour couper le bois sur les terres des colonies avant que les colons ne s'y établissent. Par exemple à Paquetville-Sud, K.F. Burns obtient des permis pour une superficie de 6 400 acres (2 592 ha) en 1881.[23] Ce phénomène n'est pas unique à Paquetville car à Saint-Isidore, des personnes voulant s'installer sur des terres se plaignent que les parcelles qu'elles désirent ont été exploitées pour le bois. Dans une lettre à l'arpenteur général, l'instituteur Charles Brison[24] plaide la cause de Louis Brideau, Henri Brideau, Henri Duguay et Chrisologue Duguay qui ont fait une demande pour des lots. De toute cette affaire, il ressort que non seulement, il y a des droits de coupe accordés avant l'établissement des colons, mais que dans le cas de Saint-Isidore, la coupe s'est faite sans permis du Département des Terres de la Couronne.[25] Ce phénomène n'est cependant pas unique à la colonisation au Nouveau Brunswick ou dans la Péninsule. Au Québec, dans l'Outaouais, dans les Laurentides et en Mauricie, la coupe du bois par les compagnies avant l'arrivée des colons est monnaie courante.[26] La coupe du bois sur les terres de colonisation ne se fait pas seulement avant que les colons s'installent. Même après, les compagnies peuvent encore obtenir des permis pour la coupe du bois, parce que le bois appartient au gouvernement tant que le colon n'a pas le titre de la terre. La loi décrète que:

> All trees growing or being upon any lots so assigned as aforesaid shall be considered as reserved from the said location, and shall be the property of Her Majesty, except that the locatee, or those claiming under him, may cut and use such trees as may be necessary for the purpose of building, fencing, or fuel, on the land so alloted, and may also cut and dispose of all trees actually required to be removed in bona fide clearing said land for cultivation; and no trees, (except for necessary building, fencing and fuel as aforesaid),

---

22 "Crown Land Report 1873", *Journal of the House of Assembly of N.B.* [*JHANB*], 1873, p. 47.

23 "McCallum à Paulin, 3 mars 1881", RG10, RS107, RNA/C/3/4/7(G), APNB.

24 Donat Robichaud, "Charles Brison", *RHSHND*, I, 5 (juin-décembre 1972), p. 118.

25 "Brison à Adams, 14 décembre 1878", RG10, RS107, RNA/C3/4/(D), APNB.

26 Gabriel Dussault, *Le curé Labelle, Messianisme, utopie et colonisation au Québec, 1850-1900* (Montréal, 1983), pp. 259-74.

shall be cut beyond the limit of such actual clearing before the issuing of the grant.[27]

Pour obtenir le titre de sa terre, le colon doit remplir plusieurs conditions, les principales étant qu'il cultive dix acres de terres et qu'il habite le lot pendant trois ans.[28] Toutefois, il y a de nombreuses critiques de l'efficacité de la loi et de l'accès facile qu'elle donne aux terres boisées. Edward Jack a souligné ce problème dans un rapport:

> Our Labor and Free Grant Acts have proved very largely failures. Not only have they to a great extent failed to attain the end which they were expected to fulfill, but they have been frequently made use of by private individuals for the purpose of obtaining timber land.[29]

Tous ces phénomènes se produisent dans la Péninsule acadienne. À titre d'exemple, en 1878 les compagnies obtiennent huit permis dans la colonie de Saint-Isidore sur des terres qui sont déjà occupeées par des colons.[30] Il s'agit donc d'une espèce de cohabitation des compagnies et des colons alors que ces derniers devaient pratiquer l'agriculture. Mais cette cohabitation n'est sûrement pas un mariage heureux puisque le bois coupé par les compagnies aurait pu être coupé et vendu par le colon. Dans une étude sur la colonisation et le curé Labelle au Québec, Gabriel Dussault explique ce conflit de la façon suivante: "L'intérêt des puissantes compagnies est de conserver le plus longtemps possible, dans les régions où elles sont installées, le monopole de l'exploitation forestière et des autres activités économiques qui sont reliés de près ou de loin".[31]

Pour sa part le gouvernement provincial ne fait rien pour changer cette situation. Cela n'est nullement surprenant car les magnats de l'industrie du bois sont bien représentés à Fredericton. K.F. Burns, J.B. Snowball, J.P. Burchill, Michael Adams et bien d'autres, liés directement ou indirectement à l'industrie du bois sont tour à tour députés à Fredericton.[32]

Malgré tous les privilèges qu'ils ont en exploitant les terres de la Couronne, les entrepreneurs cherchent toujours à obtenir de meilleurs avantages. Ceci est particulièrement évident lorsqu'un comité représentant les entrepreneurs du nord de la province et le gouvernement discutent des politiques gouvernementales concernant

---

27 "Crown Land Report 1873", *JHANB*, 1873, p. 48.

28 "Crown Land Report 1873", *JHANB*, 1873, p. 48.

29 Saint John Free Public Library, Scrapbook and MS5, no. 10, film no. 130, p. 35.

30 "Immigration Report, Saint-Isidore", *Crown Land Report, 1878*, et "Lumber Cut in Gloucester", *JHANB* , 1880, p. 84.

31 Dussault, *Le curé Labelle*, p. 261

32 James C. et Horace B. Graves, comps., *New Brunswick Political Biographies, vol. 1, 1875-1900*, Fredericton.

les terres de la Couronne. Les entrepreneurs argumentent que les taux de transport sont plus élevés dans le nord de la province que dans le sud. Ils ajoutent que leur situation est défavorable par rapport au Québec et à la Nouvelle-Écosse, où, selon eux, les avantages sont encore plus grands pour les entrepreneurs. Ils veulent une réduction des tarifs sur le bois coupé sur les terres de la Couronne. Toujours selon eux, tous les problèmes et toutes les faillites sont attribuables à la politique gouvernementale.[33] La même question est également soulevée à l'Assemblée législative par plusieurs députés de l'opposition. On utilise les mêmes arguments pour exiger encore plus de faveurs pour les entrepreneurs.[34]

La quantité de bois abattu sur les terres de la Couronne est très variable. Il faut se rappeler que les statistiques totalisent le bois coupé sur les terres ordinaires de la Couronne et le bois coupé dans les colonies où plusieurs terrains appartiennent encore à la Couronne. Un mesureur de bois employé par le Département des Terres de la Couronne parcourt les terres où les compagnies ont des permis de coupe. Il calcule la quantité de bois coupé et envoie les données à Fredericton. Voici un exemple des instructions reçues par les mesureurs pour effectuer leur travail:

> So soon as you can get a full account of the winter's operations, you will please make your returns of same. You will send the usual Scale Bills and Reports, Scaler's Book with affidavit attached, and will also return the Plans furnished you, marking on them the Licenses operated on during the season, as previously instructed. When the full accounts can be obtained, the sooner your returns can be made the better, and I trust you will furnish yours with as little delay as possible.[35]

À partir des chiffres fournis par les mesureurs de bois, nous avons constitué le Tableau II. Il illustre la quantité de bois abattu de 1884 à 1897, dans la Péninsule acadienne. Ce qui ressort de ce tableau, c'est que l'épinette est l'essence la plus exploitée. Malgré le fait que le pin soit dans la même colonne, il est certain qu'en 1870, au Nouveau-Brunswick, l'âge d'or du pin est révolu.[36] Le cèdre occupe la deuxième position, même s'il y a une énorme différence. C'est donc dire que les conifères sont les proies favorites des entrepreneurs forestiers. Malheureusement, pour les années 1895, 1896 et 1897 nous ne possédons des données que pour l'épinette et le pin.

---

33 "North Shore Lumber Interests", MNB 1889, pp. 1-35.

34 *Synoptic Report of the Proceedings of the House of Assembly of the province of New Brunswick for the session of 1890,* pp. 22-90.

35 RG10, RS107, RNA/C/3/4/7(G), APNB.

36 Burton Glendenning "The Burchill Lumbering Firm, 1850-1908, An Example of Nineteenth Century New Brunswick Entrepreneurship", thèse de maîtrise, Concordia University, Montréal, 1978, p. 101.

Les fluctuations que l'on peut constater dans la coupe sont dues entre autres à deux facteurs. Le premier est le marché. Si celui-ci n'est pas bon, il y a réduction dans les coupes de bois. Ainsi les entrepreneurs forestiers surveillent de près le marché britannique où ils vendent principalement leurs produits. Le deuxième facteur est la situation des compagnies. Par exemple, suite à la disparition de la N.B. Trading Company en 1890, on constate une baisse des coupes à partir de 1891. En 1894, lorsque la St. Lawrence Lumber Co. fait faillite, il y a une autre diminution. En 1897, avec l'apparition de la Tracadie Lumber Co. on voit une légère remontée.

La colonne des dollars dans le Tableau II indique le montant d'argent que les compagnies doivent payer pour les droits de coupe au Département des Terres de la Couronne. Les prix varient selon l'essence, mais aussi ils changent au cours des années. Les compagnies paient ,80$ de 1874 à 1884, 1,25$ de 1885 à 1889 et finalement, 1,00$ à partir de 1890 pour chaque pieds d'épinette et de pin.[37] On peut penser que la baisse de 1,25$ à 1,00$ est en partie attribuable au pressions faites par les entrepreneurs du nord de la province en 1889 et 1890.

Ce bois coupé dans la région est principalement transformé dans les scieries de Burnsville, Tracadie et Pokemouche. En 1886, 67 pour cent de l'épinette et du pin est destiné à ces moulins. Le pourcentage passe à 77 pour cent en 1887, à 91 pour cent en 1889, à 70 pour cent en 1893.[38] Le bois non transformé dans la région est transporté vers la Miramichi pour y être scié. J.B. Snowball est l'entrepreneur de la Miramichi le plus actif dans le transport du bois de la Péninsule, durant cette période. Il achète le moulin de Tracadie en 1896 et par la suite, tout le bois coupé dans la Péninsule est transformé sur place.

Toutes ces sources démontrent qu'entre 1878 et 1897, une quantité considérable de bois est sortie des terres de la Couronne pour alimenter les scieries. Cependant peut-on conclure qu'il s'agit de la coupe totale de bois? Nous avons testé ces données en les comparant aux exportations. Le moulin de Burnsville fournit un cas propice à ce test. Les compagnies exportent le bois à partir du port de Caraquet jusqu'en 1885 et en comparant le nombre de pieds exporté avec les données des coupes du bois sur les Terres de la Couronne on obtient la différence. En 1878, les coupes sont de 477 815 pieds et les exportations 2 033 228 pieds pour une différence de 1 555 413. En 1879, l'écart est de 2 043 287; en 1881 de 837 056; en 1883 de 1 738 984; en 1884 de 678 000; et en 1885 de 967 059 pieds.[39]

Il y a deux explications à cette différence substantielle. Premièrement, il y a le fait que tout le bois coupé sur les terres de la Couronne n'est pas rapporté par les mesureurs de bois du gouvernement. Ces derniers ont un grand territoire à couvrir.

---

37 Morison, *The Forests of New Brunswick*, p. 33.

38 "Scalers Returns", 1884-94, RG10, RS107, RNA/G/15/3/1-2, APBN.

39 "Lumber Cut in Gloucester", *JHANB, 1880,* pp. 83-4; RG10, RS107, RNA/C/3/6/1+2+5, 1881-3, 1884-6, 1894-7, RG10, RS107, RNA/C/15/3/1+2, 1884-94, APNB; *Miramichi Advance,* 8 novembre 1877, 1 janvier 1879, 23

Avant 1884, les districts des deux mesureurs pour la Péninsule sont composés des régions suivantes:

> James Hayden, Esq., Pockmouche. The operations of K. F. Burns Co. on Nepisiquit R. and Branches covering streams running into Bay Chaleur from below little Belledune to Caraquet inclusive. John Robertson, Esq. Tabusintac Gloucester Co., All streams from Pockmouche Sly. to Portage River all inclusive. Principal streams, Pockmouche, Big and Little Tracadie and Branches.[40]

En 1884, la description devient plus précise:

> No, 4, James Barry Jr. Pockmouche. All streams from Teagues Brooks Ely. + Sly. to and including Big Tracadie R. Principal streams being Caraquet, Pockmouche, Big + Little, Tracadie.[41]

C'est un grand territoire de travail pour une seule personne. De plus, il doit effectuer son ouvrage en plein hiver et souvent mesurer le bois enfoui dans la neige, les rivières et les lacs gelés.[42] De plus le mesureur de bois est dépendant des entrepreneurs car ces derniers doivent lui fournir son logement et sa nourriture et aussi des informations sur la coupe de bois.[43] Ces problèmes et d'autres sont mentionnés par Edward Jack dans un article retrouvé dans le *Daily Sun* de Saint-Jean, Nouveau-Brunswick. Il faut prendre note que Jack est un ancien employé du Département des Terres de la Couronne. Il explique que les compagnies cachent souvent le bois dans les rivières ou que, tout simplement, le bois a disparu quand le mesureur de bois se présente. Parlant de la malhonnêteté des mesureurs de bois, il mentionne la pratique suivante:

> The camp cook very often acts as a sort of accountant for the log hauler, as he often keeps a camps book for the boss in which he entered the number of logs which are hauled each day by the various teams; under the direction of the boss he often has two of these books in one of which he shows the boss the correct number of logs hauled with the other which gives a less quantity

---

décembre 1880, 29 décembre 1881, 31 janvier 1884, 22 janvier 1885; "J.B. Snowball's Miramichi Wood Trade Circular", 1879, 1885, Fonds Burchill, MBUII/14/3/1, APNB.

40 RG10, RS107, RNA/C/3/4/8(H), pp. 294, 296, APNB.

41 "Scalers returns", 1884-94, RG10, RS107, RNA/C/15/3/3, APNB.

42 "Lumber Cut in Gloucester County", *JHANB, 1880*, p. 106

43 *The Royal Gazette*, "Crown Land Timber Regulations", 35 (15 August 1877), p. 347.

he cheats the scaler who very often depends upon the cook's account for the quantity of logs cut.[44]

Jack soutient aussi que les mesureurs de bois ne visitent pas les camps assez fréquemment et qu'ils devraient les visiter au moins une fois par semaine.

L'autre problème affectant le travail des mesureurs de bois est le patronage politique. Au XIXe siècle, le patronage est très répandu au Nouveau-Brunswick et chaque position est donnée à des amis du gouvernement. En parlant de l'administration des terres de la Couronne, Jack déclare: "Their management is placed in the hands of the executive government instead of having been governed by a special act of the legislature, which would suffice to control the dishonest action of politicians".[45]

Tous ces éléments ressortent en 1880, lorsqu'une commission d'enquête provinciale est mise sur pied pour enquêter sur les coupes de bois dans le comté de Gloucester. À l'audience de la commission, on constate une différence entre les rapports des mesureurs de bois et un estimé fait par J.McD. Barker, un autre employé du Département des Terres de la Couronne qui visite les camps. Pour Burnsville, Barker estime qu'il y a eu 800 000 pieds coupés en 1878. Les rapports des mesureurs de bois, montre 477 815 pour la même année. L'année suivante, l'écart est encore plus accentué. La commission rapporte aussi que la même chose s'est produite à Tracadie: John Young, exploitant des camps de bûcherons, a coupé 2 020 000 pieds qui n'ont pas été déclarés par le mesureur.[46] Toute cette affaire n'a pas eu de suite, mais elle sert à démontrer que le Tableau II est un estimé minimum de la quantité de bois coupé sur les terres de la Couronne; la coupe réelle est souvent bien supérieure au montant dans les tableaux.

Pour approvisionner les scieries il est certain que les compagnies ont besoin d'une main-d'oeuvre considérable. La composition et la relation de cette main-d'oeuvre avec la société constituent un des problèmes théoriques les plus importants pour les historiens de l'industrie du bois. Plusieurs parlent d'économie agro-forestière. Notre but n'est pas de faire une analyse exhaustive de tous ceux qui ont traité de l'économie agro-forestière dans l'historiographie nord-américaine mais bien de relever deux grandes tendances.

Certains comme Normand Séguin voient le développement du capitalisme dans les régions rurales comme étant au centre de la question agro-forestière. Dans une étude sur le Saguenay et en particulier sur Hébertville, Normand Séguin montre comment, dans une région sous-développée, l'industrie forestière, qui précède lcolonisation, subjugue l'agriculture et devient le facteur dominant dans l'économie agro-forestière. Il explique aussi que, quoique l'industrie forestière constitue du développement économique, elle maintient ou perpétue un sous-développement

---

44 *Daily Sun*, 20 mars 1891, p. 1.

45 *Daily Sun*, 20 mars 1891, p. 1.

46 "Lumber cut in Gloucester", *JHANB, 1880*, pp. 99-111.

économique dans la région. Ce cadre théorique inclus la notion d'un centre développé par rapport à une périphérie sous-développée.[47] D'autres voient le problème plus en terme de développement parallèle et co-existence de l'agriculture et de l'industrie du bois ou la première peut être remplacée par la deuxième comme le facteur dominant de l'économie d'une région.[48]

Clairement la première approche me semble plus intéressante pour ce qui est de la Péninsule acadienne. La raison pour ce constat est que, ce qui est décrit précedemment dans la section sur les entrepreneurs montre le développement de l'industrie du bois dans la région comme étant central et dominant. Cependant l'industrie du bois ne précède pas la colonisation, mais arrive au même moment et se fait parallèlement. Malgré cela il y a quand même certaines réserves à apporter. Tout d'abord, quoique ces études sont fort interéssantes, elles sont plutôt de type général et pénétrent très peu la vie économique des habitants d'une région donnée. Elles manquent clairement de données quantitatives pouvant élucider quelles sont les occupations des habitants de ces régions et d'où est-ce qu'ils tirent une part importante de leur revenu. Selon nous il faut clairement établir comment la main-d'oeuvre est utilisée par les compagnies pour comprendre le problème de l'économie agro-forestière et ce qui est le plus important pour les habitants: l'agriculture ou la forêt.

Premièrement nous allons tenter d'établir quelle est la main-d'oeuvre qui coupe le bois sur les terres de la Couronne. Le recensement nominal de 1881 et celui de 1891 ont été consultés. Pour la Péninsule acadienne, on ne trouve que cinq personnes qui ont des métiers liés à l'industrie du bois en 1881. Quatre ont le métier de forestier et un a le métier de "millman". Le recensement de 1891 n'est guère plus utile car seulement dix personnes sont mentionnées comme ayant des métiers liés directement à l'industrie du bois.[49] Ensuite nous avons regardé les "Directories". Dans celui de 1889-96, on retrouve, dans la Péninsule, quatre personnes ayant comme occupation "Lumberman" et cinq personnes travaillant dans les scieries. Dans celui de 1903, il y a sept personnes oeuvrant dans les scieries et aucune autre personne n'est mentionnée.[50] Etant donné l'énorme quantité de bois exploité, on ne peut que conclure que les recensements nominaux de 1881, de 1891 et les "Direc-

---

47   Normand Séguin, *La conquête du sol au XIXe siècle. Le cas d'Hébertville* (Sillery, 1977) et "L'économie agro-forestière: genèse de développement au Saguenay au XIXe siècle", *Revue d'histoire de l'Amérique française*, 29, 4 (mars 1976), pp. 559-69.

48   Béatrice Craig; "Agriculture and the Lumberman's Frontier in the Upper St. John Valley, 1800-70", *Journal of Forest History*, 32, 3 (July 1988), pp. 125-37 et Richard W. Judd, "Lumbering and the Farming Frontier in Aroostook County, Maine, 1840-1880", *Journal of Forest History*, 28, 2 (April 1984), pp. 56-67.

49   *Recensement du Canada*, 1881, 1891, comté de Gloucester, partie nominale.

50   *McAlpine's New Brunswick Directory for 1889-1896* et *1903*, Saint John, New Brunswick (Halifax, 1896).

tories" ne tiennent pas compte de l'industrie du bois. Il est évident que si on utilise seulement ces deux sources, on commet des erreurs très graves dans l'évaluation de la main-d'oeuvre.

Il y a cependant d'autres sources qui donnent de meilleurs résultats. Tout d'abord les compagnies utilisent des sous-traitants pour faire couper le bois sur les terres de la Couronne. Dans la Péninsule il y a plusieurs sous-traitants. Le Tableau III illustre le nombre de sous-traitants pour la période de 1882 à 1897. Les sous-traitants signent des ententes avec les compagnies pour la coupe du bois sur les terres de la Couronne. Hugh Cowan, par exemple signe de telles ententes avec W.S. Loggie en 1890 et 1891. Au même moment, le recensement nominal de 1891 le considère cependant comme un fermier, démontrant encore une fois l'inexactitude de ces données.[51]

Le rapport d'une commission d'enquête, "Lumber Cut in Gloucester 1877-1878", fournit des informations sur la main-d'oeuvre pour ces années. Toutefois, les carnets annuels de visite des camps de J.McD. Barker constituent les sources les plus faibles. Barker est un employé du Département des Terres de la Couronne et il voyage dans tout le nord de la province. Durant ses excursions il visite les camps de bûcherons et il prend note du nombre d'hommes et de chevaux qui s'y trouvent. Ceci est une des entrées typiques de ses carnets: "Samuel Branch on Caraquet River. Logs for K.F. Burns & Co., 20 men plus 6 horses".[52] En utilisant ces sources, on s'aperçoit qu'il y a au moins 174 hommes et 53 chevaux dans les camps de la Péninsule en 1878-9.[53] En 1881-2, il y a 335 hommes et 92 chevaux; en 1882-3, 268 hommes et 72 chevaux; en 1895-6, 160 hommes et 37 chevaux; et en 1897-8, 269 hommes et 57 chevaux.[54]

Le Tableau IV montre les données intégrées illustrant les sous-traitants, le nombre d'hommes (H), le nombre de chevaux (C), la quantité de bois coupé en pieds et le nombre de billots coupés en 1881-2 (automne 1881 et hiver 1882). Il faut remarquer que plusieurs sous-traitants n'ont pas de camp, ou que Barker ne les a pas visités. Pour calculer le total de bûcherons en 1881-2, nous avons utilisé la corrélation suivante: 335 hommes coupent 13 411 152 pieds de bois, alors il faut donc environ 385 hommes pour pouvoir couper les 15 398 509 pieds que nous avons dans le Tableau IV. Si on prend ce nombre de 385 et qu'on le compare au total de la main-d'oeuvre de sexe masculin de 16 ans et plus, qui est de 3 095 dans le recensement nominal de 1881, nous pouvons conclure qu'un minimum de 12,44 pour cent de la main-d'oeuvre travaille dans les bois de la Péninsule en 1881-2. Ceci signifie qu'une grande partie des villages est impliquée dans la coupe du bois. En 1887 la situation est la suivante à Paquetville:

---

51 *Recensement du comté de Gloucester 1891, vol. 2* (Fredericton, 1989), p. 341.

52 "Diaries, J.McD. Barker", 1882-3, RG10, RS107, RNA/C/15/9/3, APNB

53 "Lumber Cut in Gloucester", *JHANB, 1880*, pp. 97-9.

54 RG10, RS107, RNA/C/15/7/13; RNA/C/15/9/3, APNB.

Nouvelles de Paquetville....Cet hiver nos jeunes gens travaillent presque tous dans les chantiers de M.K.F. Burns à l'ouest de Paquetville.[55]

Il faut se rappeler que Paquetville est une colonie destinée a avoir une vocation agricole. De plus, lorsqu'on considère que plusieurs personnes quittent la Péninsule pour aller dans les camps à l'extérieur, on peut conclure que l'industrie forestière a un impact important sur la main-d'oeuvre de la région.

Mais les habitants de la Péninsule ne vont pas seulement travailler dans le bois sur les terres de la Couronne pour les compagnies. Les propriétaires de lots boisés n'ont pas besoin d'investir dans la ressource, ils n'ont pas besoin de semer, de cultiver comme c'est le cas dans l'agriculture. Ils utilisent une ressource qui est présente sur leurs lots. Cela n'est pas surprenant, lorsque l'on considère qu'en 1871 65,23 pour cent des terres du district de recensement de Caraquet, Inkerman et Saumarez sont en forêt. En 1891, 78,76 pour cent des terres du district de Caraquet, Inkerman, Saumarez et Saint-Isidore sont en forêt.[56] Pour ce qui est des colonies de Paquetville, Millville et Saint-Isidore nous possédons des données annuelles pour quelques années. À Paquetville 97,1 pour cent des terres occupées par un colon sont en forêt en 1874 et ce pourcentage passe à 93,39 pour cent en 1875, à 92,16 pour cent en 1876, à 91,46 pour cent en 1877, à 90,24 pour cent en 1878, à 90,19 pour cent en 1879. À Millville le pourcentage de terres en forêt est de 93,79 pour cent en 1876, 92,32 pour cent en 1877, 91,12 pour cent en 1878 et 90,99 pour cent en 1879. À Saint-Isidore le pourcentage des terres en forêt est de 95,89 pour cent en 1874, 94,21 pour cent en 1875, 93,49 pour cent en 1876, 92,08 pour cent en 1877, 89,50 pour cent en 1878 et 88,06 pour cent en 1879.[57] Ces statistiques démontrent qu'une grande partie du territoire occupé par des habitants est couvert de bois disponible pour les habitants et les scieries.

Abattre le bois sur sa terre pour le vendre aux scieries est donc une pratique courante. Témoignant devant la commission d'enquête sur les coupes de bois dans Gloucester, un mesureur de bois déclare qu'à l'hiver de 1877 et au printemps de 1878 la situation est la suivante:

At Caraquet there are a lot of granted lands from which Burns Adams & Co. got logs. I know all these lands. To the best of my knowledge there were twenty thousand logs hauled off of granted lands which I thought would make about 1,904,76l. By every information I could get, don't think much of the twenty thousand pieces come off Crown Lands.[58]

---

55 *CPM*, 18 décembre 1887.

56 *Recensement du Canada, 1891,* vol. 2, p. 253.

57 Crown Land Report, 1875, 1876, 1877, 1878, 1879, 1880, "Statistical statement of St. Isidore, Paquetville, Millville settlement".

58 "Lumber Cut in Gloucester County", *JHANB, 1880*, p. 107.

Samuel Adams de la firme Burns & Adams Co. témoigne dans le même sens devant la commission: "In Caraquet last year we paid for about 1,800,000 logs off granted lands".[59]

D'autres exemples viennent confirmer ce phénomène. Des habitants de la région de Pokemouche vendent du bois au moulin de W.S. Loggie. Cette compagnie obtient une grande partie de son bois des habitants de la région. Ses activités sur les terres de la Couronne sont minimales puisqu'elle obtient seulement en moyenne 5,5 milles carrés (1 425 ha) en permis pour la coupe de bois du gouvernement entre 1887 et 1892.[60] W.S. Loggie signe des ententes avec des individus pour que ceux-ci lui fournissent du bois.

Nous avons retrouvé plusieurs de ces ententes dans le fonds d'archives de W.S. Loggie aux Archives provinciales du N.-B. Des ententes sont parfois faites avec plus d'un individu. Eugène Landry, Pierre Thibodeau et Philippe Thériault de Paquetville signent une entente avec W.S. Loggie en 1886 pour couper 80 000 pieds d'épinette et de pins sur des terres qui ont des titres. La compagnie va leur fournir de la farine, du porc, de l'avoine, de la mélasse, de la morue salée, du thé et du tabac pour une valeur qui ne dépassera pas 200,00$. Ils seront payés 3,50$ du mille pieds. Ceci signifie que s'ils coupent les 80 000 pieds de bois mentionnés ils recevront 280,00$. Raymond Losier de Tracadie signe une entente en 1888 òu il convient d'apporter à la scierie 250 000 pieds de bois. La compagnie accepte de lui fournir 60 barils de farine, 5 barils de farine de maïs, 4 barils de porc, 1 baril de hareng, 4 barils de boeuf, 100 gallons de mélasse, 100 livres de thé et 50 livres de tabac pour une valeur totale de 300,00$. On lui payera 5,50$ du mille pieds pour les billots de 14 pieds et plus de 11 pouces de diamètre. Pour ceux de moins de 11 pouces on lui payera 2/3 du prix. La même année John Duke signe deux ententes similaires pour produire 20 000 pieds d'épinette et 100 000 pieds de cèdre avec des provisions pour une valeur de 50,00$ dans le premier contratet 200 000 pieds de cèdre dans le deuxième.

Toujours en 1888, John Gouillette accepte une entente pour 40 000 pieds de bois avec une avance de 15,00$ de provision. George Duguay de Saint-Isidore signe une de ces ententes en 1896. Il accepte de fournir de 600 à 800 billots de bois d'épinette à la scierie de W.S. Loggie. La compagnie accepte pour sa part de lui avancer des provisions pour une valeur de 100,00$. Le contrat spécifie que Duguay sera payé au mois de juin après que le bois sera mesuré à la scierie. Bernard Ferguson signe une entente en 1895 dans laquelle il consent à vendre au moins 40 000 pieds et reçoit une valeur de 158,00$ en provisions. Pour le bois mesurant 14 pieds de long et 11 pouces de diamètre il reçoit 5,00$ du mille pieds. Pour le bois mesurant moins que cela il reçoit 2/3 de ce prix.[61] En achetant le bois des propriétaires de lots boisés et

---

59 "Lumber Cut in Gloucester County", *JHANB, 1880*, p. 114.

60 RG10, RS107, RNA/C/11/1/21, 1883-92, APNB.

61 MC1049, boîtes 13, 16 et 18, APNB.

en leur donnant des provisions à l'avance les entrepreneurs forestiers créent certainement une dépendance et ils ont une clientèle assurées pour leurs magasins. Ainsi les habitants vendent indirectement leur force de travail pour des provisions aux magasins des compagnies.

D'autres documents viennent confirmer l'étendue de ces activités avec les habitants de la région. Le gérant de l'opération à Pokemouche John Falconer écrit le 21 février 1895: "I have this day taken delivery of logs cut and hauled by Bernard D. Ferguson from his own lands, said logs now lying in landings on the Maltempec Brook and at the stump on said B.D. Ferguson land, the quantity of logs seven hundred pieces more or less".[62]

Des mesureurs de bois sont actifs pour évaluer la quantité de bois que les habitants ont coupé. Pierre A. Haché envoie une note à la compagnie en 1887 dans laquelle il explique que Joseph Paulin et Sylvestre Thériault de Paquetville ont coupé 227 billots pour un total 15 982 pieds de bois de pin et d'épinette.[63] Le mesureur de bois Simon Simpson envoie un rapport en 1896 qui indique que George Savoie a fourni 113 383 pieds de bois. Parmi ses rapports de 1897 il indique que George Duguay, Joseph Duguay et Auguste Roussel ont coupé un total de 334 050 pieds de bois destiné à la scierie de W.S. Loggie. En 1898, il envoie une facture de mesurage de bois pour John Ferguson pour 31 088 pieds de bois.[64]

Au mois d'août 1895, le moulin scie 25 143 pieds de bois apporté au moulin par Isaac Robert et John Resche. Au cours de cette même année, George et Bruno St-Pierre apportent à la scierie 8 156 pieds de bois, Bernard Ferguson 18 398, Fidèle Hébert 7 970, Olivier St-Coeur et Pierre Boudreau 18 819 pieds.[65] Pour vérifier le métier de ces individus on est allé voir dans le *McAlpine's New Brunswick Directory, 1896*. Toutes les personnes mentionnées plus haut sont inscrites comme étant des fermiers.[66] En 1898, de juillet à décembre, des producteurs de bois vendent 348 259 pieds d'épinette et 13 750 pieds de pin pour une valeur de 2 388,08$ au moulin de Loggie.[67] En vérifiant dans le même "Directory", on s'aperçoit que tous ceux que l'on a pu retracer sont inscrits comme fermiers. On peut conclure que les personnes que ces sources appellent "fermiers" tirent des revenus importants de la vente de bois aux compagnies et qu'ils sont sans aucun doute, plus des producteurs de bois que des fermiers.

---

62 MC1049, boîte 17, no. 11, APNB.

63 "Survey Bill Joseph Paulin", MC1049, boîte 13, APNB.

64 MC1049, boîte 18, APNB.

65 "Mill tally book", 1895, MC1049, Fonds W.S. Loggie, boîte 15, APNB.

66 *McAlpine's New Brunswick Directory, 1896*, pp. 707-46.

67 "Lumber books", 1898-1901, pp. 1-102, MC1049, Fonds W.S. Loggie, boîte 1, APNB

Par ailleurs, lorsqu'on regarde la main-d'oeuvre oeuvrant dans les scieries, les sous-traitants, les bûcherons qui coupent le bois sur les terres de la Couronne, ceux qui coupent du bois sur les grandes propriétés de Swinny et finalement, les propriétaires de lots boisés qui vendent aux moulins, on peut conclure que l'industrie du bois a un impact majeur sur la vie des habitants de la Péninsule acadienne. De plus la mainmise sur de vastes domaines forestiers par l'entremise de l'achat de terres comme c'est le cas pour Swinny, et l'invasion des terres de la Couronne par les entrepreneurs a d'importantes répercussions sur l'économie de la région. Ce sont les entrepreneurs forestiers qui dominent et fixent les règles du jeu dans l'économie agro-forestière de la région.

Tableau   I

Permis pour la coupe de bois, 1875-1892

Année	Nombre de permis	Nombre de milles carrés	% du total des terres
1875	19	91.5	9.29
1876	17	72.5	8.27
1877	25	100.0	11.40
1878	27	114.0	13.00
1879	19	78.5	8.95
1880	20	97.0	11.06
1881	22	101.0	11.52
1882	32	165.5	18.87
1883	25	125.5	14.31
1886	40	165.0	18.81
1887	38	158.0	18.02
1888	37	148.0	16.88
1889	35	142.0	16.19
1890	37	156.5	17.84
1891	42	154.5	17.62
1892	37	162.0	18.47

Source: RG10, RS107, RNA/C/11/1/20-21, 1872-1892, APNB.

Tableau III

Nombre de sous-traitants

Année	Sous-traitants	Année	Sous-traitants
1882	28	1890	15
1883	24	1891	13
1884	12	1892	11
1885	22	1893	—
1886	26	1894	14
1887	22	1895	13
1888	30	1896	28
1889	19	1897	46

Source: RG10, RS107, RNA/C/3/6/1+2+3+4+5, APNB.

Tableau II

Coupe de bois dans la Péninsule

Année	Epinette et pin, pied	Cèdre, pied	Pin, bois de tonne	Traverse de chemin de fer	Pruche pied	Bois franc, bois de tonne
1884	2 705 000	119 954	470	1 000		
1885	5 417 928	134 000	556			165
1886	7 116 000	108 000	26		1 200	40
1887	5 021 000	62 000	92	1 200		
1888	6 128 000	200 000	107			32
1889	5 302 000	168 000	68		32 000	25
1890	7 073 250	106 000		400	92 000	
1891	4 456 000	132 000		2 000		24
1892	4 534 000	87 000		4 340		
1893	4 245 000	357 000		900		
1894	2 525 000	18 750		12 600		
1895	2 126 000					
1896	2 771 000					
1897	3 468 000					

Année	Bois franc, pied	Poteaux de cèdre	Cordes d'écorces	Autres	Prix
1884					
1885				1 500 pé	
1886	5 000			61 tp	9 070,70$
1887	8 000	8 000	40		6 532,18
1888	234 000	16 400	5		8 342,32
1889				40 té	6 911,60
1890				60 MB	7 263,63
1891	2 000		15	75 K, 175 MB	4 622,60
1892		1 000		170 K	4 730,00
1893	9 300	700		17 K	4 654,29
1894				100 MB	2 812,00
1895					
1896					
1897					

Sources: RG10, RS107, RNA/C/15/3/1+2, 1884-1894, APNB.

pé: poteaux d'épinette, tp: tonnes de pruches, té: tonnes d'épinette, MB: Milles de Bardeaux, K: *Knees*

Tableau IV

Main-d'oeuvre dans les bois, 1881-1882

Sous-traitant	Lieu	H	C	Compagnie	Pieds bois	Billots
R. Branch	R. Caraquet	20	6	K.F. Burns	707 339	8 070
J. Thibodeau	r. Adams			K.F. Burns	563 933	650
T. Clifford	R. Caraquet	18	4	K.F. Burns	346 180	3 800
A. + J. Jago	R. Caraquet			K.F. Burns	283 251	3 600
divers	R. Caraquet			K.F. Burns	250 000	3 500
S. Branch	B.N.R. Caraquet	16	4	K.F. Burns	602 506	6 600
J. Terrio	r. Lord + Foys	28	8	J. Snowball	1 400 589	15 584
A. McLean	B.S.G.R. Traca.	25	8	J. Snowball	996 250	10 825
J. Grattan	B.S.G.R. Traca.			J. Snowball	121 105	833
An. Morrison	r. Lord + Foys	18	6	A. Morrison	1 006 511	7 460
T. Power	r. Lord + Foys	20	4	A. Morrison	563 037	3 792
Hayes + Russell	r. Lord + Foys	8	2	A. Morrison	241 822	1 450
J.A. Macdonald	B.S.G.R. Traca.	25	4	Stewart	1 100 451	11 622
A. Macdonald	r. Lord + Foys	20	6	Stewart	1 169 480	10 487
J. Woods	B.S.G.R. Traca.	22	6	Stewart	1 069 027	10 530
J. Campbell	G.R. Tracadie	24	6	Stewart	850 223	5 915
A. + P. Lebreton	G.R. Tracadie	30	12	Stewart	1 640 170	16 351
H. Lee	G.R. Tracadie	13	4	Stewart	303 458	2 000
J. Graham	r. Lord + Foys	14	4	Stewart	388 476	3 744
A. Brido	G.R. Tracadie			Stewart	36 000	425
S. Brido	G.R. Tracadie			Stewart	14 800	200
J. Brido	G.R. Tracadie			Stewart	7 900	100
R. Godfrey	r. Lord + Foys			Stewart	317 891	2 422
A. Sutherland	R. Pokemouche			A. Sutherland	6 368	35
J.M. Mazerolle	R. Pokemouche	16	4	B. Morton	556 741	4 528
J. Brine	R. Pokemouche	18	4	B. Morton	468 892	4 063
J. Whalen	R. Pokemouche			B. Morton	253 041	1 757
J. Robichaud	G.R. Tracadie			W. Ferguson	25 920	270
C. Comeau	G.R. Tracadie			W. Ferguson	107 148	1 060

Sources: RG10, RS107, RNA/C/3/6/1, 1881-1883; "Diaries J.McD. Barker", RG10, RS107, RNA/C/15/9/3, 1882-1883, APNB.

G = Grande

B = Branche

R = Rivière

S = Sud

N = Nord

r = Ruisseau

Naissance de l'industrie papetière et mainmise sur la forêt: Le cas de Bathurst

Serge Côté

Au tournant du siècle, l'apparition de l'industrie papetière au Nouveau-Brunswick entraîne de profonds changements dans l'allocation et l'exploitation de la ressource forestière. Depuis l'époque coloniale, la forêt avait constitué la première richesse de la province. Cependant, la forêt pléthorique, quasi légendaire, du début du XIXe siècle avait cédé le pas à une forêt ravagée. Des coupes intensives et répétées pratiquées sur les mêmes territoires et les fléaux que sont les incendies (souvent causés par les hommes) et les insectes avaient réduit de beaucoup la valeur commerciale des forêts.

Le pin avait presque disparu des forêts de la province. Le diamètre moyen des autres résineux, à cause de la surexploitation de la forêt, s'était réduit au cours des décennies et handicapait sérieusement les possibilités de l'industrie du sciage. Au début du siècle, on prenait un peu partout conscience du fait que la forêt ne constituait pas une ressource inépuisable.[1]

L'industrie du sciage au Nouveau-Brunswick, comme au Québec et ailleurs dans l'est du Canada, fut profondément désorganisée dans les années dix par la concurrence du bois du Pacifique. Depuis longtemps, on savait que les plus belles forêts du continent se trouvaient sur la côte du Pacifique, adossées aux Rocheuses. Parmi toutes les régions côtières, la Colombie Britannique recelait les plus vastes ressources forestières.

Jusqu'à l'ouverture du Canal de Panama, en 1914, les coûts de transport du bois du Pacifique constituaient l'obstacle majeur à son arrivée sur les marchés de l'est du continent. Une fois le Canal ouvert, le bois du Pacifique pouvait être transporté à coût abordable par bateau et il se conquit rapidement une place importante sur les marchés de l'Est, aussi bien aux États-Unis qu'au Canada.[2] Comme l'exportation

---

1   Sur la base des statistiques de 1917 et de 1918 (et la situation était la même depuis plusieurs années), une publication autorisée de l'industrie du papier conclut que la coupe de l'épinette et du sapin dans la province du Nouveau-Brunswick progresse à un taux beaucoup plus rapide que la pousse annuelle estimée. *A Handbook of the Canadian Pulp and Paper Industry* (Montréal, 1929), p. 72. *Le rapport de la Commission royale sur le bois à pâte* (Commission Picard) (Ottawa, 1924), pp. 28-40, juge que la situation est critique au Nouveau-Brunswick parce que les quantités coupées dépassent largement la capacité de régénération de la forêt.

2   A.R.M. Lower, *The North American Assault on the Canadian Forest* (Toronto et New Haven, 1938), pp. 196-8.

du bois d'oeuvre aux États-Unis constituait un débouché important pour les scieries du Nouveau-Brunswick, il s'ensuivit une certaine désorganisation de cette industrie qui favorisa la transition à l'industrie papetière.

Jusqu'en 1915, les usines de pâte et de papier au Nouveau-Brunswick furent des entreprises de taille relativement modeste, mais à partir de cette date, on assiste à la mise en place d'une deuxième génération d'usines de taille plus considérable. Ces usines se sont construites à même les dépouilles de l'industrie du sciage. La matière première, le bois, fut réorientée vers une industrie dont les perspectives apparurent bien supérieures à celles de l'industrie déclinante du sciage et qui savait se contenter de billes de bois de plus petit diamètre.

La forêt couvre environ 80 pour cent du territoire du Nouveau-Brunswick. Selon la Commission royale sur le bois à pâte qui a publié son rapport en 1924, la partie des terres boisées détenues par des propriétaires privés s'élevait alors à environ la moitié du patrimoine forestier de la province (10 675 milles carrés ou 2 766 960 ha, soit 49,7 pour cent du patrimoine). Soixante pour cent de ce total était constitué de terres petites ou moyennes (moins de 1 000 acres), détenues surtout par des individus. Quant aux autres terres (1 000 acres ou plus), elles étaient, à 95 pour cent, la propriété de sociétés.

Pour ce qui est des terres de la Couronne, elles représentaient une superficie à peu près égale à celle des terres privées (10 801 milles carrés ou 2 799 619 ha, soit 50,3 pour cent du patrimoine). La très grande majorité de ces terres (9 121 milles carrés ou 2 364 163 ha) étaient concédées à des individus ou sociétés qui les exploitaient à leur propre profit moyennant certaines redevances. Il ne restait que 1 680 milles carrés (435 456 ha) de terres boisées (7,8 pour cent de tout le patrimoine forestier) que l'état n'avait ni aliénées, ni affermées.[3]

Le régime de tenure a subi des modifications continuelles, tendant toutes à augmenter la période pendant laquelle les terres étaient concédées.[4] Avant 1874, la permission de couper le bois sur les terres de la Couronne était généralement accordée pour une année à la fois seulement. En 1874, le gouvernement du Nouveau-Brunswick institua des concessions d'une durée de trois ans. En 1877, la durée des concessions fut portée à cinq ans et, en 1883, à dix ans; en 1893, elle fut portée à 25 ans et en 1913 on créa des permis de 30 ans pour le bois destiné à être transformé en bois d'oeuvre et des permis de 50 ans pour le bois à pâte. La raison que l'on invoquait le plus souvent pour justifier l'extension des concessions était que cela favorisait davantage la protection de la forêt: le concessionnaire, disait-on, n'avait pas d'intérêt à ravager son territoire, mais plutôt à en planifier rationnellement l'exploitation pendant toute la durée de son permis.

---

3 *Rapport de la Commission royale sur le bois à pâte*, p. 29.

4 P.Z. Caverhill, "Forest Policy in New Brunswick", thèse de maîtrise en foresterie (Fredericton, 1917).

En fait, il semble que ce but de protection n'ait jamais été atteint quelle que fût la durée des permis. Les raisons de l'extension des concessions sont à chercher plutôt du côté des pressions des grands commerçants de bois et des industriels papetiers, d'une part, et du côté d'une certaine incurie de l'autorité publique, d'autre part. L'ingénieur forestier Caverhill l'a très bien vu au début du siècle :

> The preservation of our Crown timber Lands, their protection from fire and over-cutting, which was the strong argument for long term leases, seems altogether mythical, being entirely overlooked by the majority of leasees ....Our present policy does not tend to promote the best interests of our province as a whole, but rather of the lumber interests. The leasee is interested only in, relatively, immediate profit; and conservative methods of operation, the utilization of inferior products, the expenditure of money for the protection of young growth, are questions with which he has little sympathy.[5]

Il faut souligner aussi la nature spéculative des concessions. Même si, légalement, le concessionnaire n'est pas propriétaire de la terre qu'il loue, il peut vendre son bail à un tiers. Il peut aussi, en hypothéquant son droit de coupe, obtenir du crédit sur une valeur qui ne lui appartient pas. Le montant pour lequel est vendue une concession n'a souvent rien à voir avec le prix que le concessionnaire a dû débourser au gouvernement pour acquérir la concession et les sommes qu'il a dû verser pour en assurer le renouvellement annuel. Au début du siècle, le prix d'acquisition d'une concession des mains de la Couronne était de 8,00$ par mille carré (3 cents par ha). Ce montant pouvait être plus élevé seulement dans le cas où plus d'un acheteur se présentaient pour la même pièce de terre: l'on procédait alors par enchères. La consultation des rapports annuels du Departement des Terres de la Couronne indique que la plupart des acquisitions se faisaient au taux minimum de 8,00$ par mille carré. Quant aux renouvellements annuels, leur prix était fixé à 4,00$ par mille carré (1,5 cents par ha). Au tournant du siècle, plusieurs exploitants forestiers au Nouveau-Brunswick exigeaient entre 500$ et 1 000$ par mille carré (1,92$ et 3,86$ par ha) pour le bail de leur concession.[6] Les concessions étaient ainsi l'objet d'une intense spéculation.

Même lorsque les concessions n'étaient pas revendues, elles pouvaient être utilisées à d'autres fins spéculatives: par exemple, la réévaluation comptable des concessions constituait le moyen privilégié de souffler ou "mouiller" les actifs d'une société exploitant la forêt. Cette opération de soufflage permettait de présenter sous un jour favorable la situation financière d'une société et d'en stimuler l'écoulement des titres sur le marché. Cette situation tend à montrer que,

5   Caverhill, "Forest Policy in N.B.", pp. 24-5.

6   "New Brunswick's Forestry and Pulpwood Policy", *Pulp and Paper Magazine of Canada*, 4, 3 (mars 1906), p. 70.

malgré le régime légal qui faisait de l'état le propriétaire des terres de la Couronne, plusieurs exploitants se comportaient comme si ces terres étaient leur propre domaine privé.

Cette consécration par la législation en vigueur et par la réglementation étatique de la mainmise de certains intérêts privés sur une richesse naturelle de caractère public a été étudiée en détail par H.V. Nelles pour le cas de l'Ontario dont le régime de concessions forestières s'apparentait à celui du Nouveau-Brunswick. Il arrive à la conclusion que le renforcement du contrôle étatique sur les ressources n'a jamais signifié une démocratisation des décisions concernant leur affectation, mais plutôt une emprise plus grande du monde des affaires sur les richesses naturelles:

> I set out to ask some questions about the politics of natural resource development in Ontario. What determined the extent of the public sector in the resource economy? How had the state used its authority to promote and regulate the industrial process?...How did the political adjust to the new business responsibilities of government in the twentieth century?...Where did these questions lead me? To the conclusion that the positive state survived the nineteenth century primarily because businessmen found it useful. The province received substantial revenue from the development process and enjoyed the appearance of control over it, while industrialists used the government — as had the nineteenth-century commercial classes before — to provide key services at public expense, promote and protect vested interests, and confer the status of law upon private decisions.[7]

À plusieurs reprises au Nouveau-Brunswick, on entendit parler de demandes émanant de grands commerçants de bois ou d'industriels du papier, réclamant la création de concessions à perpétuité.[8] Ces concessions, qui finalement ne furent pas créées, auraient consacré la quasi-propriété que les grands concessionnaires détenaient sur les terres de la Couronne. En faveur de ces concessions à perpétuité, les industriels invoquaient invariablement les arguments de l'importance du capital investi et de l'incitation à pratiquer la conservation de la forêt. Les explications de Caverhill, qui a détenu le poste officiel de directeur du Service Forestier du Nouveau-Brunswick de 1915 à 1917, militent contre l'argument de la conservation: dans son étude historique, Caverhill n'a constaté aucun progrès de la conservation à mesure que la durée des concessions augmentait.[9]

---

7   H.V. Nelles, *The Politics of Development: Forests, Mines and Hydro-electric Power in Ontario, 1849-1941* (Toronto, 1974), pp. viii-ix.

8   *Pulp and Paper Magazine of Canada* (mars 1906), p. 69; 1er avril 1913, page éditoriale; 15 avril 1913, p. 278.

9   Notice biographique écrite par J.M. Gibson et figurant dans une réédition de 1938 de la thèse de Caverhill, "Forest Policy in N.B.".

Quant à l'argument de l'importance du capital investi, il faut dire qu'il était surtout utilisé par les promoteurs d'usines de pâte et de papier. Quand la Bathurst Lumber Company fut prête à annoncer un investissement papetier, elle joignit sa voix au concert des entreprises regroupées au sein de la Lumbermen and Limit Holders' Association of New Brunswick qui réclamaient des concessions à perpétuité auprès du gouvernement qui venait d'annoncer de nouvelles concessions d'une durée de 50 ans pour les usines de pâte et de papier:

> Mr. Angus McLean, of Bathurst, pointed out that his firm were prepared to develop one of the largest pulp and paper propositions in the Dominion, provided the Government would give them a reasonable show.[10]

À peine quelques mois plus tard, la firme de M. McLean mit en chantier sa nouvelle usine de pâte. Au fond, les concessions à perpétuité n'étaient pas indispensables au lancement de l'usine.

Le régime de tenure que le Nouveau-Brunswick a connu à partir du milieu du XIXe siècle a été la source d'un certain gaspillage, en ce sens qu'il ne favorisait ni les meilleures méthodes de conservation de la forêt, ni l'utilisation la plus rationnelle des essences. Le profit, sans être une considération exclusive, est toujours celle qui a primé. Cette exploitation en vue du profit fut le fait des grands aussi bien que des petits concessionnaires. Ce qui caractérise cependant les grands concessionnaires, c'est qu'ils ont systématiquement cherché à exercer un contrôle de fait sur la ressource forestière et ce contôle est de nature monopoliste.

La détention de concessions permettait aux grandes firmes non seulement de considérer les terres publiques comme leur propriété privée (et idéalement, c'était une propriété dont on aurait aimé jouir à perpétuité!), mais aussi d'être en mesure d'orienter toute l'activité forestière dans la région où elles étaient implantées. Ce contrôle de la ressource donnait aux grandes firmes la possibilité de planifier de nouveaux investissements (donc d'augmenter leur profit), de convertir leurs installations à des productions plus rentables, d'empêcher ou de limiter l'approvisionnement en bois des autres producteurs (généralement petits) et de reléguer ces autres producteurs dans des productions moins rentables.

Le fait que les concessions étaient spéculatives, sujettes à revente (et à profit) donnait aux grandes firmes une souplesse maximum. Cette particularité du régime de tenure rendait possible une concentration rapide de concessions adjacentes entre les mains d'une même firme. Il suffisait pour cela que la firme eût une base financière suffisamment solide et qu'elle sût profiter des moments où ses concurrents se trouvaient en difficulté.

Il vaut la peine de souligner l'importance de l'état dans la distribution de la propriété et l'application du régime de tenure au domaine forestier. Si, pour certains aspects de la question forestière, l'état a exercé un rôle surtout passif (par exemple,

---

10 "New Brunswick Lumbermen Protest", *Pulp and Paper Magazine of Canada,* 1er juillet 1913, p. 443.

en se contentant de percevoir les redevances sans se préoccuper de la conservation du patrimoine),[11] il a toujours été essentiellement actif dans le champ de la répartition de la richesse forestière. D'abord c'est lui qui a aliéné au Nouveau-Brunswick au cours des ans, environ la moitié du patrimoine forestier sous forme de terres en propriété privée. On sait que la part du lion des octrois de terre est allée aux compagnies de chemin de fer entre 1860 et 1880. La New Brunswick Land and Railway Company reçut à elle seule en cadeau 1 647 772 acres (2 575 milles carrés ou 667 440 ha) de terres pour l'inciter à construire un chemin de fer de 167 milles (267 km) de long,[12] de Fredericton à Edmundston, soit environ 15 milles carrés de terre par mille (2 500 ha par km) de voie ferrée!

Ensuite, c'est l'état qui, par ses lois et règlements, a aménagé le système de tenure des terres publiques. Dans son fonctionnement, cette tenure, tout en rapportant à l'état une grande part de ses revenus,[13] a laissé beaucoup de liberté aux concessionnaires et a favorisé la concentration des parcelles du domaine forestier aux mains de certains grands exploitants, que l'on affublait parfois du nom pittoresque de "lumber kings".[14] Avec le temps, de nombreux liens se sont tissés entre les intérêts forestiers et les partis politiques et ce, aussi bien au Nouveau-Brunswick qu'ailleurs au Canada. À la fin du siècle dernier et au début du XXe siècle, les grands commerçants de bois constituèrent une pépinière très florissante de députés, de ministres et de sénateurs.[15] Dans ces conditions, les intérêts des grands exploitants ont toujours été relativement bien servis. L'état, de son côté, a aidé, avec l'outil de la concession et du privilège, à la constitution d'un certain nombre de grandes fortunes privées.

Parmi les propriétaires ou concessionnaires de terres boisées, on peut distinguer au moins trois groupes: les colons, les petits exploitants (petits commerçants de bois et patrons de petites scieries) et les grands exploitants (gros commerçants de bois,

---

11 Caverhill, "Forest Policy in N.B.", p. 20.

12 R. Peter Gilles et Thomas R. Roach, *Lost Initiatives: Canada's Forest Industries, Forest Policy and Forest Conservation* (New York, 1986), p. 169.

13 Caverhill, "Forest Policy in N.B.", p. 22.

14 *Pulp and Paper Magazine of Canada* (mars 1905), p. 85.

15 Voir par exemple, "The Dimensions of a Client Province: Forestry in New Brunswick to 1939", dans Gillis et Roach, *Lost Initiatives*, pp. 161-88. Les deux auteurs font référence à plusieurs personnalités du commerce du bois qui ont occupé des postes politiques importants, tels le député fédéral F.B. Hale, le sénateur J.B. Snowball, le député provincial W. Currie et les premiers ministres provinciaux L.J. Tweedie et J.K. Flemming. Ajoutons à cette liste les noms de personnalités mentionnées ailleurs dans le présent article, soit les sénateurs Edwards, Burns et Burchill et le député provincial Sumner. Voir aussi Raymond Léger, "L'industrie du bois dans la Péninsule acadienne, 1875-1900", *Revue d'histoire de la Société historique Nicolas-Denys*, XVI, 2 (mai-août 1988), p. 54.

patrons de grandes scieries, propriétaires d'usines de pâte et de papier). Tous ces groupes ont été traversés de tensions diverses dont quelques-unes seront ici exposées.

Les rapports entre la colonisation et l'exploitation forestière ont fait l'objet d'analyses contradictoires. En ce qui concerne le Nouveau-Brunswick du début du XIXe siècle, certains auteurs comme Lower ont vu une incompatibilité profonde entre les deux activités,[16] tandis que d'autres comme Wynn ont plutôt eu tendance à voir une certaine complémentarité entre elles.[17] Pour ce qui est de la fin du XIXe siècle et du début du XXe, l'hypothèse d'une symbiose entre les deux activités a souvent été avancée.[18] Il n'en reste pas moins que le colon, tout en constituant une main-d'oeuvre indispensable à la coupe du bois en forêt, était très souvent mal vu

---

16 "No one can fail to observe the large proportion which land unfit for cultivation bears to the whole....There was a great deal of energy expended in fruitless efforts to advance the frontier of settlement beyond its natural limits....It also involved relations between the two occupations, lumbering and farming, which made for the good of neither. While the good timber lasted, it was in the province of New Brunswick that the harmful connection between lumbering (or more correctly, timber making) and farming stood out in the most vivid colours." A.R.M. Lower, *Settlement and the Forest Frontier in Eastern Canada* (Toronto, 1936), p. 31.

17 "Lumbering and farming were closely interconnected and to a considerable degree interdependent industries in New Brunswick". Graeme Wynn, "Deplorably Dark and Demoralized Lumberers? Rhetoric and Reality in Early Nineteenth-Century New Brunswick," *Journal of Forest History,* 24, 4 (octobre 1980), p. 178.

18 Dans une étude sur la localité de Saint-Quentin (N.-B.), l'auteure fait valoir qu'au-delà du discours agriculturiste qui a présidé à l'établissement du village vers 1910, il ne faut pas oublier cette "autre réalité apparamment très présente dès les débuts de Saint-Quentin, c'est-à-dire l'importance du bois. Dès les premières années, les moulins jouèrent un rôle de premier plan dans l'économie du village....Si les chiffres contenus dans les enquêtes du curé démontrent que l'agriculture était pendant longtemps l'activité principale à Saint-Quentin, il est évident que le bois aussi occupait une place de choix dès les débuts du village. Ces colons étaient à moitié bûcherons, à moitié agriculteurs....Saint-Quentin a eu une vie économique à deux volets. C'était bien une économie agro-forestière, et même si l'agriculture est devenue assez florissante, elle est toujours allée de pair avec l'industrie du bois et elle fut graduellement déplacée par celle-ci". Irène Landry, "Saint-Quentin et le retour à la terre, analyse socio-économique, 1910-1960", *Revue de la Société historique du Madawaska,* XIV, 4 (octobre-décembre 1986), pp. 27-8. Raymond Léger ("L'industrie du bois", p. 78) parle lui aussi d'économie agro-forestière. Le même diagnostic est émis dans une étude que René Hardy et Normand Séguin consacrent à la région québécoise de la Mauricie : "S'il est vrai que le monde rural a fourni sa base humaine à l'exploitation forestière, il n'est pas moins vrai que celle-ci a imprimé une marque profonde dans l'évolution de celui-là. En effet, la mise en valeur des forêts a apporté un appui à l'extension du domaine agricole et à l'éclosion de nouveaux cadres villageois. Des liens de complémentarité se sont établis entre

des grands concessionnaires forestiers, parce qu'il empiétait sur le domaine qui leur était traditionnellement réservé.[19]

À long terme toutefois, les habitants des régions de colonisation constituaient une réserve quasi idéale de main-d'oeuvre pour les travaux en forêt. Le commerce du bois connaissant de fortes variations cycliques, le colon constituait une main-d'oeuvre à bon marché qu'on n'avait pas besoin d'entretenir lorsque les affaires étaient à la baisse. Les coupes de bois s'effectuant principalement l'hiver, le bûcheron était un ouvrier qu'on n'avait pas besoin de payer pendant la belle saison. Le coupeur de bois a pendant longtemps été un travailleur semi-prolétaire et semi-paysan dont les revenus ont été très bas et la performance agricole assez piètre.[20] Malgré une certaine symbiose qui pouvait exister entre eux, il y avait parfois matière à conflit direct entre les concessionnaires forestiers et les colons:

> A more difficult situation to regulate, however, has arisen along the railroads, rivers and near the main boundary. Land is alloted to applicants for settlement even when timber licenses have been issued, and on each such allotment they are allowed to clear ten acres. The result has been that a man took up this and cut his ten acres, usually a little more, selling the wood for pulpwood, never actually settling on the land. Any merchantable timber cut, however, in this way was the property of the licensee of the limits before allotment. This has proven a prolific source of trouble and dispute. Again it was most annoying to such a licensee to have the best patch of spruce in his lease picked out and allowed to be used in this way.[21]

Dans ces circonstances, on comprend facilement que le colon ait été dénigré. Pourtant, à sa façon, il ne faisait que reproduire le comportement du concessionnaire: poursuivre son profit immédiat sans se préoccuper de la conservation à long terme de la forêt.

---

les activités forestières et l'agriculture principalement par le travail des paysans". *Forêt et société en Mauricie: la formation de la région de Trois-Rivières, 1830-1930* (Ottawa et Montréal, 1984), p. 146.

19 Pour le Nouveau-Brunswick, voir Gillis et Roach, *Lost Initiatives*, pp. 170, 173, et Léger, "L'industrie du bois", pp. 48-53; pour l'Ontario, Lower, *Settlement and the Forest Frontier*, pp. 103-12, et Nelles, *The Politics of Development*, pp. 16-7, 183-4 et 195-6; pour le Québec, Lower, *Settlement and the Forest Frontier*, p. 92, et Hardy et Séguin, *Forêt et société en Mauricie*, pp. 152-6.

20 Esdras Minville, "Le problème social de la forêt", dans E. Minnville, dir., *La forêt* (Montréal, 1944), pp. 331-5.

21 "New Brunswick Pulp Wood", *Pulp and Paper Magazine of Canada*, 1er février 1913, p. 89.

La principale tension existant entre les concessionnaires eux-mêmes venait des intérêts divergents des petits et des grands concessionnaires. Même si l'on a mentionné à quelques reprises qu'il existait un conflit entre le commerçant de bois d'oeuvre et l'industriel du papier,[22] ce ne fut généralement pas le cas entre le grand commerçant et l'industriel du papier, puisque, dans plusieurs cas, ces intérêts étaient parfaitement identiques: les promoteurs de la pâte et du papier furent souvent de grandes sociétés de sciage qui ont procédé à la diversification ou à la reconversion de leurs activités.

Le conflit entre grands et petits concessionnaires portait essentiellement sur l'accès à la ressource que constituait la forêt. En 1915, la concentration des concessions avait atteint un degré assez avancé. Cette année-là, il y avait environ 200 détenteurs de terres publiques au Nouveau-Brunswick. Les douze plus grands concessionnaires accaparaient 55 pour cent des concessions et, sur la base des droits de coupe payés, coupaient 65 pour cent du bois provenant de terres publiques.[23]

C'est sur des questions comme le "lobbying" à propos des concessions à perpétuité que l'on peut voir avec le plus de netteté les intérêts des deux groupes. Chaque groupe a son association qui agit comme organe représentatif de ses intérêts. Les petits concessionnaires sont regroupés au sein de la New Brunswick Lumbermen's Protective Association[24] et les gros concessionnaires, au sein de la Lumbermen and Limit Holder's Association of New Brunswick.[25] Cette dernière association regroupe aussi bien des commerçants de bois que des industriels du papier. Les grands concessionnaires, comme moyen de s'assurer plus complètement le contrôle de la ressource forestière, réclament l'instauration de concessions à perpétuité. Les petits concessionnaires, craignant de disparaître, s'opposent à la

22 *Pulp and Paper Magazine of Canada*, 1er février 1913, p. 88; 15 février 1913, p. 118.

23 Compilation effectuée à partir des listes publiées par le ministère responsable. Province of New Brunswick, *Annual Report of the Crown Land Department, 1915* (Fredericton, 1916).

24 *Pulp and Paper Magazine of Canada*, 15 avril 1913, p. 278. Les petits exploitants ont défendu leur cause devant l'Assemblée législative du Nouveau-Brunswick. Leur mémoire rapporte que dans la région de la Miramichi, 18 petits exploitants (dont les usines sont évaluées à 338 000$) se partagent 213 milles carrés (55 210 ha) de concessions; d'autre part, huit exploitants (usines évaluées à 386 000$) totalisent 2 306 milles carrés (597 715 ha) de concessions. Ces 2 519 milles carrés (652 925 ha) de concessions constituent pratiquement toutes les terres de la Couronne de la région de la Miramichi. Si les terres sont concédées à perpétuité, comme le demandent les grands exploitants, les petits exploitants perdent à tout jamais l'espoir d'agrandir leur territoire. Cet exemple montre que parfois l'ampleur des concessions (ici rapport de 1 à 10,8 entre petits et grands exploitants) a plus d'importance que le capital immobilisé dans les usines (rapport de 1 à 1,1).

25 *Pulp and Paper Magazine of Canada*, 1er juillet 1913, p. 443.

perpétuité tout en réclamant des mesures draconiennes qui soutireraient certaines terres de la Couronne des mains des grands concessionnaires: limitation de la superficie cumulative des concessions d'une même firme à 100 milles carrés (25 920 ha) (alors que certaines grandes sociétés détiennent plus de 1 000 milles carrés [259 200 ha]!), possibilité de n'obtenir à la fin du bail que la moitié des anciennes concessions à titre de renouvellement, etc. À l'occasion de ce débat, chaque partie, dans un effort pour détruire la légitimité des revendications de son adversaire, accuse l'autre partie de pratiquer des méthodes de coupe qui ne respectent pas les principes de la conservation.[26]

La nature spéculative des concessions (dont on pouvait céder le bail à un tiers) conduisait à une concentration de plus en plus poussée. Les groupes aux moyens financiers les plus importants étaient en mesure d'amener sous leur contrôle l'étendue de terres publiques qu'ils jugeaient souhaitable. Pour cela, ils n'avaient, à la rigueur, pas besoin de recevoir ces concessions directement des mains du gouvernement: ils pouvaient très bien les acheter de ceux qui les détenaient déjà. Dans ce rapport de forces, les petits exploitants étaient moins bien armés, ce qui explique qu'ils se développèrent moins vite que les gros.

Avant le début de la fabrication de la pâte à Bathurst en 1915, il existait quatre usines de pâte ou de papier au Nouveau-Brunswick. De plus, deux autres usines avaient fonctionné pendant quelques années avant d'être démantelées toutes les deux en 1910.[27] La capacité d'aucune de ces six usines ne dépassait 50 tonnes par jour et trois d'entre elles ne produisirent jamais plus de 30 tonnes par jour. Ces capacités modestes font de ces six usines une génération à part dans l'histoire papetière du Nouveau-Brunswick. La nouvelle usine de Bathurst en 1915, quant à elle, avec ses 100 tonnes de capacité quotidienne, était la première représentante de la deuxième génération. Les dates de mise en marche des usines de la première génération s'échelonnent entre 1889 et 1908. Cinq produisaient exclusivement de la pâte et une produisait de la pâte et du papier. Trois étaient situées dans l'estuaire de la Miramichi, le deuxième cours d'eau du Nouveau-Brunswick; deux se trouvaient à l'embouchure du fleuve Saint-Jean, dans la ville du même nom; une était à Saint-George sur le littoral de la baie de Fundy.

La plupart de ces usines connurent un fonctionnement erratique. Certaines changèrent de propriétaires plus d'une fois, d'autres fermèrent. La précarité marquait l'industrie papetière à ses débuts. L'une des causes les plus évidentes de cette instabilité des débuts est à chercher du côté des conditions d'approvisionnement en bois. Le contrôle de l'approvisionnement en matière première constituait un

---

26 *Pulp and Paper Magazine of Canada,* 1er mai 1913, page éditoriale.

27 Voir, Burt Glendenning, *The New Brunswick Pulp and Paper Industry, 1900 to 1930,* travail réalisé dans le cadre du cours History 622 (Prof. Richard Wilbur), Montréal, Concordia University, 30 mars 1974, 36 pp.; Georges Carruthers, *Paper in the Making* (Toronto, 1947), pp. 365-83.

élément stratégique de première importance dans la survie de toute usine de pâte et de papier au début du siècle.[28]

Or, à cette époque, la plupart des grandes réserves de matière ligneuse, que ce soit sous forme de concessions du gouvernement ou de propriétés privées, étaient détenues par des industriels du sciage ou des commerçants de bois.[29] Il n'y avait que deux possibilités pour les promoteurs des pâtes et papiers. Ou bien ces derniers étaient complètement étrangers à l'industrie du sciage et devaient alors acheter des commerçants de bois les terres forestières nécessaires à leur affaire; ou bien l'initiative de lancer une usine papetière venait des industriels du sciage. Les grands industriels du sciage qui disposaient d'importants domaines forestiers ont bénéficié d'une situation très propice pour créer des usines de pâte ou de papier. Souvent d'ailleurs, l'ampleur des concessions forestières qu'ils détenaient a permis à ces industriels du sciage de mener de front les deux activités, sciage et fabrication de pâte et de papier. Plusieurs des "dynasties" de commerçants de bois ont effectué leur reconversion dans les premières années du XXe siècle: les firmes J. R. Booth et James Maclaren de l'Outaouais, la firme Price du Saguenay et la firme Fraser du Nouveau-Brunswick sont des exemples bien connus.

Le commerce du bois, au début du XIXe siècle, s'effectuait exclusivement avec la métropole, la Grande-Bretagne. À partir de la décennie 40, le bois d'oeuvre prit de plus en plus souvent le chemin des États-Unis. Le développement des canaux et du système ferroviaire, la mise en vigueur du traité de Réciprocité (1855-1866), l'urbanisation rapide des États-Unis poussaient dans ce sens. Vers la fin du siècle, l'essor de l'industrie papetière aux États-Unis créa une demande supplémentaire pour le bois canadien. Des quantités considérables de bois à pâte étaient exportées à l'état brut aux États-Unis. On estimait que le tiers du bois à pâte utilisé au sud du 45e parallèle venait du Canada.[30]

Au Nouveau-Brunswick seulement, les quantités de bois à pâte exportées aux États-Unis atteignaient 141 500 cordes en 1913.[31] L'International Paper, qui n'avait à l'époque aucune usine de pâte ou de papier au Nouveau-Brunswick, mais qui avait commencé à collectionner des concessions qu'elle rachetait à des marchands de bois, était l'un des plus gros exportateurs.[32] Les réactions à cette situation furent

28 "The Pulp and Forestry Problem in New Brunswick", *Pulp and Paper Magazine of Canada*, octobre 1905, pp. 281-2.

29 "Industriels du sciage" et "commerçants de bois" sont des expressions à toutes fins utiles synonymes. Pour les petits exploitants, ces deux fonctions peuvent se concevoir l'une sans l'autre, mais, pour les grands exploitants, elles vont de pair.

30 *Pulp and Paper Magazine of Canada*, octobre 1905, p. 280.

31 S.A. Saunders, "Forest Industries in the Maritime Provinces", dans Lower, *The North American Assault*, p. 351. Le bois à pâte exporté représentait une quantité presque trois fois supérieure au bois à pâte transformé au Nouveau-Brunswick.

32 Glendenning, *N.B. Pulp and Paper Industry*, pp. 20, 31-3.

nombreuses et ressemblèrent à celles que l'on a retrouvées à la même époque en Ontario et au Québec, c'est-à-dire que l'on a assisté à des prises de positions diamétralement opposées selon les intérêts que l'on représentait. La solution d'un embargo a été proposée à plusieurs reprises.[33] Certains industriels canadiens, telle la famille Burchill de la région de la Miramichi (dont l'un des membres fut sénateur), espéraient que les restrictions à l'exportation favorisent un développement au Canada de l'industrie papetière.[34] Les sous-traitants qui, au Québec et au Nouveau-Brunswick, approvisionnaient les papeteries américaines s'opposèrent à toute restriction des exportations qu'aurait pu imposer leur gouvernement respectif.[35] Le gouvernement du Nouveau-Brunswick s'est finalement résolu, à l'instar de l'Ontario en 1900 et du Québec en 1910, à décréter en 1912[36] un embargo sur l'exportation du bois à pâte coupé sur les terres de la Couronne. Le bois à pâte coupé sur les propriétés privées pouvait continuer à être expédié à l'étranger sans restrictions.

En 1913, le gouvernement américain permit pour la première fois l'entrée en franchise de la pâte de bois et du papier journal canadien aux États-Unis. Plus que l'effet de l'imposition d'embargos canadiens, il faut voir dans cette décision de supprimer le tarif le résultat des pressions des propriétaires de journaux américains.[37] L'action combinée de l'entrée en franchise de la pâte et du papier journal aux États-Unis et de l'embargo canadien sur l'exportation de bois à pâte allait-elle être suffisante pour susciter l'implantation d'un grand nombre d'entreprises papetières? À court terme, cela précipita sans doute certaines décisions: c'est après 1913 que l'on vit apparaître au Nouveau-Brunswick les usines de deuxième génération, c'est-à-dire des usines de capacité sensiblement plus grande que celles du tout début du siècle. Ces usines sont, par ordre d'apparition, celle de Bathurst en 1915 (capacité de 100 tonnes par jour), celle de la Fraser à Edmundston en 1918 (160 tonnes), celle de la Fraser à Atholville en 1929 (150 tonnes) et celle de l'International Paper à Dalhousie en 1930 (225 tonnes).

---

33 *Pulp and Paper Magazine of Canada*, mars 1906, p. 69; avril 1910, p. 84; mai 1910, p. 115.

34 *Pulp and Paper Magazine of Canada*, février 1906, p. 46; avril 1910, p. 34.

35 *Pulp and Paper Magazine of Canada*, juin 1903, p. 59.

36 La mesure fut votée avant 1912, mais n'entra en vigueur que le 1er août 1912. *Pulp and Paper Magazine of Canada*, 1er janvier 1913, p. 36.

37 John A. Guthrie, *The Newsprint Paper Industry, An Economic Analysis* (Cambridge, Mass., 1941), p. 43; Louise Toupin, *L'intervention du premier ministre Taschereau lors de la crise du papier, 1927-1935*, thèse de maîtrise en sciences politiques à l'Université de Montréal (1972), p. 204. L'auteur s'appuie sur l'opinion de Hugh Aitken (*The State and Economic Growth*, p. 105) et de la Commission royale d'enquête sur les perspectives économiques du Canada (*Les perspectives de l'industrie forestière au Canada*, pp. 99-100).

L'accès à des terres forestières, dans les conditions régnant au début du siècle, constituait un élément stratégique dans la réussite de toute entreprise papetière. Les promoteurs de la papeterie de Bathurst s'installèrent au Nouveau-Brunswick en 1907 comme commerçants de bois sous la raison sociale Bathurst Lumber et procédèrent à l'agrandissement de leurs concessions forestières lorsqu'ils décidèrent, quelques années plus tard, de faire le saut dans l'industrie papetière. La grande majorité des terres forestières du nord du Nouveau-Brunswick appartenant à la Couronne et étant déjà concédées à des gens intéressés au bois d'oeuvre, il fallait pour s'y implanter faire l'acquisition de scieries et des concessions s'y rattachant.

À sa fondation en 1907, la Bathurst Lumber acquit les intérêts que la firme Sumner Company possèdait à Bathurst. Les débuts de cet établissement, dont la fondation est due à des immigrants britanniques, remontent à 1832,[38] ou 1834.[39] Dès le début, la coupe du bois fut l'une des activités de l'entreprise, qui maintint également un chantier naval et un magasin général. La famille Ferguson (dont l'un des membres fut sénateur) fut copropriétaire de l'affaire jusqu'en 1876.[40] De 1876 à 1896, l'établissement changea de propriétaire à plusieurs reprises. Vers 1896, la firme Sumner de Moncton racheta l'affaire.[41]

Les Sumner étaient des grossistes en quincaillerie et matériaux de construction et désiraient se tailler une place dans le domaine du sciage. F.W. Sumner avait été cinq fois maire de Moncton et était député de la circonscription de Westmorland à l'Assemblée législative de Fredericton. Après avoir acheté la scierie, les Sumner rénovèrent complètement l'équipement. En 1897, l'entreprise détenait 200 milles carrés (51 840 ha) de concessions forestières.[42]

En 1907, lorsque l'affaire (scierie, concessions, magasins, maisons) fut revendue par les Sumner à la Bathurst Lumber au prix de 130 000$,[43] la superficie des concessions forestières atteignait 400 milles carrés (103 680 ha).[44] Ces concessions

---

38 *The Bathurst Story*, Montréal, 18 novembre 1958, p. 1.

39 Numéro spécial consacré à la ville Bathurst, *The Busy East of Canada*, 10, 11 (juin 1920), p. 10.

40 *The Bathurst Story*, p. 1.

41 *The Wood Industries of New Brunswick in 1897* (Fredericton [Archives provinciales du Nouveau-Brunswick], 1969 [1897]), p. 22.

42 *Wood Industries of N.B. in 1897*, p. 23.

43 Document interne relatant l'histoire de la société depuis 1907 (date probable 1934), p. 1. Ce document sera désigné ci-après comme "Document interne". Deux autres sources indiquent un prix d'achat de 250 000$; cependant, comme le chiffre de 130 000$ se retrouve dans un document interne de la société, c'est ce dernier chiffre, plus fiable, qui sera retenu. Pour les deux autres sources, voir *Pulp and Paper Magazine of Canada*, octobre 1907, p. 226 et *The Maritime Merchant*, 17 octobre 1907, p. 26.

44 *Pulp and Paper Magazine of Canada*, 1er décembre 1915, p. 611.

couvraient les bassins des cours d'eau suivants: Tétagouche, Middle, Little, Millstream, Grant's Brook.[45] La transaction excluait une petite partie des concessions de la Sumner Company, soit celles situées sur un cours d'eau (Bartibog) qui ne se déversait pas dans les environs de Bathurst.[46] En 1908, la Bathurst Lumber reconstruisit la scierie qu'un incendie venait de détruire. De l'équipement moderne y fut installé.[47]

Au début du siècle, Bathurst ne comptait que deux scieries financièrement solides.[48] La première avait été acquise par la Bathurst Lumber en 1907; l'acquisition de la seconde sera complétée en 1912. Cette deuxième entreprise fut lancée vers 1870 par K.F. Burns (député aux Communes, puis sénateur): elle comprenait une scierie et un magasin général.[49] C'est ce même Burns qui construisit un chemin de fer entre Bathurst et Shippagan au "scandale" duquel Myers consacra un passage dans sa célèbre étude sur les grandes fortunes du Canada.[50] En 1890, la propriété de l'entreprise de sciage et du chemin de fer est transférée à la St. Lawrence Lumber Company, Limited, société dont la gestion est assumée par la famille Burns.[51] À la suite d'une faillite et de l'arrivée d'un partenaire américain, un nouveau groupe est mis sur pied, vers 1896, Adams, Burns and Company. La propriété fut achetée par Adams & Co., de New York, des mains de syndics londoniens. La direction générale fut assumée par T.D. Adams.[52] Après cette réorganisation, le contrôle de l'entreprise semble avoir été pris par les associés américains.[53] En 1897, la firme disposait de 250 milles carrés (64 800 ha) de concessions forestières dans la région de Bathurst.[54] En 1898, la Adams, Burns and Company projeta de fabriquer de la pâte de bois et obtint à cette fin du Conseil de comté une exemption de taxes valable pour 20 ans, exemption qui fut ensuite entérinée par une loi votée à l'Assemblée législative.[55] On ne donna pas suite au projet.

---

45 "Document interne", p. 1; D. McLaren et Myles Russell, *A Brief Report on the History of the Bathurst Power and Paper Company* (Bathurst, 1958), p. 3.

46 McLaren et Russell, *A Brief Report*, p. 4

47 *The Bathurst Story*, p. 2.

48 *The Wood Industries*, p. 22.

49 *The Busy East*, 10, 11 (juin 1920), p. 11.

50 Gustavus Myers, section sur le *Caraquet Railway*, dans son livre *History of Canadian Wealth* (Chicago, 1914), pp. 320-3. Une nouvelle édition est parue à New York en 1968 chez Argosy Antiquarian Ltd.

51 *The Busy East*, 10, 11 (juin 1920), p. 11.

52 *The Wood Industries*, p. 22.

53 Glendenning, *N.B. Pulp and Paper Industry*, p. 14.

54 *The Wood Industries*, p. 22.

55 Victoria 1899, 69. Voir *Acts of New Brunswick*, 1899, pp. 276-7.

En 1909, la Adams Burns vendit à des intérêts américains, constitués en société sous le nom de Nepisiquit Lumber Company, Limited, sa scierie et ses concessions forestières situées sur la rivière Népisiquit.[56] Apparemment, la Adams Burns garda la propriété de son chemin de fer et d'une autre scierie (avec les concessions attenantes) qu'elle possèdait à Burnsville, à environ 40 milles à l'est de Bathurst. Elle garda également la propriété de certaines concessions qu'elle possédait près de Bathurst et qu'elle céda en 1911 à la Bathurst Lumber. Ces concessions longeaient les cours d'eau suivants: Bass, Nigadoo, Elmtree.[57] Les seules concessions importantes qui échappaient encore à la Bathurst Lumber étaient celles bordant la rivière Népisiquit qui étaient aux mains de la Nepisiquit Lumber. Cette dernière société était formée de capitalistes américains de Springfield au Massachussets et de représentants de la A.S. Shermon Lumber Company de New York[58] (Sisson Lumber Company, selon une autre source).[59] Ces capitalistes new-yorkais étaient déjà actifs dans la fabrication de pâte et de papier aux États-Unis.[60]

En 1908, au moment de leur constitution en société, les propriétaires de la Nepisiquit Lumber annoncèrent qu'ils allaient faire le commerce du bois à pâte.[61] En 1909, après avoir acquis les actifs (fabrique de bardeaux et concessions forestières) d'un petit exploitant, O.F. Stacy, la Nepisiquit Lumber annonça cette fois son intention de fabriquer de la pâte.[62] Ce projet ne se concrétisa jamais. Sans doute afin d'améliorer leur position sur le marché du bois d'oeuvre, les promoteurs de la Nepisiquit Lumber, vers 1910, reconstruisirent, sur le même emplacement, la scierie qu'ils avaient achetée de la firme Adams Burns. L'année suivante la Nepisiquit Lumber était en faillite[63] et retourna à ses anciens propriétaires, la Adams Burns, qui la revendirent en 1912 à la Bathurst Lumber.[64]

À partir de 1912 donc, la Bathurst Lumber détenait toutes les concessions forestières importantes situées le long des rivières entourant Bathurst. L'acquisition des ex-intérêts Nepisiquit lui conféra le contrôle virtuel de la rivière Népisiquit, la plus importante de la région. Au total, l'acquisition en deux temps, au coût combiné de 210 000$, des anciennes concessions de la firme Adams Burns en 1911 et en

---

56 McLaren et Russell, *A Brief Report*, p. 4.

57 *The Bathurst Story*, p. 2.

58 Glendenning, *N.B. Pulp and Paper Industry*, p. 14.

59 McLaren et Russell, *A Brief Report*, p. 4.

60 Glendenning, *N.B. Pulp and Paper Industry*, p. 14.

61 *Pulp and Paper Magazine of Canada*, janvier 1908, p. 20.

62 *Pulp and Paper Magazine of Canada*, juillet 1908, p. 207.

63 Glendenning, *N.B. Pulp and Paper Industry*, p. 15.

64 *The Busy East*, 10, 11 (juin 1920), p. 11.

1912 ajouta 500 milles carrés (129 500 ha) au territoire de coupe de la Bathurst Lumber.[65]

En 1913, la société se porta acquéreur d'une dernière concession d'importance, le long de la rivière Népisiquit, celle de John et George Robertson de Bathurst, au coût de 38 500$, ce qui rajouta 150 milles carrés (38 880 ha) au domaine forestier de la société.[66] Elle avait maintenant accès à des concessions "making a total of 1050 square miles [272 160 ha], or practically all of the timber lands in the Bathurst watershed".[67] Sur une période de 16 ans, soit de 1897 à 1913, la région de Bathurst avait été témoin d'une course folle à la concentration des concessions forestières. En effet, non seulement la Bathurst Lumber avait-elle réussi à amalgamer les deux plus importantes entreprises de la région, mais ces deux entreprises elles-mêmes, entre 1897 et la date de leur acquisition, étaient parvenues à doubler, évidemment aux dépens de plus petites firmes, leur propre domaine forestier. La hantise du papier a sans doute contribué à accélérer cette concentration. L'industrie du papier connaissait un essor prodigieux au tournant du siècle. Le marché américain, affamé de papier, suscitait, partout où se trouvait de la forêt en Amérique du Nord, une ébullition sans précédent.

La concentration n'était pas une réalité nouvelle dans la forêt néo-brunswickoise. Graeme Wynn, dans son étude de l'exploitation forestière dans la première moitié du XIXe siècle, fait remarquer que quatre établissements appartenant à deux entreprises, Gilmour et Cunard, détenaient en 1836-7

> licences for approximately one third of the timber and almost 18 per cent of the lumber scheduled to be cut in the province on one-year permits. A decade later, when licences were issued on a different basis the four companies held almost 40 per cent of the licensed area in the province....The social consequences of this growing dominance of large concerns in the timber trade were profound....Throughout the province, large firms increasingly set prices and governed the terms of access to the timber trade.[68]

La Bathurst Lumber, maintenant locataire de 1 050 milles carrés (272 160 ha) de terres de la Couronne et propriétaire de deux scieries très récentes (1908 et 1911), était devenue l'une des premières firmes de sciage du Nouveau-Brunswick, en tout cas celle qui avait à sa disposition les plus grandes concessions de terres publiques (10,1 pour cent de toutes les terres publiques concédées) et celle dont la facture de droits de coupe était la plus importante du Nouveau-Brunswick (18,8

---

65 "Document interne", p. 1.

66 *Gloucester Northern Light*, 24 juin 1914; "Document interne", p. 1.

67 *Pulp and Paper Magazine of Canada*, 1er décembre 1915, p. 611.

68 Graeme Wynn, *Timber Colony: A Historical Geography of Early Nineteenth Century New Brunswick* (Toronto, 1981), pp. 125, 134.

pour cent de l'ensemble des droits de coupe acquittés au Nouveau-Brunswick).[69] L'étendue de ses terres forestières lui permettait désormais d'envisager de se lancer dans la fabrication de la pâte à papier.

Certains des associés qui avaient fondé la Bathurst Lumber en 1907 avaient déjà des propriétés dans la Baie-des-Chaleurs, du côté québécois. Ils s'y étaient même installés quelques années plus tôt, en 1904, en fondant une société en vertu d'une loi du parlement fédéral, la Cascapedia Manufacturing and Trading Company.[70] La Cascapedia allait devenir en 1920 filiale de la Bathurst Lumber et allait permettre l'adjonction de ses propres concessions forestières à celles de la Bathurst soit une superficie de 1 068 milles carrés (276 825 ha) couvrant un territoire situé dans le bassin des rivières Cascapédia et Petite Cascapédia.

En 1909, Edwards et McLean, deux cofondateurs de la Bathurst Lumber, avaient aussi acheté 450 milles carrés (116 640 ha) de concessions forestières le long de la rivière Bonaventure en Gaspésie. Ils en transférèrent la propriété à la Bathurst Lumber en 1915, au moment où la fabrication de pâte commence à Bathurst. Le bois des trois rivières gaspésiennes commença à être toué à Bathurst en 1915. Les scieries gaspésiennes qui avaient été acquises en même temps que les concessions continuèrent à fonctionner pendant quelques années, puis furent définitivement fermées.

Les acquisitions successives effectuées au Nouveau-Brunswick et au Québec ont porté en une dizaine d'années (1904-13) les concessions forestières sous le contrôle des associés de la Bathurst Lumber à un total de 2 600 milles carrés (673 920 ha) en chiffres ronds. De plus, la société détenait 15 milles carrés (3 888 ha) en propriété privée.[71] C'était plus qu'il n'en fallait pour commencer la production de pâte et de papier. Toutes ces terres avaient été rachetées de commerçants de bois (voir Carte 1).

La Bathurst Lumber fut fondée par un groupe de capitalistes américains et canadiens. Un processus assez curieux fit que l'on mit en évidence tantôt la propriété américaine, tantôt la propriété canadienne de l'entreprise, selon les époques et selon les sources. Ainsi, pendant les premières années, les journaux d'affaires présentent la firme comme étant à propriété américaine, sans autres précisions.[72] Il se peut qu'une certaine méprise ait régné puisque deux des partenaires canadiens, les frères McLean, résidaient aux États-Unis depuis longtemps

---

69 Province of New Brunswick, *Annual Report of the Crown Land Department, 1915* (Fredericton, 1916).

70 Edward VII, c. 64. Voir *Statutes of Canada,* 1904, vol. 2, pp. 89-93.

71 *Pulp and Paper Magazine of Canada,* 1er décembre 1915, p. 611.

72 *The Maritime Merchant*, 8 août 1907, p. 25 ("large American Firm") et 17 octobre 1907, p. 26 ("American concern"); *Pulp and Paper Magazine of Canada,* octobre 1907, p. 226 ("United States capitalists") et 1er janvier 1913, p. 4 ("American concern").

et y avaient lancé leur propre firme de commerce de bois. Malgré tout, un des cofondateurs était le sénateur W.C. Edwards d'Ottawa; le sénateur était une personnalité bien connue à son époque et dirigeait, entre autres, l'une des plus grandes entreprises de sciage de l'Outaouais. Il n'en reste pas moins que la présence de capital canadien n'est pas mentionnée à cette époque. Quelques années plus tard, les journaux d'affaires insistent sur le caractère hybride, canadien et américain, de la société.[73] Après 1930, toutefois, tous les documents émanant de la firme ou de ses cadres passent sous silence les copropriétaires américains pour ne mettre en évidence que le rôle des partenaires canadiens. Sans aucun doute, l'occultation de la participation du capital américain dans les premières décennies de la vie de l'entreprise procède de la canadianisation complète du capital de l'entreprise qui aura lieu pendant les années trente.

Les associés canadiens de la Bathurst Lumber furent (à l'exception d'Eckardt) les mêmes qui fondèrent la Cascapedia en 1904. Le capital de la Cascapedia était divisé en trois fractions: 40 pour cent était détenu par la W.C Edwards and Company, Limited; 40 pour cent, par la Hugh McLean Lumber Company, Limited; et 20 pour cent par A.J.H. Eckardt. Ce dernier était un magnat de l'industrie du cercueil à Toronto. Les Edwards et les McLean, quant à eux, étaient des commerçants de bois de la vallée de l'Outaouais. Edwards était originaire d'Ottawa, tandis que les McLean venaient de Thurso au Québec.

La vallée de l'Outaouais fut un des hauts lieux du commerce du bois au XIXe siècle. Dès que les canaux et les chemins de fer purent permettre un lien avec la vallée, le bois de l'Outaouais commença à être expédié sur le marché américain, à côté duquel subsista toutefois l'important marché britannique. Le capital américain abondait à Ottawa vers 1850.

Avec le temps, les firmes canadiennes se développèrent et ce furent bientôt elles qui essaimèrent aux États-Unis:

> The expansion and consolidation of these native Ottawa Valley firms were naturally accompanied by changes in their methods of financing and marketing. In the days when the Albany market dominated the Ottawa [1840-80], the American wholesalers used to have their buyers in Ottawa. Now for many years past one of the large firms has its own travelers or resident agents in the United States, selling to the wholesale houses there. A good many Canadian firms have their American sales offices.[74]

C'est ce chemin qu'allaient suivre les frères McLean en allant s'installer à Buffalo. En 1895, Angus rejoint son frère Hugh qui, déjà aux États-Unis depuis un certain temps, y a fondé sa propre firme, la Hugh McLean Lumber.

---

73 *Pulp and Paper Magazine of Canada*, 1er décembre 1915, pp. 611-2, 19 octobre 1922, p. 907; *The Busy East*, juin 1920, p. 46.

74 Lower, *The North American Assault*, pp. 168-9.

Carte 1

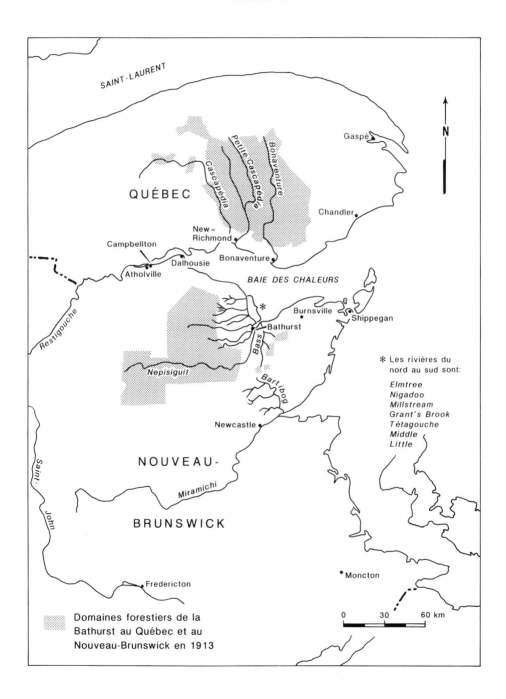

Domaines forestiers de la Bathurst au Québec et au Nouveau-Brunswick en 1913

La présence des frères McLean à Buffalo les mettait en contact avec l'un des marchés du bois les plus vastes et les plus diversifiés d'Amérique du Nord. La localité de Tonawanda, en banlieue de Buffalo, allait acquérir cette importance en devenant le point d'aboutissement du canal Erié (ouvert en 1825):

> The Erie Canal and the other canals had brought about the erection of mills at strategic points upon them, the barge system of forwarding timber, and the growth of the great lumber markets of Tonawanda and Albany.[75]

C'est sans doute à Buffalo que les McLean intéressèrent quelques Américains à venir avec eux exploiter la forêt de la Baie-des-Chaleurs. Les associés américains ne firent leur apparition qu'en 1907, lors de la fondation de la Bathurst Lumber. Les cinq personnes mentionnées dans les lettres patentes de la société en 1907 sont toutes de Buffalo (New York) et sont toutes commerçants de bois de profession. Parmi elles, les deux Canadiens Angus et Hugh McLean et trois Américains, M.E. Preisch, C.M. Carrier et Burton Fowler Jackson.[76] Même si son nom ne figure pas dans les lettres patentes, le sénateur W.C. Edwards participa aussi à l'organisation de la société.[77] La documentation disponible ne permet pas d'établir la composition du conseil d'administration de la firme pour les années antérieures à 1915. Cette année-là, les Américains occupaient sept des dix sièges du conseil d'administation, les trois autres sièges étant occupés par Angus et Hugh McLean ainsi que par le sénateur Edwards.

Les administrateurs américains en 1915 venaient tous du nord de l'état de New York et du nord de la Pennsylvanie et se partageaient en deux groupes: ceux qui étaient liés au commerce du bois et ceux qui représentaient des entreprises financières, dont le magnat Fred Kirby. Les firmes d'où venaient les premiers semblent n'avoir eu aucun intérêt dans la pâte et le papier et ne semblent pas avoir eu une envergure autre que régionale à l'intérieur des États-Unis. En effet, aucune de ces personnes ne figure dans les *Who's Who* ou les dictionnaires biographiques américains. Pour ce qui est de Kirby, c'est différent. Ce financier de Wilkes-Barre était à la tête d'intérêts considérables dans le commerce de détail (cofondateur de la firme Woolworth à laquelle il apporta 96 magasins lors de la fusion du tournant du siècle) et les chemins de fer. En 1915, au moment de se lancer dans la fabrication de la pâte, la Bathurst Lumber effectua un emprunt obligataire de 1 000 000$ dont le fiduciaire fut la Miners Bank of Wilkes-Barre que présidait Kirby. Le jeune fils de Fred Kirby, Allan, travailla comme cadre administratif à la Bathurst Lumber pendant la période de construction de l'usine de pâte en 1914 et 1915.[78] A cette époque,

---

75   Lower, *The North American Assault*, p. 59.

76   Lettres patentes de la Bathurst Lumber Company, Limited, Ottawa, Secretary of State of Canada, 14 novembre 1907.

77   *The Busy East*, 10, 11 (juin 1920), p. 46.

78   *Who's Who in America*, vol. 1 (A-K), 37e parution, 1972-1973 (Chicago, 1972), p. 1726, et *Who Was Who in America*, vol. 1 (Chicago, 5e éd.), p. 681.

on ne connaît à la famille Kirby aucun intérêt dans le commerce du bois ou l'industrie papetière. Il faut donc en conclure que pour les Kirby, la Bathurst Lumber représentait un placement parmi d'autres et qu'elle était intéressante dans la mesure où elle saurait rapporter des intérêts et des dividendes satisfaisants ou encore dans la mesure où elle permettrait la réalisation d'un gain de capital au moment de la vente des actions.

Avec le développement de l'industrie papetière au tournant du siècle, l'exploitation des forêts a connu des changements importants, tels que l'allongement des baux forestiers et l'utilisation d'arbres de petit diamètre. Un des changements les plus importants fut toutefois la concentration des terres forestières et leur monopolisation par un petit nombre d'entreprises. L'état a joué dans cette évolution un rôle de premier plan en mettant en place les mécanismes institutionnels (essentiellement le système des concessions) permettant la réalisation de ces transformations.[79]

Les entreprises qui ont été actives dans le secteur papetier au début du siècle étaient souvent des grandes firmes de sciage qui se reconvertissaient en tout ou en partie à la fabrication de pâte ou de papier. Ce fut le cas pour les propriétaires de la Bathurst Lumber qui se lancèrent en 1915 dans la fabrication de pâte de bois. Dans ce mouvement de reconversion, il ne fait pas de doute que les impératifs de marché aient tenu une place considérable: la pâte offrait des perspectives de rentabilité plus grandes que le sciage affecté par l'arrivée du bois du Pacifique sur les marchés de l'est du continent. Cependant, cette évolution, et surtout la forme qu'elle a prise, n'a pas été dictée par une fatalité imposée par les pures lois du marché.

La gestion du patrimoine forestier, l'allocation de la ressource aux industriels, le commerce lui-même du bois et des produits du bois ont fait l'objet de politiques diverses de la part de plusieurs gouvernements (régimes provinciaux de concessions forestières, embargos provinciaux sur l'exportation de bois non transformé provenant des terres publiques, droits de douane imposés par les gouvernements centraux). Ces interventions aux multiples formes ont influencé profondément la façon dont la ressource a été récoltée, transformée, transportée, etc. D'autres choix auraient pu être faits qui auraient conduit à d'autres usages de la forêt.

Les interventions étatiques ne faisaient d'ailleurs jamais l'unanimité. Sur toutes les questions cruciales reliées à la forêt, on peut relever des divergences d'intérêts et des rapports de force qui ont marqué l'adoption des grandes politiques des gouvernements. Le clivage le plus significatif dans l'avènement de l'industrie papetière semble avoir été celui qui divisait le petit capital et le grand capital. À travers la réalisation d'investissements papetiers, les grands exploitants ont renforcé leur

---

79   Gillis et Roach: "There existed in New Brunswick in the period from 1860 to 1940 almost a client state perilously dependent on its forest industry", *Lost Initiatives*, p. 163. La même expression d'"état client" est utilisée par Nelles pour qualifier l'attitude du gouvernement de l'Ontario envers les grands exploitants forestiers de cette province à la même époque. Voir *The Politics of Development,* pp. 214, 495.

emprise sur la ressource forestière. Ces grands exploitants venaient parfois de l'industrie du sciage ou provenaient parfois d'autres secteurs de l'économie. Ils étaient parfois canadiens ou parfois étrangers (surtout américains). Toujours, pour assurer le succès de leurs entreprises, ils ont cherché à déployer des stratégies visant à accroître leur contrôle de la ressource ligneuse. La concentration des terres forestières semble avoir été au début du siècle leur arme la plus efficace dans cette lutte pour le contrôle de la ressource.

Forest Policy in Nova Scotia:
The Big Lease, Cape Breton Island, 1899-1960[*]

L. Anders Sandberg

In the late 19th century, the government of Nova Scotia began to cast envious glances at industrial forest development in Ontario, Quebec and New Brunswick where large areas of Crown forest were used to attract pulp and paper mills through long-term lease arrangements. In Nova Scotia, much of the forest land had been sold off in fee simple to settlers and lumbermen; only an estimated 1,500,000 acres (607,500 ha) of relatively poor-quality and difficult-to-access Crown forest remained. Provincial politicians lamented this situation, but argued that if Nova Scotia had a lease system similar that of New Brunswick, the revenue of the Crown Land Office could increase fivefold.[1] In response to such arguments, provincial forest policy was changed in 1899. A new act, intended to promote forest management and raise revenue from Crown lands, stipulated that timber lands could be leased for 20 years, with an option for renewal, for a rental fee of 40 cents per acre (16 cents per ha) (two cents per acre [.8 cents per ha] per annum). Under these arrangements, cutting was limited to trees at least 10 inches in diameter. But a special provision, included to accommodate the burgeoning pulp and paper industry, permitted a reduction of the diameter limit to five inches upon payment of an additional 10 cents per acre (4 cents per ha). No stumpage fees were charged for trees cut, an omission criticized almost from the inception of the Act.[2] Yet despite such generous terms, when the Chief Forester of Nova Scotia reviewed the system in the mid-1920s, he found that the diameter limits on Crown leases were not enforced, lessees disregarded them, and the rent was consequently "ridiculously small".[3] And although the annual rental fee was increased over the years, one later

---

* Previously published in *Acadiensis*, XX, 2 (Spring 1991), pp. 105-28.

1 Nova Scotia, House of Assembly, *Debates*, (Halifax, 1898), p. 135.

2 Nova Scotia, *Debates* (1901), p. 74.

3 Otto Schierbeck, Chief Forester, to J.C. Douglas, Attorney-General, 20 January 1926, MG 2, vol. 597, Folder 71, no. 16150, Public Archives of Nova Scotia [PANS]. In the 1930s, officials of the Department of Lands and Forests found that in some instances, the revenue from Christmas tree sales for a single year proved greater than the revenue from rental fees for the whole duration of a previous lease. Personal interview with Wilfrid Creighton, Provincial Forester and Deputy Minister of Lands and Forests, 1934-1969, 28 October 1988.

observer concluded that, whether judged on a conservation or a revenue basis, the act was a "short-sighted and costly blunder".[4]

Nevertheless, the 1899 Lease Act constituted the beginning of a provincial policy toward pulp and paper industry development. The most significant clause in this regard offered even more generous terms to lessees interested in marginal timber land and to those who were prepared to improve and build manufacturing facilities. This clause was inserted to allow the lease of the only extensive, contiguous block of Crown land left in the province, the so-called Big Lease, covering about 620,000 acres (251,100 ha), located in the counties of Inverness and Victoria on Cape Breton Island, to a group of New England financiers for a period of 30 years[5] (see Figure 1). In return, the lessees agreed to pay an annual rental of $6,000, to build two pulp mills, expending $10,000 on each within two years, and to refrain from exporting unmanufactured wood. If, after four years, two pulp mills, each with a daily capacity of at least 50 tons had not been established, the lease would be void.[6]

This paper analyses the nature and impact of provincial forest policy by examining the history of the Big Lease from its inception in 1899 to its repurchase and re-lease by the provincial government in 1957 and 1960. Several phases are identified; during the first, from 1899 to 1917, the Big Lease constituted a speculative venture, promoted by a Gilded Age entrepreneur and supported by government. The second phase of the Big Lease, from 1917 to 1931, was exploitative. During this period of boom in the pulp and paper industry, a large international pulp and paper company harvested a limited area, exporting the pulpwood to its mill in Maine. The third phase of the Big Lease constituted a new speculative phase, in which the company, following a pattern common among American-owned pulp and paper companies of the era, purchased or held cheap woodlands in Nova Scotia for speculative purposes, kept harvesting to a minimum, and fought land tax and municipal assessments while boosting the value of its leases and freeholds to shareholders and potential buyers. The company's speculative aspirations were realized on two occasions, both at the expense of its initial benefactor, the province of Nova Scotia. In 1936, the Liberal administration of Angus MacDonald re-appropriated the poorer parts of the Big Lease to accommodate the federally sponsored Cape Breton Highlands National Park, and, in 1957, the Conservative

---

4   Wilfrid Creighton, *Forestkeeping: A History of the Department of Lands and Forests in Nova Scotia* (Halifax, 1988), p. 20.

5   Nova Scotia, *Debates* (1899), p. 78.

6   These conditions were combined with certain reservations. The lease reserved the right of settlers and squatters, the right of government to grant lots of 200 acres (81 ha) to *bona fide* settlers and state ownership of streets and roads. Nova Scotians were to be allowed to hunt and fish on the limits of the lease and settlers could continue to use the forest for firewood and construction material. Finally, all transfers of the lease were to have the approval of the Attorney-General.

Figure 1

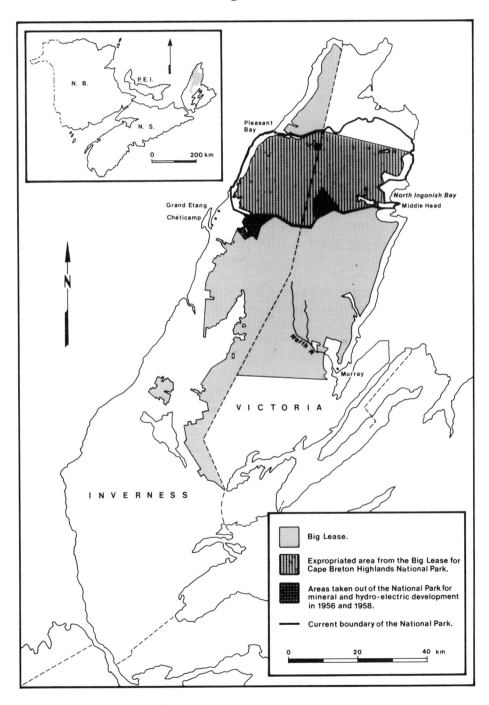

administration of Robert Stanfield, hoping to attract to the province a Swedish pulp and paper company, Stora Kopparberg, bought back the remainder.

The initial terms of the Big Lease were not unique but consistent with provincial development policy at the time. As in the case of coal and iron development on Cape Breton Island, the government looked to the big industrial promoters of New England to provide the source of investment. To the government, the Big Lease represented a marginal and difficult-to-access resource base which had to be marketed aggressively and generously. In contrast to Henry Whitney, who had asked for the most favourable terms imaginable and then settled for something less in promoting Cape Breton coal and steel, the promoter of the Big Lease asked for the most favourable terms imaginable and then settled for much more.[7] Negotiations for the Big Lease got underway in March 1898. By February 1899, a Halifax law firm, Pearson and Covert, acting in conjunction with Mr. Edwin Sanborn, a member of the consortium of entrepreneurs interested in obtaining the lease, had produced a draft document. The lease, introduced in the legislature on 18 March, passed — with one additional major concession — as first formulated.[8] The concession, outlined in a wire from Pearson and Covert to Sanborn on 25 May 1899, offered to extend the lease from 30 to 99 years. Sanborn wired back the same day: "Will accept the lease, have written".[9]

Thus the Big Lease was awarded to Daniel T. Emery, merchant, of Portland, Maine, Edwin L. Sanborn, merchant, of Boston, Massachusetts, and Robert H. Blodgett, manufacturer, also of Boston.[10] It was generally known, however, that Frank John Dixie Barnjum, an industrial promoter and operator, who would later become a self-styled forest conservationist, was the leading player in the consortium. Barnjum controlled two industrial ventures in Victoria and Inverness counties,

---

7   Don MacGillivray, "Henry Melville Whitney Comes to Cape Breton: The Saga of a Gilded Age Entrepreneur", *Acadiensis*, IX, 1 (Autumn, 1979), pp. 44-70.

8   Nova Scotia, *Debates* (1899), p. 164ff. Although Premier George Murray had consulted J. M. Gibson of the Department of Crown Land in Ontario, concerning the practice of issuing Crown leases in that province, he did not follow the Ontario example. Gibson had admitted that "pretty liberal concessions" seemed necessary to attract pulp ventures but noted that Ontario was aiming to require lessees to establish manufacturing facilities in the province. He enclosed an 1888 agreement between Ontario and the Sturgeon Falls Pulp Company which required production of at least $5,000 of pulp per annum, as well as the building of a $1 million paper mill in return for the use of 75 square miles (19,440 ha) of Crown lands for 21 years at a stumpage rate of 20 cents per cord for spruce and hardwood and 10 cents per cord for other wood. J.M. Gibson to George Murray, 17 April 1899, RG 7, vol. 130, PANS.

9   RG 10, vol. 130, PANS.

10 Emery was also a backer of the Rumford Falls Paper Company, the predecessor of the International Paper Company, and the Great Northern Paper Company, International Paper's major competitor in Maine. David Smith, *Lumbering in Maine 1861-1960* (Orono, Maine, 1972), pp. 250, 252.

the North American Paper and Lumber Company, which had been granted the Big Lease, and the North River Lumber Company, which owned 8,000 acres (3,240 ha) of forest lands in the area.[11]

The extension of the term of the lease to 99 years was justified on the grounds that the shorter term "was not sufficiently long to ensure...a sufficient permanency for the investment of the large amount of capital required for the effectual carrying out of the purposes intended by the said lease". This concession, along with others which followed, and which were all aimed at making the lease more acceptable to potential buyers, served to dilute the terms of the lease in subsequent years.[12] Thus, in 1900, the time limit for initiating the construction of the pulp mills was extended to three years and the limit for completion of the mills to five years. In 1901, these limits were extended to five and seven years respectively. The same order proclaimed that "all wood cut and shaved ready for being made into pulp shall, for the purposes of the said lease, be considered as manufactured". In 1904, the condition requiring the establishment of two pulp mills was rescinded after the company claimed it had expended a considerable sum of money but found it impracticable to operate a pulp industry in the area.

The 1901 concessions allowed Barnjum to limit his manufacturing operations to a small rossing mill, which merely stripped the bark off the logs. Such a mill was built and operated, along with five camps in the woods, four on the East branch and one on the Middle branch of the North River in 1902. Two dams were also constructed. The mill operation, however, was a half-hearted effort. The leaseholders proved reluctant to invest sufficient money and in 1907, after only 15,000 cords of log-length choice lumber had been harvested, the operations were closed. In the same year the mill burned. Barnjum's woodlands manager at the time, Thomas Bateman, later emphasized that the mill was never meant as a viable industrial operation, its main function being to make the Big Lease more attractive to poten-

---

11 The names of these companies were used interchangeably in the debates of the local legislature. Nova Scotia *Debates* (1911), p. 187. Barnjum (1858-1933) was born in Montreal but launched his business career in Maine by opening a sawmill and acquiring some timber limits. By 1898, Barnjum had become a major industrial promoter. From clippings in MG 100, vol. 108, no. 12, PANS. For a more detailed discussion of various aspects of Barnjum's career, see: Peter Gillis and Thomas Roach *Lost Initiatives: Canada's Forest Industries, Forest Policy and Forest Conservation* (Westport, Conn., 1986), pp. 199-203; Thomas Roach and Richard Judd, "A Man For All Seasons: Frank John Dixie Barnjum, Conservationist, Pulpwood Embargoist and Speculator!", *Acadiensis*, XX, 2 (Spring 1991), pp. 129-44; J.M. Beck, *Politics in Nova Scotia, Volume Two: 1896-1988* (Tantallon, 1988), p. 110; and Thomas Raddall's novel, *The Wings of Night* (London, 1961 [1957]).

12 These concessions, contained in a series of Orders in Council, were conveniently recorded in the Nova Scotia, *Debates* (1905), pp. 152-3.

tial buyers. A lease with associated manufacturing facilities was always easier to sell profitably.[13]

Barnjum also employed a series of professional forest inventories or cruises to promote a sale. Reports from 1904, 1908, 1915 and 1916 estimated the amount of softwood at 12 to 14 million cords.[14] B.E. Fernow, later Dean of Forestry at the University of Toronto and a renowned and respected professional, also cruised the area for a syndicate interested in the purchase of the lease. Shortly thereafter, he was employed by the Commission of Conservation to conduct an independent forest inventory of the whole of Nova Scotia. Fernow estimated that the plateau portion of Victoria and Inverness counties (the Big Lease) contained about 10 million cords of pulpwood, while the rest of Cape Breton held two million cords and mainland Nova Scotia 10 million cords.[15] Yet while Fernow's estimates appear to confirm Barnjum's figures, it should be noted that cruisers applied several standards when performing forest inventories. One was speculative and aimed at boosting the financial standing of the company for its shareholders, bankers and potential buyers; another was based on biological principles, the species available and their suitability for pulpwood regardless of cost and delivery to the mill; a final standard was based on the narrow economics of forest exploitation by the pulp companies, the cost of getting the wood out of the forest and delivered at the mill. Barnjum, interested in selling the lease, no doubt biased his inventories in the direction of the highest possible figures, and although the volumes reported may well have been an accurate inventory of total softwood stands,[16] they were greatly exaggerated with respect to merchantable volumes. Barnjum's own woodlands manager, for example, estimated the amount of merchantable wood at a mere 3.5 million cords.[17]

By 1913, Barnjum had interested new partners in his speculative venture, and they approached the government to negotiate new terms. The old lease was cancelled and a new one issued to Rene T. Paine of Brookline, Massachussetts, and

---

13 Evidence of Thomas Bateman, RG 10, Series B, vol. 204, pp. 1378-82, PANS.

14 "In re Expropriation of Lands of the Oxford Paper Company, Decision of Doull, J. sitting as Arbitrator", RG 39, Series "C", vol. 905, Halifax, 1940, SC 10438, PANS [hereafter cited as Doull Decision, 1940], pp. 6-7.

15 B.E. Fernow, *Forest Conditions in Nova Scotia* (Ottawa, 1912), pp. 24-5. For a history of the life of Fernow, see Andrew Rodgers III, *Bernhard Eduard Fernow: A Study of North American Forestry* (Princeton, 1951). In the concluding remarks of the company report, Fernow wrote: "I do not know of any better located, more compact and promising pulpwood proposition on the market". RG 10, Series B, vol. 204, Exhibit L/57, PANS.

16 The provincial forest inventory of 1956, for example, came up with similar figures to Fernow. The softwood volumes for Fernow and the provincial inventory were as follows: Cape Breton Island, 14 versus 12.5 million cords; mainland Nova Scotia 35.9 versus 42.5 million cords. Lloyd Hawboldt and R.M. Bulmer, *The Forest Resources of Nova Scotia* (Halifax, 1958), pp. 31-2. See also Creighton, *Forestkeeping*, p. 24.

17 Doull Decision, 1940, pp. 6-7.

Clarence Hale of Portland, Maine, both associates of Barnjum. Two years later the Big Lease was assigned to the Cape Breton Pulp Company, Limited, which had been formed in 1913 by a merger of the North American Pulp Company and the North River Lumber Company. One of the provisions in the 1915 lease prohibited the export of unmanufactured timber, but defined wood that was "barked, rossed or hand-peeled ready for manufacture into pulp" as manufactured lumber. This convenient clause would, in the future, allow leaseholders to phase out manufacturing operations altogether, while still retaining the lease and the right to export pulpwood. In April 1915, the lease was ratified and confirmed by an act (Chapter 84) of the Nova Scotia Legislature.[18] The new lease required the expenditure, within two years, of the modest sum of $20,000 in the erection of mills and machinery for the manufacture of wood products or pulp. The term was 20 years (from 1913) and subject to renewal for two terms of 20 and 25 years respectively.[19] With a new lease sanctioned by a legislative act, Barnjum began construction of a new rossing mill with a shipping pier, completing the venture the following year. The new mill's capacity was 80 cords per 10-hour day and its cost was estimated at $125,000.

In January 1917, Barnjum finally succeeded in selling the lease, realizing a "commission" estimated at $1.5 million, 250 years worth of rental fees at $6,000 per year! The purchasers, Hugh J. Chisholm and his wife Sarah, sold it, later in the same day, to the Cape Breton Pulp and Paper Company of which Hugh was president. In April 1920, the Big Lease changed hands for the last time when the Cape Breton Pulp and Paper Company was sold to the Oxford Paper Company, over which Hugh Chisholm also presided.[20] Oxford retained the lease until it was bought back by the government in 1957. By peddling the lease between the Cape Breton Pulp and Paper Company and the Oxford Paper Company, Hugh J. Chisholm also realized a handsome personal profit, receiving 3,000,000 common shares, $500,000 in bonds and $651,996 in cash.[21] And, through these financial transactions, the province realized its own objective of selling the Big Lease to a large American pulp and paper company.

18 The Act of 15 April 1915 also noted that the owners of the former lease had expended a sum of $185,000 and paid to the province the sum of $78,000 in rentals since the lease was first issued in 1899.

19 A copy of the lease is contained in RG 10, Series B, vol. 206, PANS.

20 Hugh Chisholm's father had been the first president of International Paper, a position he resigned in 1909 to take up the presidency of the Oxford Paper Company. When he died in 1912, his son took over the presidency and retained it until 1957. *Hugh J. Chisholm, A Man and the Paper Industry, 1847-1912* (New York, 1952) and John Leane, *The Oxford Story: The History of the Oxford Paper Company* (Rumford, 1958).

21 Doull Decision, 1940, p. 7; RG 10, Series B, vols. 200-6, PANS; and Ralph Johnson, *Forests of Nova Scotia* (Halifax, 1987), p. 118.

The government exhibited a remarkable and unqualified support for Barnjum's speculative machinations. In response to criticism from the opposition, Premier George Murray referred to the lands as unprofitable and claimed that in the past nobody had wanted them. In this situation, argued the premier, the government had no choice but to grant Barnjum the concessions requested. "Personally, he [the premier] would extend the time for building mills for ten, fifteen, or twenty years. What else was he to do? If he did not, the lease would be forfeited and ended". In justifying the lack of pulp mill development on the Lease, he pointed to the poor quality of the timber and the lack of water power in Inverness and Victoria counties, hinting that these conditions had been known from the beginning of the lease.[22] Finally, by asserting that he regretted being forced to discuss these issues publicly since his statements were likely to "interfere with the value of the property rights" of the leaseholders, the premier tacitly sanctioned the Big Lease as a speculative venture.[23]

When the legality of the concessions granted by Orders in Council was called into question, the premier acted to correct the problem.[24] According to Murray, the legislative Act of 1915 was "intended to cure a technical point which had been raised in England and elsewhere", no doubt in response to Barnjum's various attempts to sell the Lease, as to "the power to surrender Crown Lands". The new act settled the legality of the lease, while giving credence to the opposition's contention that the government was more concerned about maintaining the confidence of the international financial community, and the image of Nova Scotia as a speculative haven and secure place of investment, than about challenging the company on the terms of the lease.[25]

The interdependence of government and big business extended towards the counties and the electorate of the Big Lease. On the one hand, the premier might have expected to gain some personal credibility from the Big Lease. He represented Victoria County in the provincial legislature and took a personal interest in negotiating and defending the lease. In reciprocating, the company named its little

---

22   Nova Scotia, *Debates* (1905), p. 156.

23   The speculative nature of the Big Lease was widely recognized in other than government circles. In 1913, the names of Paine and Hale figured in the Boston newspapers as the owners of pulp tracts in Cape Breton worth "several million dollars". Members of the Opposition charged that these newspaper articles provided proof that "the lease was not given for the purpose of development, and the Government must have known that it was not to be developed by the lessees but trafficked from country to country with a view to put it on the market". Nova Scotia, *Debates* (1913), pp. 414, 417.

24   This issue had first been raised as a potential problem in 1905. Nova Scotia, *Debates* (1905), pp. 156, 159-61.

25   Nova Scotia, *Debates* (1915), pp. 222-3.

mill settlement "Murray", after the premier, and openly "encouraged" its employees to support the "proper" political party. A letter to a local newspaper following the federal election of 1904 provides effective testimony concerning Barnjum's active support for the government in that campaign. He thanked "all my employees for the loyal support which they gave me for D.D. McKenzie, Esquire", noting that "that not a single man out of my whole force violated his pledge to me is probably a record seldom before equalled".[26] The government, in its turn, supported Barnjum. The leaseholders, as well as local politicians and the electorate, benefited from a 1912 law which stipulated that the rental money paid by the leaseholders was to go to road building in the counties of the lease. When challenged by the opposition, the premier defended the law on the grounds that there were no railways in the counties of Inverness and Victoria.[27] Barnjum was clearly a favoured client of the province. The statement by one of the members of the opposition that "if any Company that was ever formed had a friend in court in Nova Scotia, a friend in the Government today occupying the treasury benches, it was the North River Lumber Company",[28] appeared to hold true. Barnjum not only received various concessions and favours, he also used his political connections in attempting to market the Lease. Thomas Bateman, his woodlands manager, testified that "Mr. Chisholm told me...that Barnjum told him that...in Nova Scotia...there would never be any embargo [on the export of pulpwood]...and he was...not a member of the Government but good friends with the Government, and Mr. Chisholm said he told him, in that case I will give you so many shares of stock and you will always be on the Board of Directors".[29]

With the sale of the Big Lease to the Oxford Paper Company, the provincial government realized its original development strategy, the attraction of a major pulp and paper company to the province. But the Oxford Paper Company, which concentrated on the finer grades of paper, was unlikely to move its operations to Canada, a practice confined to the large integrated newsprint mills.[30] Its purchase of

---

26 Quoted in Nova Scotia, *Debates* (1905), p. 154. Barnjum's support of the federal Liberals continued for some years. In 1922, he wrote Mackenzie King offering his full support in a by-election: "If there is anything I can do, do not fail to call on me as we must now win every by-election". Barnjum to King, January 31, 1922, King Papers, vol. 69, C2242, National Archives of Canada [NAC]. Thanks to Bill Parenteau for this reference.

27 Nova Scotia, *Debates* (1913), p. 457.

28 Nova Scotia, *Debates* (1913), p. 421.

29 Evidence of Thomas Bateman, RG 10, Series B, vol. 204, p. 1388, PANS. It is interesting to note that even when Nova Scotia did impose an embargo on the export of pulpwood from Crown lands in the late 1920s, the last province to do so, the embargo did not apply to the Big Lease.

30 In the late 1920s, American branch plants, mainly integrated newsprint mills, represented 76 per cent of the capital invested in the Canadian pulp and paper industry.

the Big Lease had been prompted by the motive of securing a wood reserve for its paper mill in Rumford, Maine. By 1913, the company had already acquired the stumpage rights on 119,500 acres (48,398 ha) of Crown lands and on 53,000 acres (21,465 ha) of land owned by a seminary in Montmorency County, Quebec, and was shipping about 25,000 cords of rossed pulpwood annually from that province to its mill in Rumford, Maine.[31] In New Brunswick, Oxford acquired 51 per cent control of the Nashwaak Pulp and Paper Company with a mill at Fairville, as well as 230,000 acres (93,150 ha) of freehold forest lands and stumpage rights on 140,000 acres (56,700 ha) of Crown lands in 1916. From 1910 to 1939, the company received 54 per cent of its spruce and fir pulpwood from Canada. Between 1920 and 1931, Cape Breton became the most important source, supplying an annual average of 42 per cent of all softwood to the Rumford mill.[32]

During this exploitative phase of the Big Lease, the Oxford Paper Company was involved in a major expansionary phase of its mill facilities in Maine. From

J.W. Shipley, *Pulp and Papermaking in Canada* (Toronto, 1929), p. 125. In 1937, 73 per cent of all newsprint consumed in the United States came from Canada and almost all pulp produced in Canada was used in the production of newsprint for the American market. The production of newsprint in the United States declined from 1,618 thousand tons in 1908 to 832 thousand tons in 1937. P.J. Reinertsen, "The Pulp and Paper Industries in Sweden and Canada", Ph.D. thesis, University of Chicago, 1958, p. 37. The developing scarcities of pulpwood in the United States and the economies of scale afforded by integrated newsprint industries were important factors in the establishment of such mills in Canada. Other factors were the removal, in 1913, of the $3.75 per ton duty on newsprint imported into the United States, a victory for the American newspaper lobby (L. Ethan Ellis, *Newsprint: Producers, Publishers, Political Pressures* (New Brunswick, N.J., 1960)), the large Crown leases and other generous benefits awarded to the newsprint mills by the Dominion and Provincial Governments, and the several acts prohibiting the export of wood cut on Crown lands. The economics of production and the uniformity of newsprint, however, were the main incentives for locating in Canada. John A. Guthrie, *The Newsprint Paper Industry: An Economic Analysis* (Cambridge, 1941), p. 222; Nathan Reich, *National Problems of Canada: The Pulp and Paper Industry in Canada* (Montreal, 1926), p. 55ff; T.J.O. Dick, "Canadian Newsprint, 1913-1930: National Policies and the North American Economy", *Journal of Economic History*, 42 (September 1982), pp. 659-87. Many newsprint producers closed their American operations and moved northward, but others converted to finer types of paper whose mills benefited from being close to consumers and whose products were protected by tariffs. In contrast to the integrated newsprint mills, it was, therefore, less likely for a paper mill specializing in the finer grades of paper to move to Canada.

31   Leane, *The Oxford Story*, p. 22.

32   RG 10, Series B, vol. 204, no. 13, Exhibits L/28 and L/29, PANS. By 1926, the merchantable pulpwood in Quebec was inaccessible due to the provincial export embargo on pulpwood from Crown lands and the holdings were sold to the Anglo-Canadian Pulp and Paper Company.

1920 to 1929, paper production at the Rumford mill increased from 79,155 to 100,345 tons. The company also acquired a subsidiary company, the Oxford Miami Company, of West Carollton, Ohio, in 1926. As a result of this expansion, considerable investments were made in the Big Lease. The capacity of the rossing mill was upgraded from 80 to 250 cords per ten-hour day by the addition of a barking drum.[33] A total of $626,164 was expended on dams, camps, river improvements, roads, fire towers, telephone lines, machinery, buildings, booms, floating equipment and an auto truck. Opportunities for employment reached their height in 1920 when 885 men were working in the woods and 136 at the mill.[34] Yet, even so, the work remained seasonal, employing mainly farmers, and operations were suspended during the haying season.[35] Moreover, by 1931 the number of men employed had fallen to just 84 in the woods and 39 at the mill.

Later that year, the Oxford Paper Company closed down its mill operations altogether, justifying its decision on the grounds of the declining competitiveness of Cape Breton pulpwood.[36] The closure, when it finally came, was not unexpected. During the boom of the early 1920s, the company had adopted a policy of using its own stumpage. Although the machine-rossed pulpwood from the Big Lease proved relatively expensive, continued production was necessary to meet the company's wood requirements at that time. By 1926, however, the company had begun to purchase some rough and sap-peeled wood from contractors and jobbers. This carefully organized winding-down process corresponded to the industry's convention of keeping wood reserves while buying wood from private producers.[37] Eventually, only sap-peeled wood was purchased. This shift to the use of sap-peeled wood, which is lighter, resulted in the reduction of transport costs. At the mill, it obviated the need to replace costly barking equipment which was practically worn out, or renew dilapidated conveyors. By purchasing wood, while at the same time selling off equipment, the company managed to reduce inventories considerably by the time it finally closed operations in 1931.[38] Remaining equipment which was not antiquated, such as electric motors, was shipped to the company's operations on the Nashwaak River in New Brunswick. By then, the forest at the North River site had

---

33   G. Harvey, "Oxford Paper Company, Cape Breton Division, Report on Cape Breton Properties", MG 10, vol. 203, no. 43, PANS. Unless otherwise stated, all subsequent information on the Murray operations are gathered from this document.

34   An interesting description by workers at the woodlands and mill operations at Murray is given in "In the North River Lumber Woods", *Cape Breton's Magazine*, 7 (1974), pp. 2-9.

35   "The Resources of North Inverness", RG 12, vol. 1958, File 3508-19, vol. 3, p. 18, NAC. Thanks to Danny Samson for this reference.

36   RG 10, Series B, vol. 204, Exhibit L/44 and MG 100, vol. 203, no. 43, PANS.

37   Evidence of Charles A. Gordon, RG 10, Series B, vol. 203, p. 6, PANS

38   Harvey, "Oxford Paper Company".

been stripped and in 1933 a company spokesman observed that the area was "very clean cut and any wood standing was practically worthless".[39]

The closure of the Cape Breton operations was also related to the Depression of the 1930s, for the Oxford Paper Company did not prove immune to the problems of overproduction and diminishing profits which plagued the industry as a whole. The company's production of paper fell from 100,345 tons in 1928 to 64,536 tons in 1932.[40] Profits, calculated on the basis of the difference between manufacturing costs per ton of paper and its average net selling price, fell from $22.71 to a low of $6.80 by 1932.[41] At this stage, the company started to purchase wood locally in Maine for half the price of the pulpwood produced in Cape Breton, and the production and export of pulpwood from the Big Lease was almost abandoned.[42]

The exploitative phase in the history of the Big Lease, which depended on seasonal wage labour to cut the wood on the North River watershed, was a function of the economic boom and the wood scarcities of the time. Recruitment of labour on the wage principle was not difficult. Wages offered by the Oxford Paper Company were considered good and both the Royal Commission investigating the lumber industry and the Workmen's Compensation Board praised the company for its fine safety record in the woods.[43] The wage nexus no doubt contributed to the high cost of the pulpwood. In 1923, Hugh Chisholm testified that "the farmer can produce wood cheaper than the company can. This is a well known fact, I do not know why, but it is so". Chisholm would willingly have bought all the farmers' wood had they been able to deliver it to the shipping piers at Murray.[44] The purchase of pulpwood from farmers and contractors had to await the development of a physical and social infrastructure consisting of roads, railroads, jobbers and contractors, a system which grew in importance during the Depression of the 1930s and beyond.[45]

---

39 Harvey, "Oxford Paper Company".

40 Leane, *The Oxford Story*, pp. 26, 29.

41 RG 10, Series B, vol. 204, no.13, Exhibit L/106, PANS.

42 Doull Decision, 1940, p. 12.

43 Carl D. Dennis, *Royal Commission on the Ratings of the Lunenburg Fishing Fleet and the Lumber Industry as Applied to the Workmen's Compensation Board* (Halifax, 1927)

44 Royal Commission on Pulpwood, Evidence, vol. 1, p. 145, RG 39, vol. 593, NAC.

45 This was a complex process. During the 1930s, when pulpwood was exported to Germany, and during the immediate post-World War II period, when Marshall dollars promoted overseas trade in pulpwood, small producers were reluctant to produce pulpwood and contract labour, often Acadians and Québécois, had to be imported. Interview with Wilfrid Creighton, 11 April 1990. In a region, such as Sweden, where forest workers were strong and unionized, terms of work progressed from contract to

The 1920s constituted an exploitative but also challenging phase in the history of the Big Lease. After over 44 years of Liberal rule, the Conservative government of E.N. Rhodes gained office in 1925. In their drive to victory, the Conservatives charged that the Liberal administration was a "corporation government dominated by an invisible Government...kept in office by designing groups and corporations; who for years have been exploiting the people of this province for their own private gain".[46] The Big Lease was repeatedly referred to in this connection.[47] In 1926, the new government merged the Department of Crown Lands with the Department of Forests and Game to form the Department of Lands and Forests.[48] Ironically, F.J.D. Barnjum, who had switched party affiliations and was now a Conservative MLA, had a major influence on the new department.[49] Barnjum was instrumental in the appointment of Otto Schierbeck, whom he had previously employed as a "public forester" for Nova Scotia, as Chief Forester of the Department of Lands and Forests and in the appointment of W.L. Hall, legal representative for his own extensive timber holdings and a former leader of the Conservative party, as Minister of Lands and Forests.[50]

Once established, the new department faced two major and conflicting objectives: on the one hand, how to remedy the shortfalls of past forest policies, and, on the other, how to attract wood-producing industries to the province. Hall and Schierbeck, with Barnjum's support, became ardent opponents of the Big Lease. Schierbeck argued that not only were the larger provincial freeholds and Crown leases held by United States corporations, but also that they were, in most cases, "idle, kept by the Company as a reserve".[51] Schierbeck lamented the fact that the Oxford Paper Company had cut only 281,500 cords in 12 years. Characterizing this

---

sub-contract to industrial wage work in the 1920s and 1930s. On Cape Breton Island, as in many other areas of North America, development regressed from industrial wage work to the contract system

46 *Halifax Herald* quoted in E. Forbes, "The Rise and Fall of the Conservative Party in the Provincial Politics of Nova Scotia, 1922-1933", M.A. thesis, Dalhousie University, 1967, p. 26.

47 See, for example, *Morning Chronicle*, 20 June 1925.

48 Creighton, *Forestkeeping*, pp. 29ff.

49 Beck, *Politics in Nova Scotia*, p. 109. Barnjum had changed political affiliation in 1923 when the Liberal government failed to implement a national export embargo of Canadian pulpwood. Elected as a Conservative in 1925, the following year he resigned his seat in the legislature, having failed to build a pulp mill promised in the election campaign.

50 Roach and Judd, "A Man For All Seasons"; Forbes, "The Rise and Fall of the Conservative Party", pp. 58, 103.

51 Schierbeck to J.C. Douglas, Attorney-General, 20 January 1926. MG 2, vol. 597, Folder 71, no. 16150, PANS. In 1923, Crown lands constituted a mere 8.5 per cent of all forest land and 75 per cent was covered by the Big Lease.

as "hoarding", he urged that "the remaining...wood on the Big Lease...be cut as soon as possible before it deteriorizes [sic]".[52] He claimed that the Big Lease entailed a considerable loss to the province and recommended that the Oxford Paper Company, along with other American corporations, be required to work their leases or turn them back to the Crown for re-lease to other parties. As well as the re-possession of Crown lands, Schierbeck advocated a prohibition on the export of pulpwood from Crown lands and large private holdings.[53] In 1930, in response to these recommendations, the government introduced Bill 151, which would give the Governor in Council power to ban pulpwood exports from holdings of more than 1,000 acres (405 ha). If proclaimed and enforced, the bill would have forced the large landowners or leaseholders to sell their lands or build pulp and paper mills in the province.[54]

At the same time as Hall and Schierbeck were arguing in favour of the promotion of industrial development through tougher legislation, other factions in the provincial government pressed for a continuation of the well-worn policy of concessions. Upon its election in 1925, the new government was deluged with proposals for pulp and paper industry development. Local as well as international promoters sought guaranteed access to pulpwood from the province's Crown lands, but, given the very limited amount of Crown lands available, only one enterprise could be considered. The successful bidder was the Royal Securities Corporation. I.W. Killam, the company's major investor, started building the Mersey Paper Company's newsprint mill at Liverpool in 1928. The company, which received generous concessions in the supply of power to the mill, was guaranteed 1,000,000 cords of pulpwood, at an initial rate of $1 per cord stumpage, from selected Crown lands in Guysborough County and on Cape Breton Island. Hugh J. Chisholm, the holder of the Big Lease, and one of the unsuccessful bidders, expressed no hard feelings.[55] Instead, he visited Rhodes to give evidence of the worth of the Big

---

52   "Memorandum regarding the Big Lease", 13 March 1930, RG 20, vol. 749, no. 5, PANS

53   Slightly over 40 per cent of all forest land was held by large landholders and corporations. Canadian ownership constituted 83 per cent while three American pulp companies held the rest. In total, it was estimated that 17 to 20 per cent of all pulpwood resources were controlled by American interests. Canada, *Royal Commission on Pulpwood*, Sessional Paper No. 310, 1924, pp. 14-6. In 1926, Schierbeck noted "the alarming rate in which the American pulp and paper producers are buying Nova Scotian freehold land for the export of pulpwood. Over 2,000,000 acres [810,000 ha] of the best timberlands of the Province are in the hands of American pulp and paper companies who have no manufacturing plans in the Province and are only concerned in the export of pulpwood". Nova Scotia, Department of Lands and Forests, *Annual Report*, 1927 (Halifax, 1928), p. 42.

54   Bill 151 was preceded by a bill that would tax all pulpwood cut but not manufactured in the province, but that bill was stymied by the legislative council. Beck, *Politics in Nova Scotia*, p. 119.

55   MG 2, vol. 629, file 85, PANS.

Lease, possibly pointing to the poor reserves and the monies expended on development, rental fees and taxes.[56] And, at a meeting with Hall and MLA Percy Black in January of 1928, he managed to negotiate some further concessions with respect to the Big Lease.[57]

In the struggle between regulation and concession in forest policy, concession prevailed. Hall and Schierbeck met fierce resistance from the large foreign holders of forest lands and their political supporters. Premier Rhodes believed that the finances of the province would not allow the purchase of the forest reserves of American absentee pulp companies. And he thought any other, more drastic act presented "a very grave problem, involving as it does a question of property rights which will have to be dealt with as a matter of general policy effecting [sic] the whole Province".[58] Therefore, in the end, the premier refused to support Bill 151, arguing that it was not within the competence of the province "to pass legislation by way of embargo upon wood cut on lands owned in fee simple".[59] Strongly opposed in the local legislature, protested by the large holders of forest lands, and lacking the solid support of government leaders, the bill was never proclaimed.

Once Bill 151 had failed, the days of regulatory forest policies were numbered. Hall was appointed Justice of the Supreme Court of Nova Scotia in 1931 and John Doull, the new Minister of Lands and Forests, bluntly opposed Schierbeck's attempts at regulation of the industry.[60] In 1933, Barnjum died and Schierbeck was dismissed.[61] In the same year, the first 20-year term of the Big Lease expired, but it was renewed by Doull for an additional 30 years. Shortly thereafter, following the defeat of the Conservative government in the provincial election of 1933, the entire staff of the Department of Lands and Forests was dismissed and the department reorganized.[62]

---

56 MG 2, vol. 597, Folder 71, nos. 16145-6, PANS.

57 No details are provided of these concessions. R.P. Bell to E.N. Rhodes, 29 January 1928, MG 2, vol. 629, file 85, PANS.

58 Isaac C. Spicer to E.N. Rhodes, 14 November 1925, and E. N. Rhodes to Isaac C. Spicer, 23 November 1925, MG 2, vol. 597, Folder 71, nos. 16162, 16164, PANS

59 He did feel, however, that a tax on felled timber, refunded if the wood was manufactured in the province, could be levied, but not until a "local market is provided sufficient to take care of the supply of pulpwood". Rhodes to Dan Chisholm, 1 March 1926, MG 2, vol. 598, Folder 85, no. 16894, PANS.

60 John Doull to O. Schierbeck, 20 January 1932, RG 20, vol. 739, no. 9, files 4-6, PANS.

61 Schierbeck had, by that time, become embroiled in a number of controveries, including a dispute with the Mersey Company. Creighton, *Forestkeeping*, pp. 31-3, 38.

62 "for the worse" according to Creighton, *Forestkeeping*, p. 40. On the national level, the period from 1926 to 1939 has been characterized as a time of "retreat and disaster" in forestry matters. The Dominion Forestry Service lost its western forest

By the time the term of the Big Lease was renewed, the Oxford Paper Company no longer considered it useful as a source of pulpwood, but sought to retain it as a speculative venture. On the company books the lease was assessed at a value of $1,650,874.27. It had long been an important asset on prospectuses for the issue of bonds and preferred shares, providing the security behind the bond issue of the Cape Breton Pulp and Paper Company, Limited, assumed by the Oxford Paper Company in 1920. In two prospectuses dated 1922, the company had stated: "These holdings are virgin forests and contain...at least 6,000,000 cords of high grade pulpwood, sufficient to supply Oxford Paper Company for more than 100 years at its present rate of consumption of spruce and fir".[63] Beginning in the 1930s, the Oxford Paper Company took on the role of speculative seller, keeping their operations to a minimum, and fighting provincial land tax and municipal assessments.[64] On the latter point, the double standard with respect to forest inventories continued to prevail. As early as 1921, the Oxford Paper Company had conducted a cruise of the Big Lease, and concluded that the Lease contained a mere 3,083,499 cords of merchantable wood, about 25 per cent of the volume reported by Barnjum's cruises, and 50 per cent less than stated in the company's own prospectuses. Nonetheless, the property possessed a speculative value in view of future economic recovery, new harvesting and transport techniques and continued scarcities of woodland reserves.[65] Meanwhile, the company could sell stumpage to local contractors and

reserves through their transfer to the provinces; at the same time the Service lost funding and its staff was reduced drastically. The transfer of forest reserves to the provinces was politically motivated, an attempt to rally western support for the King administration. In commenting on the provincial situation, Gillis and Roach note that, "While it is not correct to suggest that the provinces slavishly followed the federal lead in paring back their forestry administrations, it is fair to say that neglect and underfunding led to the same end". Gillis and Roach, *Lost Initiatives*, ch. 9, p. 229.

63 Doull Decision, 1940, p. 10. These statements were exaggerated for reasons elaborated below.

64 The company did have some grounds for complaint. There is no doubt that the wood volumes of the Big Lease declined in the 1910s and 1920s. The major species on the Big Lease, balsam fir, although excellent as pulpwood, is also prone to insect damage and early natural death. The Big Lease stands were, at the time of Fernow's early cruise (1904), ripe for cutting. Fernow, *Forest Conditions in Nova Scotia*. In 1936, Provincial Forester Creighton claimed that a pure stand of balsam fir which is mature to overmature "will actually go back...In 1936...I was struck by the quantity of dead timber...it was my opinion that there had been more wood 10 to 20 years ago than there was in 1936". Evidence of Wilfrid Creighton, RG 10, series B, vol. 204, p. 2395, PANS. In 1965-71, the balsam fir stands on Cape Breton Island were estimated at 12,125,000 cords. By the mid-1980s, six million cords had been destroyed by the spruce budworm. Johnson, *Forests of Nova Scotia*, p. 338.

65 The claim that woodland was scarce was a clear exaggeration. Seventeen years later the Oxford Paper Company readily acquired title to undivided interests of approximately 70 per cent in 203,000 acres (82,215 ha) in northern Maine. Oxford also

jobbers; here, the Big Lease, along with other company lands, served to maintain a low price of wood to contractors.[66] In 1934, for example, the Oxford Company bought 5,000 cords of wood from small holders and jobbers in Cape Breton, and the price was competitive with New England.[67] The government, rather than oppose such practices, joined forces, however cautiously, by implementing a buy-back programme of Crown lands in the 1930s.[68] The price offered sellers was notoriously low and never a serious challenge to other interested buyers.

Oxford's first speculative "sale" was unusual. In 1914, a group of "prominent citizens" had begun lobbying for the establishment of a federal park in Nova Scotia. The year 1928 brought the first proposal that a national park be established on Cape Breton Island, but plans were suspended in 1932 because of the troubled finances of the federal government. By January 1934, the Yarmouth Fish and Game Protective Association, headed by Seymour Baker and supported by other conservation-minded organizations, rekindled the lobby for a national park in Nova Scotia. The Ministry of Interior sponsored a series of talks on the advantages of national parks in several cities and towns in Nova Scotia. In May 1934, Premier Angus MacDonald requested that the ministry inspect areas suitable for a park; three areas were chosen and a Cape Breton site was recommended and agreed upon in February 1935.[69] In 1936, the federal government and the province negotiated the boundaries and the area delineated for park purposes included Crown lands

---

purchased 23,100 acres (9,356 ha) of woodlands north of Rumford, Maine. This meant that over 50 per cent of the area constituted by the woodlands of the Big Lease sold back to the Nova Scotia government in 1957 was immediately replaced by wood reserves of much better quality and accessibility in the state of Maine. Leane, *The Oxford Story*, pp. 37-8. Nonetheless, on two occasions (1929 and 1937-8), the Mersey Company had offered to buy the Big Lease from Oxford. Evidence of C. Gordon, RG 10, Series B, vol. 203, p. 7, PANS

66 Crown stumpage was not only considered low on the Big Lease but also on other Crown lands. As a result, pulpwood prices in Nova Scotia were relatively low. In the 1930s, the price of pulpwood piled at roadside dropped $5 per cord when passing the boundary from New Brunswick to Nova Scotia. Creighton, p. 52. This discrepancy still prevails. For the poor position of the small woodlot owner in other areas of North America, see Thomas Roach, "The Pulpwood Trade and Settlers of New Ontario, 1919-1938", *Journal of Canadian Studies*, 22 (Fall 1987), pp. 78-88; Bill Parenteau, "Pulp, Paper and Poverty", *New Maritimes*, VII (March/April 1989), pp. 20-6; and William C. Osborn, *The Paper Plantation: The Nader Report on the Pulp and Paper Industry in Maine* (Washington, 1973).

67 Evidence of G. Harvey, RG 10, Series B, vol. 203, p. 1023, PANS.

68 Creighton, *Forestkeeping,* p. 47. The objective was to refurbish and manage these lands, but in the end they were merely used as development tools to attract foreign pulp and paper mills to the province.

69 William Lothian, *A Brief History of Canada's National Parks* (Ottawa, 1987), p. 97

under the terms of the Big Lease and some 300 private holdings, including 70 homes (see Figure 1).

The expropriation of part of the Big Lease was not a mere matter of passing Orders in Council. The Oxford Paper Company engaged experts to cruise the property to determine the potential financial loss which would be caused by the expropriation. Based on forest inventories provided by the reputable Maine forester and cruiser, James Sewall, and its own calculations, the company claimed compensation amounting to a fantastic $10.17 per acre ($4.12 per ha).[70] In response, the provincial Department of Lands and Forests engaged its own experts to check the company's figures. The re-lease was settled in 1940 after six weeks in court, presided over by Judge John Doull, the man who had, in his previous capacity as Lands and Forests Minister, renewed the Big Lease in 1933. The expropriated area was 178,648 acres (72,352 ha), a little less than one third the original lease. The settlement was $398,500, of which $346,500 was for lands expropriated and $52,000 for lands injuriously affected.[71] The compensation translated into a price of $2.23 per acre (90 cents per ha), far from the amount requested by the Oxford Paper Company. But at a time when the Department of Lands and Forests was charged to buy back Crown lands for no more than 25 cents per acre (10 cents per ha), it was a very good price. Moreover, one of the company cruisers, overheard discussing the expropriated lands, admitted that: "I have cruised a lot of country; some of it was good and some of it bad, but of all the country I ever saw, this is the worst...."[72]

The private holders of land were less fortunate. Total payments to the expropriated were $72,051.01 and only eight of the 70 parties received sums exceeding $1,000. One, from Rockport, Maine, received by far the largest payment, $40,000. Eight parties resided in the United States.[73] The stories of the expropriated

---

70 Doull Decision, 1940, p. 3. As a comparison, the lands of the Annapolis Lumber Company and the McLeod Paper and Power Company sold to the Mersey Paper Company at a price of $6.94 and $4.63 per acre ($2.81 and $1.88 per ha), respectively. These well-stocked and accessible lands were cruised by the buyers and sellers, with James Sewall as arbiter. "Reports on and Valuations of MacLeod Paper and Power Co. Ltd. and Annapolis Lumber Co., Ltd. Lands, N.S." (1937), MG 1, vols. 2643, 2645, PANS.

71 Doull Decision, 1940, pp. 30-1. The cruiser hired by the Oxford Paper Company estimated the whole quantity of softwood, operable or not, at 644,144 cords. Judge Doull considered 450,000 cords as a "fair estimate" for the operable softwood on the expropriated area (p. 15).

72 Quoted in Evidence of W. Creighton, RG 10, Series B, vol. 204, p. 204, PANS. One Dominion government report of the Big Lease described it as containing 240,000 acres (97,200 ha) of barren and 270,000 acres (109,350 ha) of small growth, mostly fir. Johnson, *Forests of Nova Scotia*, p. 364n.

73 Orders in Council, 4 February 1941, RG 3, vol. 95, PANS. The $40,000 property was owned by the widow of H.C. Corson, a wealthy industrialist of Akron, Ohio, who had used the site as a summer estate. Lothian, *A Brief History of Canada's National Parks*, p. 98.

families are invariably bitter. Some make reference to the settlements as "take-it-or-leave-it-deals" and others liken the resettlements to the clearances of the Scottish Highlands or the expulsion of the Acadians. Nor was there any provision made for the loss of numerous subsistence uses of the forest contained within the park. The bitter memories of those expropriated undoubtedly contributed to the successful local opposition to the northward extension of the park in 1970.[74]

The role of the government may seem contradictory but it was, in fact, consistent with the state of society and the economy at the time. The federal system of national parks defined areas set aside as public heritages or trusts, to preserve, forever, outstanding examples of Canada's scenery, wilderness, geology, natural phenomena or native flora and fauna. The promotion of national pride and a concept of national greatness through the development of a national parks system found favour with the federal government. At the provincial and local government levels, such parks were attractive as potential generators of tourism and political plums to be bestowed on local constituencies.[75] For Nova Scotia, suffering from postwar depression and industrial decline, the Cape Breton National Highlands Park was attractive for additional reasons. The local MLA for Victoria County explained that the national park system was a Dominion undertaking which Nova Scotia had "the right to share in", noting, as well, that this may relieve the province of policing and protecting forest lands and building roads.[76] The only concern of the provincial government, that rights to surface and sub-surface resources be retained, did not prove to be an insurmountable obstacle.[77]

Prior and subsequent to the expropriation in 1940, the Oxford Company conducted very few operations on the Big Lease. The company continued to sell stumpage to local contractors who cut sawlogs for local mills, but it is not likely that this cut contributed much to the total pulpwood cut in the counties. Gordon Harvey and his son Leonard were responsible for the "management" of the lease

74 "Stories from the Clyburn Valley", *Cape Breton's Magazine,* 49 (1988), pp. 1-20. For documentation of the unsuccessful expansion in 1970, see MG 1, vol. 1768, no. 16, PANS. Creighton, who was involved in the settlements, writes that while "the setting aside of a large wilderness area for park purposes appealed to me, forcing people from their homes to make a playground for summer visitors seemed harsh and in many cases unnecessary. The work was interesting, sometimes funny, often frustrating and more often distasteful". Creighton, *Forestkeeping,* p. 58.

75 See, for example, Nancy Colpitts, "Alma, New Brunswick, and the Twentieth Century Crisis of Readjustment: Sawmilling Community to National Park", M.A. thesis, Dalhousie University, 1983, ch. 4

76 *Halifax Herald,* 5 April 1934, p. 3.

77 In 1956, a section in the southeast of the park was withdrawn for mineral development at the request of the province. In 1958, an additional section of Cheticamp Lake was withdrawn to accommodate a provincial hydro-electric scheme (see Figure 1). Lothian, *A Brief History of Canada's National Parks,* pp. 97-8.

but probably only built sufficient roads and cut and sold enough stumpage to pay themselves a salary, and cover the taxes as well as the rental fee.[78] The company continued its opposition to municipal assessments, taking the Municipality of the County of Inverness to court in 1947, protesting the assessment of its properties and lands in the county. The local assessor valued the real and personal property of the company at $193,750. Judge J. Archibald heard the case in County Court and, in spite of recognizing there were "reasonable grounds for objection", he dismissed the case on a technicality.[79] The company did not give up, however, but continued to challenge provincial land tax and municipal assessments, processes abandoned only when it became known that the province was interested in a repurchase of the lease.[80]

Meanwhile, pulpwood production was becoming firmly established in Inverness and Victoria counties. Before the Second World War, local contractors bought stumpage from private woodlot owners and exported it to Europe. After the war, Marshall dollars encouraged a similar trade.[81] One German company, the Mariana Company, was active in the export trade. The Mersey Paper Company was active in purchasing pulpwood from local contractors and woodlot owners. Mersey also cut about 5,000 cords annually from a Crown lease at the Crowdis Mountain portion of the Cape Breton Highlands south of the Big Lease.[82] From 1940 to 1957, 487,182 cords of pulpwood were produced in the two counties. Sixty-nine per cent of that production was concentrated in the six years (1952-7) before the repurchase of the Big Lease. In 1956 and 1957, Inverness County topped all counties in pulpwood production in Nova Scotia.[83] Much of the activity occurred in anticipation of the establishment of a new pulp and paper company, an event opposed by Mersey.[84]

The final speculative phase in the history of the Big Lease ended with its termination and the government's purchase of the lease in 1957. The repurchase was occasioned by a series of factors. In 1956, after 23 years of Liberal rule, the Conservatives, under Robert Stanfield, gained power in Nova Scotia. The province was suffering the effects of a major depression in the steel and coal industry and un-

---

78 Personal interviews with Wilfrid Creighton, 11 April 1990, and David Dwyer, 27 September 1989.

79 *Maritime Provinces Reports* (1948), pp. 405-9.

80 Personal interview with Wilfrid Creighton, 14 May 1991.

81 Personal interview with Wilfrid Creighton, 11 April 1990.

82 Johnson, *Forests of Nova Scotia*, p. 273.

83 Calculated from Nova Scotia, Department of Lands and Forests, *Annual Reports* (1940-1958).

84 Mersey, which had a good deal of political clout, argued that there was not enough wood in the province for two pulp companies. Personal interview with Wilfrid Creighton, 28 October 1988; E. Haliburton, *My Years With Stanfield* (Windsor, 1972), p. 18.

employment was high. The previous government had failed to entice a pulp and paper company to establish a mill in the province.[85] And the promotion of industrial development had been a key plank in the Conservative election platform. Determined "to do something" for the province, the government decided to pursue a Swedish pulp company, Stora Kopparberg (hereafter Stora), one of several companies which had already been approached by the previous government. But if this effort was to be successful, a major tract of Crown land had to be made available for lease to the Stora venture. The government buy-back programme of Crown lands, begun so cautiously in the 1930s, had, by 1957, resulted in the recovery of almost 25 per cent of the province's forest lands. The ungranted portions of these lands, however, were still not sufficient. The Big Lease was an obvious additional source. The government now played an active role in repossessing the lease.[86] Negotiations with the Oxford Paper Company, initiated in March 1957, were concluded in May of that year. Although Stora's promoter and the provincial officials had kept their negotiations secret in order not to affect the negotiations with Oxford, the desire to attract Stora placed the government under considerable political pressure to settle with Oxford. The difference between the 1940 expropriation agreement and the 1957 negotiated settlement reflects that pressure; in 1940 the government paid $5.84 per acre ($2.37 per ha) while in 1957 the rate was $12.02 per acre ($4.87 per ha), despite the elapse of a further 17 years on the lease.[87] When the government reported to the local legislature that they had agreed to pay the Oxford Paper Company $3,750,000, they faced strong criticism. In response, Premier Stanfield echoed a now familiar theme: "We took the position from the start...that it

---

85 Creighton, *Forestkeeping*, pp. 101-2.

86 The urgency of cutting the balsam fir stands was critical. The first signs of budworm infestations were visible and the local foresters were frustrated and angry by the lack of activity on the lease. Personal interview with Allister Fraser, District Forester for Cape Breton Island in the 1950s and 1960s, 21 June 1990.

87 These are 1971 dollars. Statistics Canada, *The Historical Statistics of Canada* (2nd ed., Ottawa, 1983). Table K8-18, Consumer Price Index for Canada Classified by Main Component 1913-1975 (1971=100). The 1940 and 1957 dollar values were $2.23 and $8.50 (90 cents and $3.44 per ha), respectively. In the 1930s, the Department of Lands and Forests was charged with buying back Crown lands at a cost not to exceed 25 cents per acre (10 cents per ha). From 1942 to 1955, the price ranged from 72 cents to $3.92 an acre (29 cents to $1.59 per ha). In the mid 1950s however, with the prospects of Stora entering the province, the Department acquired 32,532 acres (13,175 ha) for an average of $7.11 per acre ($2.88 per ha) in 1955; 5,074.6 acres (2,055 ha) for an average price of $11.50 ($4.66 per ha) in 1956; and 57,317 acres (23,213 ha) for an average price of $5.57 an acre ($2.26 per ha) in 1957. Once the Stora agreement was signed, the average price for buy-back land dropped to under $5 ($2.05 per ha) for the next three years. Calculated from Nova Scotia, Department of Lands and Forests, *Annual Reports* (1940-1958) and Nova Scotia, *Public Accounts* (1958-1962).

was essential to the good name and good reputation of the province of Nova Scotia that we must regard any rights of the Oxford Paper Company as legal rights which could be terminated or modified only by agreement, or under the provisions...of our law which relates to property rights in Nova Scotia".[88]

In July 1957, Karl Clauson, the sales representative of the Stora Kopparberg Corporation in New York, formed the Nova Scotia Pulp Limited (NSP). The company was capitalized at $2,000 Canadian and wholly owned by Clauson, who acted both as Chairman of the Board and President. Clauson's solicitors in Nova Scotia, Arthur Gordon Cooper and Hector McInnes, were also partners in NSP. NSP and the Nova Scotia government signed the Nova Scotia Pulp Limited Agreement, leasing 1 million acres (520,000 ha) of Crown lands on Cape Breton Island and the three eastern counties of Pictou, Antigonish and Guysborough to the company. The agreement was remarkable in that Stora made no formal commitment to build a pulp mill in Nova Scotia until July 1959, when the company took over NSP.[89]

By that time Clauson had wrested several concessions from the government. Cooper, serving as mediator, formulated the agreement, virtually rewriting the tax laws of Nova Scotia in response to Clauson's requests. Stumpage rates were set at $1 per cord, the same rate given the Mersey Company 30 years earlier, and $2 per cord less than Clauson had been prepared to pay.[90] The government also acquired a 323 acre (131 ha) site for the mill and undertook, at a cost of $30,000, to carry out special surveys for NSP. Spending under the provisions of the Nova Scotia Pulp Limited Agreement Act exceeded $2.27 million from 1959 to 1962.[91] The assurance of transferability of the new lease was another feature which the government approved.[92] The premier considered himself forced to comply with this concession to Stora: "It seems to me it's going quite a distance, but the solicitors of the mortgagee are insistent that the provision is essential".[93] The premier's major concern during this period was to secure a commitment from Stora and the content of the agree-

---

88 Nova Scotia, *Debates* (29 March 1960), p. 2019. The Oxford Paper Company initially asked for $6,400,000 but this was reduced to a payment of $3,750,000. Beck, *Politics in Nova Scotia,* p. 264.

89 Dietrich Soyez, "Stora Lured Abroad? A Nova Scotian Case Study in Industrial Decision-Making and Persistence", *The Operational Geographer,* 16 (September 1988), pp. 11-4.

90 The Deputy Minister of Lands and Forests at the time, Wilfrid Creighton, also felt that the province could have obtained more for stumpage. Personal interview with Wilfrid Creighton, 11 April 1990.

91 Nova Scotia, *Public Accounts* (1957-1962).

92 Nova Scotia, *Laws* (1960), Chapter 58, p. 230.

93 Nova Scotia, *Debates* (1960), p. 2016.

ment seemed secondary.[94] The opposition predicted "that the type of agreement, as regards to the price, which was negotiated with NSP will be a millstone about the necks of the people of Nova Scotia for many years to come, and will serve to depress, not only the price received for pulpwood off the Crown lands of the province, but by analogy off the lands owned by small wood-lot owners in the province, for 30 years to come, because that's the duration of the agreement".[95]

Throughout its history, then, government timidity and extreme dependence on business coloured the changing terms and conditions of the Big Lease. Yet the property rights of the leaseholders could have been changed or modified. At various times local companies called upon their government to make the foreign absentee pulp and paper companies work their idle leases and freeholds. Chief Forester Schierbeck's policy proposals in the 1920s similarly challenged such property rights. The establishment of the Cape Breton Highlands National Park showed that expropriation could be invoked. In a different context, Conservative MP John Haggart stressed that governments had the legal power to interfere with existing, almost perpetual leases; "the question of whether or not to use the power was solely a moral issue".[96] Other countries, and even other provinces, had introduced effective forest management legislation to regulate both private and public forests.[97]

In Nova Scotia, by contrast, accommodation rather than challenge characterized government response to the demands of leaseholders. Yet the nature and implications of such accommodation did change over time. In the early period, in spite of company demands eroding the stipulations of the lease, large speculative profits realized from its sale, a meagre $6,000 rental fee collected, and thousands of cords

---

94 The premier was, however, concerned about the sequence in which the concessions would be announced. Haste characterized the agreement and at one point a pending visit by Queen Elizabeth and Prince Philip to the construction site of the mill added to the urgency. This information was gathered from N.S. *huvudserie*, Series F, no. 780 at Stora's archives in Falun, Sweden. See especially, Clauson to Abenius, 16 September 1957; 15 December 1958; 16 March 1959; and 30 March 1959. I am indebted to Direktor Håkan Vestergren of Stora for permission to examine these records. I am also grateful to Sven Rydberg, formerly head of Stora's Information Department, and Sture Kristiansson, Stora's archivist.

95 Nova Scotia, *Debates* (1960), pp. 73-4. In 1991, the price of pulpwood for Nova Scotia small woodlot owners remains the lowest in Canada.

96 Referred to in Gillis and Roach, *Lost Initiatives*, p. 64.

97 See, for example, L. Anders Sandberg, "Swedish Forestry Legislation in Nova Scotia: The Rise and Fall of the Forest Improvement Act, 1965-1986", in D. Day, ed., *Geographical Perspectives on the Maritime Provinces* (Halifax, 1988). Embargoes on the export of pulpwood from Crown lands were imposed by Ontario in 1900, Quebec in 1910, New Brunswick in 1911 and British Columbia in 1924. Reich, *National Problems of Canada*, pp. 48-9.

of unprocessed pulpwood shipped abroad, the province retained a certain degree of autonomy. With the formation of the Department of Lands and Forests in 1926, the Big Lease was challenged by the proposed export embargo on pulpwood from Crown leases and freehold lands, a policy which also threatened well-established sawmillers, pulpwood exporters, and large absentee holders of forest land. The challenge, however, was defeated and overshadowed by the establishment of the Mersey Paper Company in 1928, which signified a new era of state support through stepped-up concessions in the forest industry. Mersey received concessions in the supply of power and guarantees of 1,000,000 cords of pulpwood from Crown lands. At the time, the importance of Crown reserves in attracting foreign pulp mills to the province reached new heights, as the province barely possessed enough Crown lands to accommodate Mersey. In Mersey's wake, the government embarked on a programme of buying back Crown lands as a future locational incentive to foreign pulp and paper companies. In 1957, the buy-back of the Big Lease (178,748 ha) by a newly elected provincial Conservative government, and its re-issue along with an additional 341,252 ha of Crown lands, signified yet another stage in the province's quest for pulp and paper industry development.

The generous and stepped-up concessions of provincial Crown land policy over the years were not made merely because politicians were timid. Instead they should be seen in the context and history of dependent development and state reliance on foreign capital. Dependence on foreign corporate capital meant that the government required a good international credit rating, and such a rating could only be maintained by treating the "property rights" of increasingly powerful corporate players as more or less exclusive, transferable and subject to state favours and collaboration. In the era of transnational capital in the 1950s and beyond, the province was forced into a closer partnership with corporate capital, through the provision of generous leases and other subsidies. By then, the state-corporate partnership had been institutionalized. In the future, it was to influence all political decisions on provincial forest matters.

In the final analysis, it is difficult to justify the Big Lease on the same principle as that used by Hiller in the case of the Newfoundland pulp and paper industry. The Newfoundland government also issued generous leases for 99 years, but, Hiller argues, in spite of all the drawbacks, this was necessary to obtain a pulp and paper industry.[98] In Cape Breton, by contrast, the Big Lease resulted in all the drawbacks of a long-term lease but no pulp and paper mill. Instead, the Big Lease was part of a system which kept the price of purchased pulpwood low, and the lease may even have blocked the development of a pulp and paper industry on Cape Breton Is-

---

98 James Hiller, "The Origins of the Pulp and Paper Industry in Newfoundland", *Acadiensis*, XI, 2 (Spring 1982), p. 68. For a more critical assessment of the Newfoundland system, see John A. Gray, *The Trees Behind the Shore: The Forest and Forest Industries of Newfoundland and Labrador* (Hull, 1981).

land.[99] Once a pulp and paper industry was induced to come to the Island, the provincial government had to buy back the Big Lease and then enter into a new generous deal at considerable cost, both at the time and for the future.[100]

---

99 In 1951, for example, the Nova Scotia government was approached by the Chief Chemist of the Bathurst Power and Paper Company with a proposal for the establishment of a pulp mill on Cape Breton Island. The government was hesitant because of the "lack" of pulpwood. "The greatest supply of pulpwood from a single landholder...is the Oxford Lease. It is quite possible that a Company could buy from the Oxford Company, but this is a question that could be answered only by the Oxford Company itself". As a result, the Bathurst initiative faltered. Angus L. MacDonald Papers, MG 2, vol. 962, Folder 21-11, PANS. In 1954, a report written by William Woodfine of St. Francis Xavier University argued that unless the Big Lease was rescinded "pulp and paper industries will be unwilling to come into the four eastern counties". *Chronicle Herald*, 29 April 1954.

100 These costs not only include the revenue foregone as a result of low stumpage rates. It can also be argued that forest management has since been shaped to serve the pulpwood economy (at the expense of other uses), and that the organizational efforts of small woodlot owners have been undermined for the same reason. See Glyn Bissix and L. Anders Sandberg, "The Political Economy of Nova Scotia's Forest Improvement Act, 1962-1986" and Peter Clancy, "The Politics of Pulpwood Marketing in Nova Scotia, 1962-1985", in this volume.

Sawmills to National Park:
Alma, New Brunswick, 1921-1947

Nancy Colpitts

When Murice Martin told the story of the sawmilling industry in Alma, New Brunswick, he began with an event in January 1921 that he considered to be a turning point in the history of the community (Figure 1).[1] Murice, his brothers and his father Owen were in the woods making a small contracted cut for the area's major lumberman, Garfield White, when Bill Gildard, the cruiser for Whites', arrived and said to Murice's father: "Owen, hell's to pay. They sent me to knock you off. Whites' have sold out".[2] It was a hard blow to the sawmilling industry in Alma, but it was not the end. In spite of obstructions on every front, the sawmilling industry continued to function with some success, especially after 1933, until the area became the site of Fundy National Park in 1947.

The most common view of the New Brunswick sawmilling industry during this period, however, is one of decline.[3] Sawmilling is seen as having been a last resort for the desperate, with large sawlogs depleted, only smaller trees suitable for pulp remaining, markets irrevocably damaged, and international competition growing.[4] The alleged result was an irreversible loss of viability for sawmilling, leaving the pulp and paper industry as the only hope for forestry in New Brunswick.[5]

This view can, however, be challenged. The 1921 crisis and the depressed markets of the 1920s and early 1930s were problems, but after a 1933 low, when lumber production was less than one-fifth of that in 1921, New Brunswick's production of lumber consistently increased (Table I). Following the record lows in provincial cuts, averaging approximately 115 million board feet in 1931, 1932 and 1933, the cuts for 1934 and the remainder of the decade were above the 200 million

---

1   References made to the Alma sawmilling industry include the stationary mills in Alma and Point Wolfe and the portable mills in the watersheds of the Point Wolfe and Upper Salmon rivers (Figure 1).

2   Letter from Murice Martin (former Alma forest worker), 15 September 1981.

3   See in particular A.R.M. Lower, *The North American Assault on the Canadian Forest* (Toronto, 1938) and in the same volume, S.A. Saunders, "Forest Industries in the Maritime Provinces", pp. 347-71.

4   Lower, *The North American Assault*, ch. 15.

5   Lower, *The North American Assault*, p. 194.

Figure 1

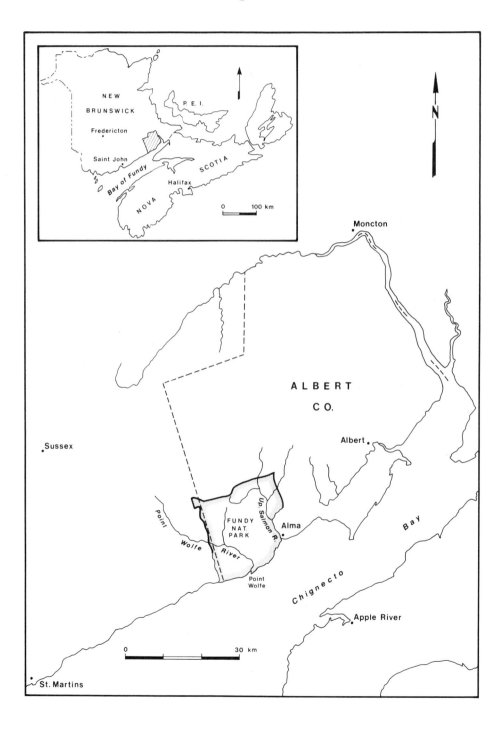

board feet mark. The Second World War threw the industry into a boom that was limited only by a shortage of workers.[6] The subsequent postwar trend was for demand to exceed supply.[7] Despite growing competition, New Brunswick sawmillers held their own, although other countries may have done better.[8] Indeed, the revival of sawmilling in Alma was even more impressive than in New Brunswick as a whole.

In this paper, using the sawmilling industry in Alma as a case study, I argue that restricted access to forest resources and capital, as well as the persistence of a merchant-dominated marketing system, set important limits to the restructuring and revival of the New Brunswick sawmilling industry.[9] I also argue that these constraints were not only market-driven, but actively promoted by government policies in support of the pulp and paper industry at the expense of sawmilling. Finally, I argue that patron-client relations provided both the opportunities for, and limits to, the revival of the sawmilling industry in Alma after the 1920s.[10] Such relations were hierarchical; individuals unequal in socio-economic status exchanged material favours, such as jobs and contracts, for loyalty and political support.[11] Class consciousness and class organizations were absent. Industrial and political patrons, often one and the same, were in command and benefited the most from the allocation of public resources, yet helped sustain a structure of limited opportunity for all. Patron-client relations were typical in the rural politics of sawmilling in the first half of 20th-century New Brunswick. Sawmillers and merchants entered politics or used political connections to obtain leases, licences and public funds to expand their businesses and reward supporters with sub-contracts and jobs.[12]

---

6   B.S. Keirstead, *The Economic Effects of the War on the Maritime Provinces of Canada* (Halifax, 1944), p. 103.

7   Gerrit Hazenberg, "An Analysis of the New Brunswick Lumber Industry", M.Sc. thesis, University of New Brunswick, 1966.

8   Nova Scotia, Department of Lands and Forests, B.F.A. Hektor, *Comparison: Forestry in Nova Scotia and Sweden* (Halifax, 1974).

9   For more on these factors see Nancy Colpitts, "Alma, New Brunswick and the Twentieth Century Crisis of Readjustment: Sawmilling Community to National Park", M.A. thesis, Dalhousie University, 1983, pp. 16-73.

10 R.A. Young, "'and the people will sink into despair': Reconstruction in New Brunswick", *Canadian Historical Review*, LXIX, 2 (1988), p. 128.

11 Young, "Reconstruction in New Brunswick", p. 128. For the situation in 19th-century New Brunswick, see Graeme Wynn, *Timber Colony* (Toronto, 1980).

12 Hugh Thorburn, *Politics in New Brunswick* (Toronto, 1961); for Nova Scotia, see D. Campbell and R.A. McLean, *Beyond the Atlantic Roar* (Toronto, 1974).

Alma, with poor soil for agriculture and a cool, foggy Bay of Fundy climate, was the last part of Albert County to be settled.[13] Settlers arrived in the 1830s when the rich marshes further up the Fundy coast and the farms of the Annapolis Valley across the bay were fully occupied. The influence of the lumber industry was present from the start. Early settlement was limited by grants to lumbermen who controlled the virgin forests on the two strategic driving rivers, the Point Wolfe and the Upper Salmon. These lumbermen, primarily Saint John merchants, were the patrons who controlled the river mouths and the large tracts of Crown land that form the drainage basins.

Two small communities with sawmills, Point Wolfe and Alma, appeared at the mouths of the two rivers. The farmland between the communities was soon occupied. Later settlers were forced inland to accept grants with fine stands of spruce but with poor soil for farming. The population of the parish of Alma reached a peak of 1,263 in 1881 and then declined until the 1930s.[14] The decline reflected the departure of the inland settlers whose subsistence from the farm, forest and sawmill failed to meet household needs.

Those who stayed in Alma and on the coast were in a better position. They were the original settlers who held the best of Alma's scanty farmlands.[15] They engaged in some fishing and farming and worked in the forest and in the nearby sawmills. The village of Alma grew. In the early 1880s, the population was 200, with four business establishments. By 1892, the population was 500, and no decline was recorded for the next 50 years. At the same time, nine business establishments were present, including a railway and telegraph station.[16]

Charles (known as C.T.) White was the patron in the Alma sawmilling industry. White, a Baptist (the dominant religion in Albert County) and a United Empire

---

13 Background information on the early years of settlement in Alma can be found in Parks Canada Atlantic Regional Library, Gilbert Allardyce, "The Salt and the Fir: Report on the History of the Fundy Park Area" (1969) and also in several less-academic accounts. See *The Busy East,* Albert County Number, XV (April-May 1925); Albert W. Smith, "Essay on the History and Resources of Albert County", in R.F. Fellows, ed., *The New Brunswick Census of 1851, Albert County, N.B., Canada* (1970), Appendix I, pp. 9-10; Mary Maijka, *Fundy National Park* (Fredericton, 1977).

14 Canada, *Census Reports,* 1901, 1911, 1921, 1931, 1941, 1951.

15 The process of rural stratification in the Maritime Provinces is only beginning to be documented. For an excellent beginning, see Rusty Bittermann, "The Hierarchy of the Soil: Land and Labour in a 19th Century Cape Breton Community", *Acadiensis,* XVIII, 1 (Autumn 1988), pp. 33-55. For a recent review, see Catharine A. Wilson, "'Outstanding in the Field': Recent Rural History in Canada", *Acadiensis,* XX, 2 (Spring 1991), pp. 177-90.

16 R.G. Dunn and Co., *Reference Books for the Dominion of Canada* (New York, 1882-1922).

Loyalist descendant, was part of the political and economic elite in New Brunswick. He resided in the town of Sussex some 40 miles from Alma, where his property bordered that of his nephew, Supreme Court judge Albert Scott White, 16 years his junior, who served as an MLA, speaker, solicitor and attorney-general in the New Brunswick legislature from 1890 to 1900. C.T.'s sons Simeon H. White and G. Harley White, who likewise ran lumber businesses, were also neighbours.[17] C.T. was a "true lumberman", practising vertical integration in the sawmilling community.[18] He operated a sawmill in Apple River, Nova Scotia. In 1895 he bought the sawmill in Point Wolfe. One year later his older son, S.H. White, bought the Alma mill. Over the next 12 years, C.T. not only took over the Alma concern, but also acquired smaller mills on the nearby Goose and West rivers, and at St. Martins. By 1908, he owned the largest store in Alma, controlled all the area's major rivers, dams and sawmills, and had purchased the large grants of land on the rivers as well as several smaller private grants inland. In addition, he held licence to the large blocks of Crown land on the upper reaches of the rivers. White controlled most of the valuable lumber in the area as well as the means by which it was processed.

When C.T. White died in 1915 he left a small fortune. His real estate holdings amounted to $54,500, including 19,000 acres (7,695 ha) of forest lands in Kings and Albert counties. His Crown leases, valued at $9,750, amounted to 20,807 acres (8,427 ha). His total assets stood at $211,512.95.[19] These assets increased when the business was left to his son Garfield. By 1922, C.T. White and Sons was reported to possess lands in Albert, Kings and St. John counties as well as 35,903 acres (14,541 ha) in Cumberland County, Nova Scotia. White's credit rating remained stable and a new hotel, another grocery store and two garages were opened in Alma between 1912 and 1922.[20] In spite of these signs of stability, the White business collapsed quite suddenly in 1921. No doubt the depression in the lumber market was a major factor of the decline. Local opinion attributes the collapse to Garfield White's undue trust in shipping, shipbuilding and the First World War bull market in lumber.[21] In 1921 the White company could not finance the winter's cut, and on 18

---

17   Graves Papers, MC 1156, vol. 6, Provincial Archives of New Brunswick [PANB] and RS-66 Kings County Probate - 1915, Micro. 11728, PANB.

18   Allardyce, "The Salt and the Fir", p. 138.

19   Kings County Probate - 1915.

20   Dunn, *Reference Books*, 1912-1922.

21   White built two ships, *Vincent White* and *Meredith White*, registered in 1918. Four more ships were built and registered in 1919 and 1920, the *Bessie A. White*, *Whiteson*, *Whiteway* and *Whitebell*. The demand for shipping declined shortly after the First World War, and *Whiteson* was lost in 1921 on its second voyage and *Bessie A. White* went down in 1922. Interviews with Bob Hickey, Murice Martin and Frank Sinclair (all former forest workers in Alma), 1981. Also John P. Parker, *Sails of the Maritimes* (Great Britain, 1960).

May 1922 the firm's holdings were sold to the Hollingsworth and Whitney Paper Company of Maine.[22]

The Hollingsworth and Whitney takeover of the forest lands in Alma was part of a larger process. In the 1920s, forested freeholds and Crown leases in New Brunswick were rapidly taken over by pulp and paper companies. The two largest, the Fraser Company and International Paper, controlled 70 per cent of all Crown lands by 1930.[23] Their Crown leases were long term in order to give security to their heavily capitalized mills. The leases were also issued not by auction but through mere negotiation between government officials and licensees. Where a substantial company was involved, it was unlikely for government to refuse the granting and renewal of leases.[24]

The terms of the Crown leases to the pulp and paper industry were very generous. Government powers to control corporate mismanagement on Crown leases were never used.[25] Taxes and holding fees were kept low and did not discourage accumulation of large tracts of land.[26] Stumpage rates were used as a mere

---

22 Interviews with Murice Martin and L.R. Colpitts (nephew of Fred Colpitts), 1981; "Brief Outline of History of Hollingsworth and Whitney Ltd. and Scott Paper Co. in Nova Scotia", MG 1, vol. 2861, no. 16, Provincial Archives of Nova Scotia [PANS]. Hollingsworth and Whitney was not one of the largest American pulp and paper companies, but nevertheless operated two mills in Maine and, in 1938, constructed a third in Mobile, Alabama. The company's land holdings spilled across the Canadian border at about the same time that other pulp and paper companies expanded into the Maritime Provinces. During the 1920s they acquired 550,000 acres (222,750 ha) in Nova Scotia, making them one of the province's major landholders and arousing concern in some circles as to what use would be made of the land. In New Brunswick, the company occupied 56,000 acres (22,680 ha) of freehold land and 53,000 acres (21,465 ha) of Crown lands, the largest part of which was in the Alma area. *New York Times*, 15 April 1938, 7 Aug. 1954, 11 Sept. 1954; Saunders, "Forest Industries", p. 360; RG 39, vol. 594, file 10, p. 270, National Archives of Canada [NAC].

23 C.H. Jones, "The Lumber Industry in New Brunswick and Nova Scotia", M.A. thesis, University of Toronto, 1930, p. 7. For another case, see Serge Côté, "Naissance de l'industrie papetière et mainmise sur la forêt: Le cas de Bathurst", in this volume.

24 Interviews with John Bigelow (former Secretary of the Maritime Lumber Bureau) and Harold Hoyt (retired forester of the New Brunswick Department of Natural Resources), 1981.

25 For example, see the preamble to *New Statutes* (1926), c. 41, s.246, or New Brunswick Department of Natural Resources Library, Murray B. Morrison, "The Evolution of Forest Policy in New Brunswick", 1936, p. 10.

26 K.B. Brown, *Taxation of Forest Land in New Brunswick: A Brief Presented to the Royal Commission for Revision of the Rates and Tax Act* (n.p., 1951), p. 7.

tax and not as a means to regulate the province's annual cut.[27] Minimum cut stipulations were small and did not discourage the speculative holding of forest land because the minimum cut required could be averaged over a period of time or over the licensee's entire holdings, so that a very heavy cut in one small area could make any operations in the rest of the province unnecessary. Maximum cut stipulations failed to restrict cuts to estimated annual growth because lack of surveys made the annual growth impossible to calculate.[28] Minimum diameter regulations aimed at preventing the cutting of young sawlogs were ignored by the pulp and paper industry's indiscriminate quest for pulpwood.[29] Special management plans for specific areas came into use but failed because government lacked the bureaucratic machinery to administer them.[30] In short, government was rapidly transferring the bulk of the Crown land forest reserve into the hands of a few pulp and paper companies under an arrangement where government was reduced to a client spectator.[31]

Sawmillers were thus in a poor position with respect to sawlog supplies. The granting of land was uncommon and, when allowed, made to promote farming rather than lumbering.[32] Temporary permits, though common, offered little security for a long-term milling operation. As well, the vast majority of desirable forest land in New Brunswick was either owned privately or already licensed and therefore unavailable for temporary permits. As large and small logs were ground up for pulp or left to rot on the large Crown leases, sawmillers and independent pulp cutters were forced to overcut private lands.[33] Sawmillers' access to sawlogs was clearly restricted.

---

27 H.M. Babcock, "Some Economic Aspects of New Brunswick's Crown Land Stumpage", M.Sc. thesis, University of New Brunswick, 1957.

28 New Brunswick Department of Natural Resources Library, J.M. Gibson and K.B. Brown, "A Memorandum Regarding Forest and Forest Policy in New Brunswick with Special Reference to Crown Lands", (1937), pp. 8-15.

29 Gibson and Brown, "Memorandum", pp. 1-7.

30 Gibson and Brown, "Memorandum", p. 7.

31 Peter Gillis and Thomas Roach, *Lost Initiatives: Canada's Forest Industries, Forest Policy and Forest Conservation* (Westport, Conn., 1986).

32 Petrie, "The Regional Economy of New Brunswick", pp. 18-9, 47.

33 On control and use of reserves see Keirstead, *The Economic Effects,* pp. 106-7; William L. McKillop, "Forest Land Ownership in Relation to Forest Management in Gladstone Parish, Sunbury County, New Brunswick", M.Sc. thesis, University of New Brunswick, 1959, part 1; New Brunswick, Royal Commission on Primary Forest Products in New Brunswick, *Report,* 1964, pp. 51-5, 61-5; William C. Osborn, *The Paper Plantation: The Nader Report on the Pulp and Paper Industry in Maine* (Washington, 1973), ch. 5.

The position of the sawmilling industry was further worsened by restricted access to capital. After the crisis of the early 1920s, the large Canadian banks did not usually allow small loans at standard interest rates to local rural enterprise. Even large companies had to rely less on banks and more on sale of securities to acquire capital, while banks were more concerned with government securities and, later, with personal short-term loans. The small producer existed in a no-man's land where sale of securities was not possible and bank loans were increasingly difficult to get.[34]

In those rare cases where loans for small businesses continued to be made, the average sawmiller had difficulty meeting the criteria for collateral. He could not use forest inventories, nor real or fixed property, as security before the mid-1930s. Even the loosening of restrictions on the use of primary products as collateral in the 1930s did little to help New Brunswick lumbermen, who at this stage had been stripped of their forest lands and forced to take sub-licences from the pulp and paper companies. Also, when the lumbermen sought capital before embarking on the winter's cut, they were usually not in possession of the previous year's cut. In short, they often had no inventory to offer as security.

Given the restricted access to forest lands and capital, the persistence of a marketing system dominated by merchant exporters worsened the position of the sawmilling industry. Most lumber passed through the hands of one of the Maritime's half-dozen large-scale exporters. Operating out of the region's major ports, they acquired wood from producers or small agents, chartered ships and dealt with buyers in the country to which the lumber was being shipped. These exporters were of such size and importance as to be a fair match in bargaining with the province's leading lumbermen, although some large millers could switch exporters if agreement on price and grading of merchandise could not be reached. When dealing with small producers, however, the exporters had a distinct advantage. Because of the problems involved in shipping a bulk staple in small lots, small lumber producers could only deal with one exporter at a time. When profit margins were low and markets weak, small producers had little choice but to accept whatever the exporter offered.[35]

The exporters' powers were multiplied in the areas where they also acted as financial backers. The producers' flexibility to bargain with the exporters was thus lost and any benefits from an improved market accrued to the latter. Even more serious for the lumbermen was the fact that financing from the exporters was never assured on a long-term basis. Most exporters had nothing invested except the price of one year's stumpage, and often dropped producers when the market was poor.

---

34 John T. Sears, *Institutional Financing of Small Business in Nova Scotia* (Toronto, 1972).

35 Interviews with John Bigelow and Murice Martin, 1981.

The creation of the Maritime Lumber Bureau, a co-ordinating agency for marketing and standardization of prices and grades in 1939, did little to challenge the hegemony of the exporters. There was no fundamental attack on the credit system, resource control, or the old system of private exporters and buyers, and many small producers remained distrustful and were hesitant to join.[36] They were fearful that the organization's accent on grading would put the cost of reform on their shoulders, just as the cost of poor markets had been borne by them in the past. The setting of grading standards was not matched by an easing of the pressure involved in finding capital and a supply of logs.

A full understanding of sawmillers' difficulties in Alma in the 1920s, their sudden recovery in the 1930s and their lack of resistance to the national park in 1947, is only possible through reference to the rise of hegemony and state support of the pulp and paper industry. Sawmillers only succeeded to the extent that they could negotiate cutting rights from the reserves of the major licence holders. It was a tenuous system. The pulp companies, being under no obligation to sub-license, could weigh the pros and cons of such arrangements and accept or reject applications without being required to offer any public explanation. As taxes and licence fees were low and government regulations easy to meet, the holder was in no real need of sub-licensing, and yet had little to lose from the business. In this situation, cuts might be allowed, but only if the conditions were pleasing to the holder. In some cases, economics was the primary concern, and larger sawmill operators were favoured because they had the capital to guarantee the payment of stumpage fees and the successful marketing of the lumber.[37] In other cases, political concerns played an important role in the gaining of access to licensed Crown lands. A sawmiller with friends in government could encourage his local member and the minister to use their influence to ensure that the Crown land licence-holder viewed an application favourably. In this way sub-licensing acted as a vehicle for a form of petty patronage that was all the more useful because names of sub-licensees were never made public, as were the names of direct licensees.

After the Hollingsworth and Whitney takeover in 1922, some Alma residents hoped for a pulp and paper mill in Albert County.[38] The company, however, made it clear that it had sufficient manufacturing capacity and raw materials in Maine to make a Canadian plant an "unnecessary duplication".[39] Rather, Hollingsworth and Whitney viewed the White property as a "reserve for the protection of [their] American Plant".[40] Shortages of raw material at the Maine mill did not result in

---

36   Interviews with John Bigelow, 1981.

37   Little has been written on this process of "sub-licensing". Information was gleaned from personal interviews with lumbermen and retired government foresters such as Harold Hoyt, Burtt Smith and Murice Martin.

38   Interview with Murice Martin, 1981.

39   RG 39, vol. 594, file 10, p. 270, NAC.

40   RG 39, vol. 594, file 10, p. 274, NAC.

pulpwood cuts in Alma, lending support to the local belief that Hollingsworth and Whitney was satisfied to leave Alma's major lumber land untouched in expectation of some highly indefinite future need.[41]

The monopolization of forest lands by Hollingsworth and Whitney was a serious obstacle to the lumbermen in Alma as they attempted to recover from the 1921 crisis. By contrast, it was easy to find milling facilities to replace the dismantled White mills. Prior to the 1920s, cheaper portable sawmills had been growing in popularity. White had realized the value of using these mills to reach trees that were too far from the river to be transported to the stationary mills in the usual manner, and also to mill the dense and less-buoyant hardwoods. Though portable cuts remained a very minor activity in comparison to the stationary mills, they did generate enough business to encourage John McLaughlin, one of White's employees, to purchase a portable mill and accept White company contracts. Thus when the White mills were dismantled in 1921, the McLaughlin portable mill remained intact.[42]

Another group was formed to buy a second-hand portable mill, probably from the McLennan Company in the nearby town of Albert. The original partnership consisted of Jack Strayhorne, who had been an edgerman in White's mill; Edward Hickey, a mill-steam engineer; Fred Hickey, a tallyman and surveyor; Hantford Keirstead, who had also been involved in lumbering; and "Big Jack" McLaughlin, a cousin of the previously mentioned John McLaughlin. Each of the men had held responsible positions under White and no doubt possessed savings which could be reinvested in the portable mill. Eventually McLaughlin, Keirstead and one of the Hickeys became involved in other phases of the local lumber industry, leaving Strayhorne and Fred Hickey as the two major owners and operators of the mill. Although the Strayhorne-Hickey mill and the McLaughlin mill were the two most active sawing operations in the area, from time to time cuts were made using saw-

---

41 This was not unusual in the pulp and paper industry. Pulp and paper companies established a tradition of controlling far larger amounts of forest than they needed because such reserves served a purpose, even if never actually used. On one hand, they were protection for the companies' large capital expenditures and insurance against natural disaster. On the other hand, they were often virtual gifts from governments to entice industry into an area. These lots of land then became a source of power in negotiating not only with governments, but also in negotiating with small woodlot owners and "independent" woodsmen who cut from company land on contract. Interview with John Bigelow, 1981; Osborn, *The Paper Plantation,* chs. 4, 5; New Brunswick, *Report,* 1964, pp. 51-2, 60-5. The same situation prevailed in Inverness and Victoria counties on Cape Breton Island, Nova Scotia, where the Oxford Paper Company held a large Crown lease without developing or exploiting the forest resource. See L. Anders Sandberg, "Forest Policy in Nova Scotia: The Big Lease, Cape Breton Island, 1899-1960", *Acadiensis,* XX, 2 (Spring 1991), also in this volume.

42 Interview with Jim McLaughlin, 1981.

mills brought in from other parts of the province. Such non-local names as Berryman, Duffy and Bourque appeared in the area during years when cuts were especially large.[43]

Generally, these portable mill owners were responsible only for the sawing operation while the cutting and hauling was carried out by separate parties. The men who organized the logging operations were usually permanent residents and small landholders, whose surnames can be found repeatedly among the names of original land grantees in the parish.[44] The composition of the crews was also heavily based on kinship, with the head man's own sons and cousins often being members. Occasionally, as the cuts increased in size, people from other parts of the county, as well as Acadians, Prince Edward Islanders and Nova Scotians, worked in Alma, although the majority of the labourers continued to be from local families.[45]

The major problem was not the logging and milling arrangements, but finding backers who could capitalize operations and pry stumpage from Hollingsworth and Whitney. This was very difficult. Apart from some clean-up operations and survey work for Hollingsworth and Whitney in the 1922 season, there were few cuts allowed on the company's Alma holdings in the 1920s. There were, however, some other stop-gap methods of finding capital and stumpage.[46] Before his death (reportedly by suicide)[47] in 1930, Garfield White appears to have been able to use his personal funds and his connections with Hollingsworth and Whitney to back John McLaughlin for a few cuts on the company's lands. However, Garfield represented the last attachment to a company that was unlikely to expand and re-establish after the 1921 catastrophe.[48] Many lumbermen were financed for cuts on inferior private woodlots. The Bonnie River Lumber Company of Charlotte County, New

---

43 Letter from Murice Martin, 21 Oct. 1981; interview with Bob Hickey, 1981; Department of Natural Resources, "Chief Scalers Reports", 1920-47, RS 107 15/3/7 to 15, PANB.

44 Some of those organizing the "logging" were Wallie Alexander, Owen Martin, Alfred McQuaid, Bill McKinley, Henry Butland and Tom Elliot.

45 Letter from Murice Martin, 28 Sept. 1981.

46 The tracing of these backers is difficult because transactions were often casual and based on verbal agreements. Most of the information on the Alma cuts between 1921 and 1935 was taken from three letters from Murice Martin (20 and 28 September and 21 October 1981) and interviews with Murice Martin, Norvil Martin (former partner of Fred Colpitts), L.R. Colpitts, Bob Hickey and Jim McLaughlin, 1981.

47 Interview with Murice Martin, 1981.

48 Garfield White's operations ceased completely in 1928, and no cuts were made on Hollingsworth and Whitney's lands in 1926-7 and 1927-8. In Nova Scotia, by contrast, large volumes of pulpwood were harvested by contractors and then sold. In 1926-7, the company cut 31,645 cords of pulpwood, with a market value of $379,751, and paid its contractors $232,820. In 1927-8, the company cut 50,690

Brunswick, contracted Alma portables to mill local cuts, but Bonnie River had no permanent investment in the area and disappeared when markets tightened. Scattered backing from other small and insufficiently capitalized buyers often ended in bankruptcies and unpaid stumpage fees.[49] When the Depression hit, all of these sources dried up and Alma was left dependent on one last method of backing — the Saint John exporters, primarily the MacKay Lumber Company. As the major supplier of credit and the major buyer in the area, MacKay was able to offer low prices with the assurance that his would be the only bid. MacKay, like Bonnie River, had no investment in Alma beyond annual loans and was therefore free to withdraw support at any time.

On the whole, the 1920s were difficult years for the Alma samilling industry, although the portable sawmills maintained some activity (Table I). As a result, between 1921 and 1931 the population of the parish fell from 674 to 495.[50] White's stationary sawmills were junked and any valuables left were sold in Saint John. What was left of the mills fell into disrepair as did the dams, thus removing the rivers from use as transportation for the logs. In the early 1930s, the New Brunswick sawmilling industry faced a chaotic international market with demand and prices for sawn lumber at their lowest point. In Alma, backers were hard to find and, without backing, the resource was closed to lumbermen. The gradual increases in size of cuts made during the 1920s came to a sudden halt in 1930. Nevertheless, over the next few years production in the community increased. In 1932 the cut was 2.5 million board feet; in 1933, 4 million board feet; then, in 1934, production doubled and maintained at least that level every year until the creation of the park in 1947 (Table I).[51]

The recovery of the Alma sawmilling industry in the 1930s was in large measure due to a crisis in the pulp and paper industry, which, after the boom of the 1920s, was seriously affected by the Depression of the 1930s. As pleas for employment filled department files, government was active in encouraging large Crown land holders to allow cuts on their leases. Ironically, the government was asking for public access to land that was defined as public property. The large licence holders of Crown lands showed a willingness to co-operate and accept government recom-

---

cords, total selling value $608,282.62, and paid its contractors $392,756.37. Since very little money went into managing these lands, and taxes were low, forest lands were clearly a good source of profit.

49 Colpitts, "Alma, New Brunswick and the Twentieth Century Crisis of Readjustment", pp. 113-6.

50 Canada, *Census Reports,* 1921 and 1931.

51 These estimates of size of cuts in Alma were compiled from Hollingsworth and Whitney Papers held at the Dalhousie University Archives, New Brunswick Chief Scaler's Reports and Fundy National Park Land Assembly files.

mendations on allotment of "sub-licensees", but not without something in return: lower stumpage fees and less-stringent forest regulations.[52]

Two backers in Alma managed to access wood through the new arrangement between government and the pulp and paper industry. Through their efforts, the two river systems were reopened and the stationary mills re-established. Operations on the Upper Salmon River were guided by Hartford Keirstead and Judson Cleveland until 1939, when Keirstead left the partnership and Cleveland became the dominant party. The sawmill on the Point Wolfe River was run by Strayhorne and Hickey and a new backer, Fred Colpitts.

Judson Cleveland was a member of a prominent Alma family and had been White's superintendent before the 1921 failure. It was Cleveland and Keirstead who took over what was left of White's company operations in 1928. They operated one portable sawmill but soon expanded to several more. Capital employed increased from $2,000 to $8,000. Then, in 1935, when Cleveland was in his mid-seventies, the partners built a stationary sawmill, boosting their employed capital to $14,000.[53] This expansion was perhaps inspired by an awareness of the problems of unstable and insufficient capital, the limited use of the portable mill and the gap that could be filled by backers seeking to expand in the industry.[54]

The patron-client relations in woods and sawmill operations are clearly illustrated in the case of the Cleveland and Keirstead mills. The harvesting, transporting and even some of the sawing was done on a contract basis. In 1932, Cleveland and Keirstead employed 11 contractors to cut on Hollingsworth and Whitney lands. The total amount paid was $10,740, with a low of $256 and a high of $2,412. Cuts were made in the winter, employing from 40 to 50 men, with operations beginning in November or December and ending in April of May. The portables employed from 10 to 15 men and operated mainly in the winter, from January to March.

---

52 For samples of correspondence between major licence holders and government, see "Minutes of Meeting of Lumbermen and Government", 26 Sept. 1934; River Valley Lumber Co. to the Minister, 6 Oct. 1931; "Possible Lumber Cut 1932-33", 17 Oct. 1932; Nashwaak Pulp and Paper Co. to the Minister, 29 Sept. 1932, Records of the Department of Natural Resources, RG 10, RS 106, boxes 46 and 47, PANB. To quote from one, "Concerning our discussions in Saint John on the 28th, should you decide to reduce crown land stumpage for the 1932-33 operating season to $1.00, $1.25 or $1.50 per thousand feet spruce, fir, pine, etc. in promoting production of lumber for relief of unemployment, we will cooperate". The popular protests directed against the pulp and paper industry also forced the provincial government to pass minimum wage legislation for woodsmen. The industry, however, found "innovative" ways of minimizing the effect of the legislation. See Bill Parenteau, "Pulp, Paper and Poverty", *New Maritimes*, 7, 4 (March/April, 1989), pp. 22-4.

53 This information was gathered from Timber and Sawmill Records, Micro-F11309, PANB.

54 Interview with John Bigelow, 1981.

When the stationary mill was established, the work force increased and work pattern changed. Fifty to 60 men worked in the woods during the winter, while the sawmill employed from 30 to 40 men in the summer. Some evidence suggests that the mill was idle in the early spring and late summer to accommodate the ploughing and harvesting of crops. The seasonal pattern of work and the local competition for stumpage, contracts and jobs, coupled with the indifference of Hollingsworth and Whitney to selling stumpage, were factors that wedded the sawmilling industry to local politics. Local people lined up behind traditional parties as the parties were seen, quite correctly, as a source of help in securing a wood supply.

Fred Colpitts started the sawmill on the Point Wolfe River in 1934. Colpitts was the son of an Albert County farming family whose transition from comfortable mixed farmer to sawmiller was achieved via the fox ranching industry. Influenced by successes in fur farming on Prince Edward Island, Colpitts, while in his early twenties, formed a company, raised money by local sale of stocks and started a small ranch. By 1936 he operated what was reputed to be the largest fox ranch in the British Empire. However, the fortunes of fox ranching were tied to the vagaries of the fashion industry. Perhaps for this reason, Colpitts diversified, building a beef herd, hiring crews to cut pulp and pit props, buying a store, looking into investing in Alberta and putting money into the sawmilling industry.[55] His reasons for choosing sawmilling were probably quite similar to Cleveland's. It was a business he knew, his family having logged as well as farmed. Like Cleveland, he apparently saw the need to centralize the mills again and also realized that gaps had been left by the fall of old lumber barons and the retrenchment policies of former backers. One other motive might be added. Colpitts was a Liberal MLA, representing Albert County from 1930 to 1939. While the financial outlay for the Point Wolfe operation was not too great, he might have considered it to be worthwhile in terms of the political value of goodwill created in Alma.

On one level, Colpitts and Cleveland appeared to play roles quite similar to each other and indeed to White, or even to the backers who had existed during the years intervening between the fall of White and the reorganization of the stationary mills in the 1930s. They arranged stumpage, found capital, distributed contracts, organized company crews and negotiated sale of the product. In some respect, their operations held more promise than the portable sawmills of the 1920s, since both Cleveland and Colpitts reopened the rivers and invested in stationary sawmills. However, they were different from White in that their control of the resource and of the town was much weaker. They did not own the forests or local stores.

At another level, Colpitts and Cleveland functioned differently in their methods of finding capital, buying stumpage and marketing. Colpitts worked from a rather stronger position, which stemmed in large part from his superior access to capital in the form of earnings from the fox industry and bank loans that that collateral made

---

55 Ian Sclanders, "You Take Two Foxes", *Maclean's Magazine,* LX (1947), p. 18.

possible.[56] Cleveland relied more heavily on MacKay for backing on a year-to-year basis. On at least two occasions between 1936 and 1947, MacKay refused credit to Cleveland, who was then forced to acquire capital from his "rival" on the Point Wolfe River.[57] To this was added another problem: because Cleveland relied heavily on MacKay for capital, he could not simply change exporters if grading and prices did not appeal to him. Though both Colpitts and Cleveland dealt for much of the period with MacKay, Colpitts retained greater manoeuvrability, reportedly switching exporters at times to improve his bargaining position.[58]

There is also some evidence that Colpitts may have had an advantage in the acquisition of timber. In the late 1940s, Cleveland's mill was listed in a Department of Lands and Mines report that recorded New Brunswick sawmillers who had been suffering from a shortage of stumpage.[59] Cleveland's problem may have been caused by the fact that Colpitts was a better credit risk, but it is also possible that any pressure government was exerting on Crown land holders to increase cuts was acting in favour of Colpitts, a Liberal MLA. When his involvement with the Point Wolfe operation became evident in 1934, the Liberals were in opposition, but in the election of 1935 the Conservative government was defeated. Cleveland vocally supported the Conservative Party, and the consequent loss of political friends in Fredericton may have made it more difficult to pry stumpage from Hollingsworth and Whitney. It may also have tied Cleveland even more tightly to MacKay, as the exporter operated a business of a size to be less affected by the shifting tides of provincial politics.

Hollingsworth and Whitney was not responsible to the public for its decisions on how to distribute stumpage sales from its Crown land leases and, therefore, no official record exists expressing its motivation for being party to such practices. It is possible, however, to speculate on the reasons. No doubt pressures applied from Fredericton tipped the balance in the direction of selling stumpage. As stated earlier, government was not reforming the industry, but was encouraging licence holders to allow cuts in order to reduce unemployment. Hollingsworth and Whitney could not expect much profit from allowing sawmillers to cut on its land. In fact,

---

56 Interview with L.R. Colpitts, 1981. The banks favoured big business but, as Sears suggests, small business loans could be made, and indeed sometimes were, if the applicant was either well established in the business or possessed a "good account". A "good account" was defined as "an applicant who can exert significant pressure on the bank". More bluntly, "an endorser could pressure a bank into making a loan it would prefer not to make". Sears, *Institutional Financing,* pp. 51, 85n. Such pressure was often political, and Colpitts, as a Liberal MLA from 1930 to 1939, possessed such power.

57 Interview with Murice Martin, 1981.

58 Interview with L.R. Colpitts, 1981.

59 Department of Natural Resources, Deputy Minister's Office Records, RG 10, RS 106, vol. 46, PANB.

stumpage revenues never exceeded $10,000 per year.[60] On the other hand, the costs to Hollingsworth and Whitney were small. The company kept only one agent in the area, with scaling and inspection of cuts being done by government employees at a minimal cost.[61] The risk of fees owed Hollingsworth and Whitney not being paid was removed once stable backers appeared on the scene to guarantee stumpage. Such sales, made in large units, involved little administration and bookkeeping. Hollingsworth and Whitney had little in terms of profits to either lose or gain by the sale of stumpage.

The reorganization of the sawmilling industry in the 1930s did not result in general ease and prosperity, yet the community showed signs of success. The size of the cuts grew, averaging over 10 million board feet a year. In the late 1930s the Point Wolfe mill burned, and one of the partners died shortly thereafter; another mill was later constructed on the site. A new partnership of Strayhorne, Wortman and Colpitts was formed and again broken by death. Colpitts took on new partners who managed the cut and the mill until its closure in 1947. The population of Alma climbed from 495 in 1931 to 657 in 1941, an increase of 32 per cent. Of the other five parishes in Albert County, one declined in population by one per cent, another by seven per cent, two increased by eight and 14 per cent, and only one parish, the one across the river from the city of Moncton, even approached Alma's rate of growth.[62] The benefits of improved production and increased population not only took the form of widening the profit margin at the upper end of the industry's hierarchy, but also served to sustain those employed and remaining in the county. County council records, census materials and park land assembly papers leave the impression that living standards in Alma compared favourably with those in the rest of the county and in rural Canada in general.[63] Department of Lands and Mines employees who visited the town during the period depicted it as "having hard times but not bad in comparison with other parts of New Brunswick", "...not well off at all, but comfortable for those times — certainly not slave labour".[64]

However successful the community of Alma was in dealing with the Depression, it nevertheless remained based on an unsound foundation. The stationary sawmills had not removed the industry's major problems, but rather had provided, in the person of two backers, tools with which the industry could continue to exist in the shadow of unresolved difficulties. Though solid backing and political influence

---

60 Department of Natural Resources, Fundy National Park Land Assembly Records, RG 10, RS 145, Hollingsworth and Whitney file, PANB.

61 Interview with Holly Gildart (the son of Hollingsworth and Whitney's agent in Alma), 1981.

62 Canada, *Census Reports*, 1941, vol. I, Table 7, p. 317.

63 Colpitts, "Alma, New Brunswick and the Twentieth Century Crisis of Adjustment", p. 129.

64 Interviews with Harold Hoyt and Burtt Smith, 1981.

might have encouraged Hollingsworth and Whitney to continue selling stumpage indefinitely, the pulp company was under no obligation to the sawmillers beyond an agreement renewed on a yearly basis. The mills' supply could be legally cut off at any time. For Cleveland at least, capital was still a periodic problem, and if the re-establishment of his stationary sawmill in 1934 gave him slightly more negotiating power with exporters, it did nothing to combat market problems such as grading, price and international reputation, all of which still plagued the province.

The revival of stationary mills in the 1930s merely gave the industry another management level, absorbing profits in exchange for powers that could exert some degree of influence on the government, Hollingsworth and Whitney, the bank and the exporter. The backer's role was largely to deal with obstacles that could have been more efficiently removed by basic changes in resource control, credit and marketing.

Ultimately, the success of sawmilling in Alma was dependent on Hollingsworth and Whitney, an inactive absentee landlord accessible to local people only through government and local political strongmen. Colpitts (and Cleveland, to a lesser extent) acted as backers-cum-politicians-cum-entrepreneurs and, therefore, relied on the goodwill of both the corporate landlord and the government. Thus the mutual indebtedness of government and the pulp and paper industry was manifested at the local level by the entrepreneur's indebtedness to the political party. Within the community, workers depended on the management levels above them to obtain contracts and wage work. Ironically, the industry's survival was predicated on a self-perpetuating system that offered no mechanism for major reform. There was no easily identifiable point at which pressure for change could be applied without bringing down the entire structure. The essential weaknesses of the industry remained beneath the veneer of relative prosperity.

The changing position of the people of Alma was not resolved by reforms in the forest industries but by the 1947 announcement that the community would be the site of a national park. In the 1920s the government began to promote tourism via the creation of national parks as a method of providing service-sector jobs for Canadians displaced by the introduction of modern capital-intensive industries. The 20-year process of selecting a site for New Brunswick's first national park is yet another story.[65] Perhaps it is enough to mention a few of the most striking aspects of that process. The selection of Alma was the result of a long political wrangle during which the community was never the parks branch's first choice.[66] No socio-economic studies of the area were done, though some parks employees warned

---

65   For more on the funding of the National Park see Colpitts, "Alma, New Brunswick and the Twentieth Century Crisis of Adjustment", ch. 4.

66   RG 84, vol. 483, Fundy National Park Site Selection. See especially "Report of J. Smart, Chief Inspector National Parks re: Examination of Proposed National Park, Province of New Brunswick, 1937", Parks Canada, National Parks Branch Archives.

about disruption of local industry.[67] Hollingsworth and Whitney, which held the land virtually free of charge for 25 years, received the largest expropriation payment, while people who owned no land in the park but relied on the resource for a living got nothing.[68] No consideration of future earnings was made in expropriation.[69] Finally, the park itself did not prove to be the source of economic growth that some hoped it would be and, indeed, as a source of income it shared many of the disadvantages of the sawmilling industry.[70]

In spite of these problems, Alma residents did not voice objections or act collectively to negotiate for better terms. Hollingsworth and Whitney had little real interest in the land and thus settled amicably early in the expropriation negotiations.[71] Cleveland lost his source of wood supply but was not compensated because his mill, though rendered worthless by the park, was outside park boundaries. Perhaps because of his advanced age or perhaps because he expected no help from the Liberal Party, his objections were confined to a few angry letters. Colpitts was unlikely to argue too vocally with the Liberal government he had been part of or with Hollingsworth and Whitney, which he relied upon for supply of timber.[72] Perhaps he was also tired of the insecurity and instability of the unreformed industry and had hopes for a new type of prosperity based on tourism. For the Alma small lumber producers, the same fear of loss of capital and timber supply existed, as did the feeling that these problems were beyond their ability to correct. During the decade before the creation of the park the community had prospered, but the memory of the 1921 crisis had not faded.

The village of Alma itself, being just outside park boundaries, still exists today but with a reduced population. Within the park, the farmhouses, barns, mills, churches and all other traces of past human history are gone, having been bulldozed following expropriation for the park. Yet, to forget the history of sawmilling com-

---

67 Colpitts, "Alma, New Brunswick and the Twentieth Century Crisis of Adjustment", p. 184.

68 Department of Natural Resources, Fundy National Park Land Assembly Records, RG 10, RS 145, PANB. The people expropriated in the establishment of the Cape Breton National Highlands Park in the mid-1930s experienced a similar fate. See Sandberg, "The Big Lease".

69 Department of Natural Resources, Fundy National Park Land Assembly Records, RG 10, RS 145, PANB.

70 See for example, Atlantic Area Consultants Ltd., *Preliminary Economic Study of the Municipality of Albert County*, ca. 1965, p. 76.

71 In the 1950s, the company merged with Scott Paper, an American pulp and paper company, which now operates in Nova Scotia.

72 Department of Natural Resources, Fundy National Park Land Assembly Records, RG 10, RS 145, PANB.

munities like Alma in the years following 1921 is to assume an inevitable transition from sawmilling to pulp and paper without regard for the obstacles created by government and financial institutions with respect to resource and capital access, and market reform. Local sawmillers in Alma preserved the local industry through the manipulation of government, credit systems and the pulp and paper landlord. Paradoxically, the very weapons used to perpetuate the sawmilling industry also served to block any attack on its fundamental problems. The continued presence of obstacles to the access of wood and capital, and an inequitable marketing system, made the people willing to accept the arrival of government support in the form of a national park.

Table I

Lumber Cut in New Brunswick and Alma, 1922-1947

Years	New Brunswick cut in thousand board feet	Estimated Alma cut in thousand board feet	Alma cut as a percentage of the New Brunswick cut
1922-23		3,120	
1924		3,310	
1925	405,203	3,160	.78
1926	381,673	3,460	.91
1927	335,395	2,000-4,000	.60-1.2
1928	283,738	5,500	1.9
1929	363,114	6,500	1.8
1930	275,626	4,500	1.6
1931	130,412	2,500	1.9
1932	112,314	2,500	2.2
1933	100,568	4,000	4.0
1934	204,065	6,500-9,000	3.2-4.4
1935	230,751	7,500-11,000	3.2-4.8
1936	213,564	6,500-8,000	3.0-3.7
1937	306,823	11,500-15,000	3.7-5.0
1938	223,384	8,000	3.6
1939	210,919	no data	no data
1940	309,844	13,500-16,000	4.4-5.2
1941	369,988	9,500-11,000	2.6-3.0
1942	386,206	7,000-8,000	1.8-2.1
1943	340,170	8,000	2.4
1944	335,228	8,000	2.4
1945	292,443	8,000	2.7
1946	351,302	8,000	2.3
1947	389,042	8,000	2.1

Sources: Petrie, "The Regional Economy of New Brunswick", Appendix A, *Report of the New Brunswick Committee on Reconstruction* (1944), p. 96; Dominion Bureau of Statistics, *The Lumber Industry* (1926-1947) and *Operations in the Woods, Revised Estimate of Forest Produce* (1940-1947); Hollingsworth and Whitney Papers, Chief Scaler's Reports; and Fundy National Park Land Assembly Files.

"In Good Faith":
The Development of Pulpwood Marketing for
Independent Producers in New Brunswick, 1960-1975

Bill Parenteau

Farmers, small pulpwood contractors, truckers and woodlot owners throughout New Brunswick began to protest against the low prices they were receiving for their forest products in the early 1960s. The protest was touched off by a recession in the paper industry — a downturn in the world paper market that translated into shrinking markets and low prices for the wood of small producers. The immediate crisis, however, cannot fully explain the militant response of the farmers, contractors and woodlot owners; there had certainly been hard times for small wood producers before the 1960s without such a concerted and organized protest. The timing and direction of the small wood producers movement was shaped by ongoing structural changes in the rural farm economy and the market for woodlot products. Not coincidentally, the rhetoric of many of the young organizations that appeared during these years was laden with appeals to save the farming communities and the rural way of life. Many people who relied on the forest for their livelihood placed blame for the deteriorating economic and social conditions in rural communities of New Brunswick squarely on the pulp and paper companies of the province.

In the early 1960s wood producers in New Brunswick began a long struggle for government action to improve their position in the pulpwood market. Few tangible gains were achieved. This failure was partly a result of the producers' inability to speak with a unified voice, but it was also due to the unwillingness of the Liberal government to act on the recommendations of a royal commission, appointed in 1963 to deal with the problems of small wood producers. When the pulpwood market improved in the mid-1960s, the young associations could not sustain the level of popular participation necessary for applying pressure on the state; however, when the industry went into another recession in 1970, the movement re-emerged with vigour. At this point producers did speak with one voice, and they demanded state-controlled, mandatory collective bargaining for the price of pulpwood and a provincial government strategy of using Crown land leases as a lever to ensure that the mills bargained "in good faith". The provincial government passed legislation to facilitate the creation of a controlled marketing system for privately produced wood in the early 1970s. The decision of the Conservative Hatfield adminstration was a response to the demand of independent producers, but it was also in keeping with the government's forest-management agenda, aimed at meeting the deepening crisis of the pulp and paper industry in New Brunswick. Although the marketing system helped the small producer in some respects, it also upheld and legitimated the traditional power relationships between forest capital, the wood-producing classes and the state.

Agricultural associations and private wood producer groups began to protest against the low price of pulpwood during a period of major transformations in New Brunswick agriculture. Between 1941 and 1961 the number of farms in the province dropped from 31,889 to 18,331 and the area of farms from 3.5 to 2.2 million acres (1,417,500 to 891,000 ha).[1] To some degree the decline in the number of farms was due to attrition — the rising expectations and unwillingness of farm children to take up farming as an occupation. But other forces were also turning rural people away from farming and pushing them out of farm-commodity markets. The 42 per cent decrease in the number of farms and disproportional 37 per cent decrease in the area of farmland reflected the growing trend toward mechanization, commercialization and specialization, particularly in the potato and dairy farming sectors.[2] Production of agricultural commodities in New Brunswick was becoming more capital intensive and concentrated on larger farms in specific areas of the province. As in other provinces in Eastern Canada, the agricultural crisis of the post-Second World War period was experienced unevenly among regions of New Brunswick and economic strata of the farming population. It was the "small scale" sector of the farm economy — farms enumerated in the 1941 census as producing less than $1,200 surplus — that was being most harmed by technological, market and consumer changes.[3] Broad statements on the structure of agriculture in New

---

1 Canada, Dominion Bureau of Statistics [DBS], *Census of Agriculture*, 1961, vol. 5, no. 1, Bulletin 5.1-5, p. 1-1. The figures on both number of farms and acreage of farmland have been adjusted to allow for the 6,545 farms and 489,483 acres (198,241 ha) that were eliminated by a definitional change in the 1961 census.

2 Thomas Murphy, "The Structural Transformation of New Brunswick Agriculture, 1951-1981", M.A. thesis, University of New Brunswick, 1982; Arthur C. Parks, "New Brunswick Agriculture, 1945-1955", M.A. thesis, University of New Brunswick, 1957; *Report of the Royal Commission on the Potato Industry*, (Fredericton, 1962); G.C. Retson and P.C. L'Ecuyer, "A Study of Rural Problems in Madawaska County, New Brunswick", Economics Division, Canadian Department of Agriculture, 1963.

3 The term "Eastern Canada" includes Ontario, Quebec and the Atlantic Provinces. See M. Wilman, "Changes in Farm Size and Numbers in Canada", *Canadian Farm Economics*, 2 (1967), pp. 21-7; Murphy, "Transformation of New Brunswick Agriculture"; Retson and L'Ecuyer, "Rural Problems in Madawaska"; Peter Sinclair, "From Peasants to Corporations: The Development of Capitalist Agriculture in Canada's Maritime Provinces", in John Fry, ed., *Contradictions in Canadian Society*, (Toronto, 1983); Bernard Bernier, "The Penetration of Capitalism in Quebec Agriculture", *Canadian Review of Sociology and Anthropology*, XIII, 4 (1976), pp. 422-34; and John Warnock, "The Farm Crisis," in Laurier LaPierre, ed., *Essays on the Left*, (Toronto, 1971), pp. 121-33.

Brunswick cannot capture the complexity of these changes; they can, however, help to explain why protest against the paper industry frequently contained wider appeals to save and revitalize the rural communities of New Brunswick.

Although farmers and small woodlot owners in New Brunswick had supplied a large proportion of independently produced pulpwood for the provincial and export markets at least as far back as the 1920s, cash income from the sale of pulpwood became more important to these groups after the Second World War. The average percentage of total farm income generated from the sale of forest products in New Brunswick climbed from 16.2 per cent in the years 1941-5 to 25.9 per cent in 1951-5 and the total production of pulpwood on farms increased from 188,059 to 295,791 cords between the 1941 and 1951 censuses.[4] In part these increases were due to farmers being squeezed out of farm commodity markets; the high prices paid for "farm wood" from 1950 to 1952 also undoubtedly stimulated production. Indeed, the average return from pulpwood for farms that reported the sale of forest products rose dramatically, from $48 in 1941 to $245 in 1951. The latter figure was at least twice as high as for any other province in Eastern Canada.[5] Comprehensive data on the size and financial structure of the farms and other private woodlots was not compiled by census takers, but during the 1950s a Department of Agriculture study classified 30 areas where farming was undertaken in New Brunswick, and designated five of these as forest products areas, where 50 per cent or more of gross farm revenue was from the sale of wood. The 2,960 farms in these areas were located in parts of seven counties; they had an average size of 100 acres (41 ha), compared with the provincial average of 131 acres (53 ha); and 91 per cent sold less than $1,200 of farm commodities in 1951, whereas the average for all of New Brunswick was 48 per cent.[6] As in the pre-Second World War period, dependence on the production of forest products was thus most evident among less prosperous farmers in the marginal farming areas of the province.[7]

---

4   Eugene Grasberg and Hugh Whalen, *The New Brunswick Economy*, (Fredericton, 1959), p. 69; Canada, DBS, *Census of Agriculture*, 1951, vol. 5, pt. 1, New Brunswick, p. 6.1.

5   Restrictive Trade Practices Commission, Canada Department of Justice, *Report Concerning the Purchase of Pulpwood in Certain Districts of Eastern Canada*, (Ottawa, 1958), pp. 2-6.

6   The seven counties were Charlotte, Carleton, York, Sunbury, Northumberland, Restigouche and Gloucester. E.P. Reid and J.M. Fitzpatrick, *Atlantic Provinces Agriculture*, Economics Division, Canada Department of Agriculture (Ottawa, 1957). pp. 2-6.

7   This was also the conclusion of the New Brunswick Forest Development Commission. See John S. Bates, Director, *Report of the New Brunswick Forest Development Commission* (Fredericton, 1957). For the dependence of small farmers and settlers on the production of pulpwood in the 1920s, see Evidence taken at "Royal Commission on Pulpwood", 1924, in Records of the Canadian Forest Service, RG 39, vol. 593, nos. 4, 5 and 10, National Archives of Canada.

Changes in the market for woodlot products in the 1940s and 1950s also raised the dependence level of parts of rural New Brunswick on pulpwood. In 1910, on the eve of large scale pulp industry development, the value of farm wood sold for lumber products was several times that of pulpwood.[8] With the expansion of the export market in the 1910s, pulpwood became the leading forest product on New Brunswick farms, and the erection of large-scale pulp and paper mills in the 1920s assured that it would remain the most valuable farm forest commodity. Produced in four-foot lengths, pulpwood was easy to handle, and, with the development of sophisticated buying networks by the mid-1920s, it was also easy to market. Cumulative resource depletion, as well as the lack of markets for sawlogs and high returns on pulpwood, particularly after the Second World War, also contributed to the shift toward pulpwood.[9] The Census of Agriculture suggests that the major transition came during the 1940s. In 1940 the respective values of pulpwood and sawlogs produced on farms in the province were $1,157,389 and $925,529; by 1950 the value of pulpwood had risen substantially to $4,495,024 and, despite much higher prices for all farm wood, the value of sawlogs advanced only modestly to $1,011,537. Although changes in the enumeration of the census prevent further comparisons with 1960, successive commissions on the New Brunswick forest industries in 1957 and 1964 reported that the production of sawlogs on farms did not change materially after 1950.[10] Thus by 1960 the production of sawlogs on farms was considerably less significant than it had been even in 1940.

The production and sale of fuel wood from New Brunswick farms also declined sharply after 1940. Traditionally, farmers produced a large proportion of the fuel wood sold to consumers in the province.[11] With the development of alternative

---

8   Canada, DBS, *Census of Canada*, 1921, vol. 5, p. 679.

9   For the decline of saw milling and the rise of pulp and paper manufacturing see Bill Parenteau, "The Woods Transformed: The Emergence of the Pulp and Paper Industry in New Brunswick, 1918-1931", *Acadiensis*, XXII, 1 (Autumn 1992), forthcoming; Gerrit Hazenberg, "An Analysis of the New Brunswick Lumber Industry", M.A. thesis, University of New Brunswick, 1966; New Brunswick Resources Development Board, *The Development of the Forest and Forest Industries of New Brunswick*, (Fredericton, 1950); *Report of the New Brunswick Committee on Reconstruction* (Fredericton, 1944); Bates, dir., *Forest Development Commission*.

10 Canada, DBS, *Census of Agriculture*, 1951, New Brunswick, vol. 6, pt. 1., p. 6.1.; Bates, dir., *Forest Development Commission*; Louis Seheult, dir., *Report of the Royal Commission on Primary Forest Products in New Brunswick* (Fredericton, 1964).

11 The movement of farmers out of the market to take advantage of the higher regulated prices for sawlogs and pulpwood precipitated a crisis in the fuel wood supply during the Second World War. It is interesting to note that because of the labour shortage in the forest industries and wage and price controls, farmers and small woodlot owners were able to exert some influence over commodity prices by shifting production. See John D. Kennedy, *History of the Department of Munitions and Supply: Canada in the*

home heating fuels after the war, the market for firewood deteriorated. Again, the census figures note, at least in general terms, the pattern of decline. In 1940, 112,316 cords of fuel wood were sold from farms with a total value of $551,549; in 1950, 53,030 cords were sold, for a return of $556,815; and by 1960 the sale of fuel wood from farms had dropped to 16,155 cords, with no value recorded.[12] Combined with the falling production of wood for lumber, the collapse of the fuel wood market meant that most of the wood produced for sale on farms by the end of the 1950s — more than 80 per cent — was destined for the pulp mills.

Farmers were not the only members of the rural population affected by structural changes in the forest products industry. Throughout the period 1940-60 small non-farm holdings were steadily becoming an important source of forest production in New Brunswick. By 1960, in fact, they had surpassed farms in volume of production. The pattern of cutting on non-farm woodlots was more diverse than on farms, involving a complex web of productive relations between woodlot owners, contractors, wood cutters, truckers and buyers. At one end of the spectrum were the increasingly numerous small landowners, who were concerned only with selling stumpage.[13] At the other end were owner-operators who, like most farmers, cut and sold wood at roadside landings. Many in this group were distinct from farmers only at the whim of bureaucrats. Of the 14,645 fewer farms enumerated in the 1960 census, 6,545 were eliminated by a definitional change, and many in the larger group of 14,645 were producing forest products before and after they were dropped from the Census of Agriculture.[14] Thousands of New Brunswickers on non-farm woodlots produced primary forest products and were affected by the changes in the rural economy in the same way that farmers were.

It is difficult to compare production on farm and non-farm woodlots, because there were no statistics compiled on the latter until 1959. Information on the 1959-63 period shows that there were some differences between the two groups, but also that both were dependent mainly on pulpwood. In 1964, non-farm small holdings cut a higher percentage of sawlogs (25 per cent) than did farm holdings (13 per cent), and farms cut twice as much fuel wood, most of it for personal consump-

---

Second World War, (Ottawa, 1950), pp. 243-69; and Donald Gordon, Chairman, Wartime Prices and Trade Board to J.B. McNair, 12 November 1942; F.W. Pirie, Minister of Lands and Mines to John Baldwin, 19 December 1942; Memorandum to F.W. Pirie, re: Fuelwood, 1 May 1943, RS 106, box 34, Deputy Minister's Office Records, Department of Lands and Mines, Provincial Archives of New Brunswick [PANB].

12 Canada, DBS, *Census of Agriculture*, 1961, New Brunswick, vol. 5, pt. 1, Bull. 5.1-5, p. 8.1.

13 Seheult, dir., *Primary Forest Products*, pp. 12-25.

14 For an explanation of the change and number of farms affected, see Canada, DBS, *Census of Agriculture*, 1961, New Brunswick, vol. 5, pt. 1, Bull. 5.1-5, p. vii.

tion.[15] Figure 1 and Table I illustrate the production of sawlogs and pulpwood on all small private holdings from 1959 to 1963 in the five forest districts of the province. The wide variation in production on small holdings between regions was in large part due to the pattern of land tenure in the province. Sections 1 and 2 were dominated by large tracts of Crown land, while the southern forest areas, Sections 3 and 4, were mostly freehold land. Section 5 was in large part freehold land as well, although a tract of more than 1 million acres (405,000 ha), located in Madawaska and Victoria counties, was owned by paper companies. The higher volume of production in Sections 3 and 4 did not necessarily signify that small landowners in southern New Brunswick were more reliant on the sale of wood, only that there were more of them.[16] Independent wood producers on the narrow strip of freehold land along the North Shore and in parts of Madawaska County, for example, depended on the sale of forest products at least as much as did their counterparts in other areas of the province.[17]

Increased dependence on the pulpwood market after the Second World War intensified and highlighted the unequal relationship between small producers in New Brunswick and the province's pulp and paper companies. The ability of pulp mills to tightly control the price paid for independently produced pulpwood has been generally recognized by forest economists. Because of high capital costs and the vital importance of securing a guaranteed long-term supply of wood, it was common for individual mills to "achieve geographical isolation from competition for raw materials".[18] Prices for pulpwood were openly published and often fairly uniform throughout a region, even without agreements between companies. However, collusion was not uncommon, as was the case in Eastern Canada during the 1950s. In 1958 the Restrictive Trade Practices Commission of the federal Department of Justice, reported that paper company executives from Ontario, Quebec and

---

15 Seheult, dir., *Primary Forest Products*, p. 25.

16 The acreage and percentage of stocked forest land in small holdings — less than 500 acres (203 ha) — by district was as follows: District 1: 462,000 acres (187,110 ha), 16%; District 2: 424,000 acres (171,720 ha), 16%; District 3: 1,333,000 acres (539,865 ha), 46%; District 4: 1,165,000 acres (471,825 ha), 36%; District 5: 372,000 acres (150,660 ha), 18%. Seheult, dir., *Primary Forest Products*, p. 13.

17 Retson and L'Ecuyer, "Rural Problems in Madawaska"; Forge and Acadian Federations in Northern New Brunswick, brief submitted to Seheult, dir., *Primary Forest Products*.

18 Paul B. Huber, *Promoting Timber Cropping: Policies Toward Non-Industrial Forest Owners in New Brunswick* (Montreal, 1985), p. 43; Albert C. Worrell, *The Economics of American Forestry* (New York, 1959); D.S. Curtis, *Woodlot Owner Organizations in Eastern Canada: Historical Development, Legislation, Structure, Financing and Services, Information Report*, Canadian Forest Service-Maritimes (Fredericton, 1987).

Figure 1

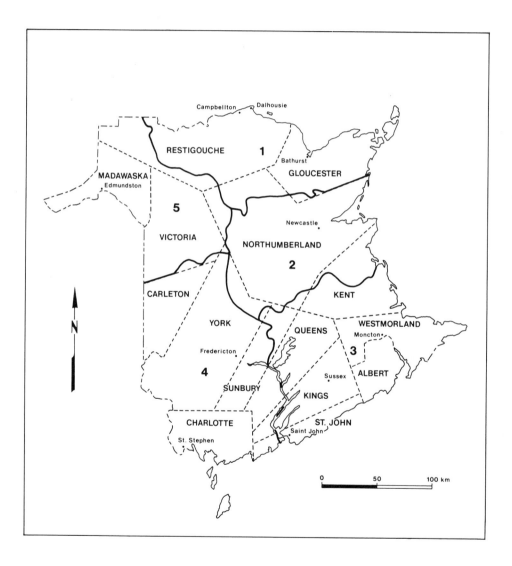

New Brunswick were meeting regularly between 1948 and 1954 to fix prices paid to farmers and other small producers of pulpwood. The participating companies had divided Eastern Canada into zones, set prices in each, and agreed upon how the anticipated production would be distributed.[19] These practices, the commission concluded, "had a depressing effect on the prices paid for such pulpwood". It urged a "complete abandonment of arrangements and practices among pulp and paper companies which restrain competition among them with respect to the purchase price of farmers wood".[20] The figures from the Bathurst Power and Paper Company's woodlands department in Table II suggest the extent to which companies in New Brunswick controlled the price of independently produced wood. Despite significant fluctuations in supply and demand, and rising costs of production, the Bathurst Company was able to hold prices remarkably stable for most of the 1950s and early 1960s.

A key factor in the industry's ability to dictate prices was ownership or control over large tracts of forest. New Brunswick paper companies held long-term leases over 70 per cent of the provincial Crown lands in 1955 — more than 7,500 square miles (1,944,000 ha) — mostly in the northern half of the province. In addition they owned 36 per cent of private forest land, concentrated in southern and western New Brunswick.[21] A perpetual supply of pulpwood allowed mills to use independently produced pulpwood as a residual source of supply to reduce the overall cost of pulpwood procurement. In practical terms, the mills bought wood from small producers because it was less expensive than producing it on company land. Small producers in New Brunswick sold pulpwood to the mills at a deflated price because they had little choice.[22] The ability of paper companies to use Crown lands as a

19 The rationalization of production during the Second World War may have had an effect on the attitude of woodland managers toward purchased wood. That is, the Munitions and Supply Board demonstrated that the production and procurement of farm wood could be, to some degree, controlled. Some of the industry members of the board were affiliated with companies that participated in the price fixing meetings after the war. *Report Concerning Purchase of Pulpwood*, pp. 140-2; Kennedy, *History of Munitions and Supply*, pp. 243-69.

20 *Report Concerning Purchase of Pulpwood*, p. 214. For an analysis of the practice of price fixing in the 1980s see Huber, *Timber Cropping*, p. 43.

21 Bates, dir., *Forest Development Commission*, p. 336.

22 For a discussion of similar relationships between primary producers and large enterprises in the farming and fishing industries, see Henry Veltmeyer, "The Capitalist Underdevelopment of Atlantic Canada", and R. James Sacouman, "The Differing Origins, Organization and Impact of Maritime and Prairie Co-operative Movements to 1940", in R. Brym and R.J. Sacouman, *Underdevelopment and Social Movements in Atlantic Canada* (Toronto, 1979); Wallace Clement, "Property and Proletarianization: The Transformation of Simple Commodity Production in Canadian Farming and Fishing", in Clement, *Class, Power and Property: Essays on Canadian Society* (Toronto, 1983).

means of reducing the price paid for independently produced wood was central to the struggle of small wood producers in New Brunswick for economic justice.

It was in the context of accelerating rural decline and increasing domination by the paper industry that farmers, woodlot owners, contractors and others involved in the independent production of pulpwood in New Brunswick began to organize. The early 1960s were not good years for the paper industry or, consequently, for the small pulpwood producers in the province. After an unprecedented decade of expansion at the end of the Second World War, the paper industry entered one of its periodic slumps in the late 1950s, marked by excess capacity and falling prices on the world market.[23] As most of the paper produced in the province was for export, New Brunswick felt the full force of the recession. By the end of 1961 the effects of the slump had filtered down through the production process to the raw materials end. The total volume of pulpwood produced in New Brunswick fell from 1.1 million to 770,000 cords between 1961 and 1962; the 1962 figure was the lowest total since the Depression.[24] Farmers and woodlot owners shared in the ill fortunes of the industry; in fact, they absorbed more than their share of the drop in pulpwood production. While production fell off by 25 per cent on company operations, the corresponding figure on farms and small woodlots was 45 per cent (see Table I). Some mills simply stopped receiving wood; others shut down and started up deliveries of wood according to their needs. "This discrepancy", commented one official, "shows clearly the marginal position of the woodlot owners and their vulnerability to any weakness in the market".[25] By this time producers understood very well the extent of their vulnerability in the market. The decreasing demand for wood in the 1960s — after more than a decade of stagnant prices and more than two decades of rural decline — unified all of the groups that had a stake in the independent production of pulpwood, in an effort to improve the position of the small producer.

The organization of small wood producers in the New Brunswick pulpwood industry began in the first months of 1962 and spread quickly; by the end of 1963 there were producer associations representing nearly all producers who wished to participate. The early rhetoric of the movement appealed to a sense of community and was also marked by open hostility toward the paper industry. Newly formed producer associations and existing agricultural societies — the institution through which rural primary producers traditionally voiced their opinions — conveyed the concern and dissatisfaction of the rural population. One farmer expressed the view among small producers when he declared: "We must do something. It is not a ques-

---

23 Newsprint Association of Canada, *Newsprint Data,* yearly report, (Montreal, 1958-65); 1958, pp. 9-13; 1959, pp. 9-11; 1960, pp. 12-15; 1961, pp. 3-12; 1962, pp. 10-14.

24 Seheult, dir., *Primary Forest Products,* p. 29.

25 Seheult, dir., *Primary Forest Products,* p. 24.

tion of whether we will or we won't. It is either root, hog, or die now. We either have to organize or be wiped out".[26]

At its most basic level, the organization of independent producers was a reaction to low mill prices. The common denominator among farmers, woodlot owners, small contractors, woodsworkers, truckers and other interested parties — who up until this time had expressed very little common interest — was the sting of low wood prices and unequal exchange relations with the paper industry. They contended that paper companies could afford to pay more for the wood of private producers, and that they should be paid an amount per cord equal to the cost of company wood produced on Crown lands.[27] Although there was no consensus on what the price of wood should be, all small independent producers agreed that prices had failed to keep up with rising production costs, and that the paper industry was dealing unfairly with them.

Even before the height of the market crisis in 1963, pulpwood producers in some areas of the province had begun to recognize the importance of organization. At the annual meeting of the New Brunswick Federation of Agriculture in December 1961, a resolution asking the provincial government to force paper companies to buy from woodlot owners before cutting on Crown lands "stirred up a hornet's nest". It was, delegates agreed, "the most important resolution to come before the meeting in years", and after heated discussion passed unanimously.[28] In February 1962 the Southern New Brunswick Pulpwood Producers Association (SNBPPA) was formed in Kings County to promote higher prices for pulpwood and better management of woodlots, and to "encourage the formation of other associations of pulpwood producers and co-operate with them". Like other organizations representing primary producers in Atlantic Canada, the association's leadership represented a cross section of the rural population.[29] The president of the association, Anglican clergyman William Hart, and the vice-president, James Thompson, became key figures in the province-wide movement. By as early as 1962 the *Maritime Farmer*, of which Thompson was editor, was acting as a mouthpiece for the organization; Hart became the first president of the New Brunswick Federation of Wood Producers when it was founded in December 1965.

In May 1962 the small wood producers movement was given further encouragement by the formation of a marketing board in Madawaska County. Formed under the Natural Products Control Act (1952), the Madawaska Forest Products

---

26 *Maritime Farmer* (Sussex), 7 July 1964.

27 See, for example, Madawaska Forest Products Marketing Board, brief submitted to Seheult, dir., *Primary Forest Products,* p. 13.

28 *Maritime Farmer*, 2 January 1962.

29 The executive committee included, in addition to a clergyman and an editor, a bank manager, two farmers, a woods operator/trucker and a carpenter. On the complex class formation of lower-class social movements in the region, see Brym and Sacouman, *Underdevelopment and Social Movements*, pp. 1-15.

Marketing Board was given jurisdiction over making joint contracts for all of the independent producers in the county. The formation of this organization was heavily influenced by developments in Quebec, where Bill 41 was passed in 1961, requiring pulp and paper companies to negotiate with small wood producer marketing boards. If an agreement could not be reached in Quebec, the producers had recourse to compulsory arbitration, and companies were required to honour contracts arrived at by the government or face the suspension of cutting rights on Crown lands.[30] While the Natural Products Control Act enabled the Madawaska Board to fix pulpwood prices within the county, it did not compel acceptance by the paper companies. The Madawaska Board and other small producer associations in New Brunswick lobbied for provincial legislation with the same force as Bill 41 for the next 20 years. They were unsuccessful; however, the Madawaska Forest Products Marketing Board did serve as a model for the modified province-wide marketing system that developed in the 1970s.[31]

As conditions in the pulpwood market deteriorated, the movement for province-wide organization gathered steam. By the beginning of 1963 there was a growing list of organizations agitating for higher prices. Producer groups such as the Central New Brunswick Pulpwood Producers Association and the Charlotte County Woodlot Owners Association were formed specifically to meet the crisis in the pulpwood market. Previously established farmer associations such as the Miramichi Federation of Agriculture and the Forge and Acadian Federation of Northern New Brunswick also focused their energies on promoting higher wood prices. Six of these organizations came together in 1965 to form the New Brunswick Wood Producers Association.[32]

The issue of pulpwood prices made it to the provincial legislature in late February 1963. H.H. Williamson, an MLA from Gloucester County, proposed that a Forest Products Board be established in New Brunswick for the purpose of regulating pulpwood prices. In the grand tradition of Canadian politics, Liberal premier Louis Robichaud appointed a royal commission to investigate the problem before debate was opened and Williamson withdrew his proposal. The Royal Commission on Primary Forest Products was established by Order-in-Council on 10 April 1963 under the chairmanship of University of New Brunswick forestry professor Louis Seheult.[33] If the move by Robichaud was designed to deflect criticism from his government, it also provided farmers and woodlot owners with a

---

30   Quebec, Order-in-Council #2026, cited in Forge and Acadian Federation of Northern New Brunswick, brief submitted to Seheult, dir., *Primary Forest Products*, Appendix.

31   Valerie Fowler, "The History of Forest Products Marketing Boards in New Brunswick", New Brunswick Federation of Woodlot Owners (Fredericton, 1984), copy in possession of author.

32   Fowler, "History of Marketing Boards".

33   *Synoptic Report of the Proceedings of the Legislative Assembly of the Province of New Brunswick*, first session, 1963, pp. 153, 267.

forum in which to focus their efforts. The more than one dozen briefs submitted by agricultural societies and producer associations were testimony to the widespread dissatisfaction of New Brunswick independent pulpwood producers.

The briefs sent to the Seheult Commission revealed that many of the organizations, particularly the agricultural societies, viewed the pulpwood situation in the broader context of the continuing deterioration of rural New Brunswick. "Current prices", commented Walter Cameron of the Miramichi Federation of Agriculture, "limit average income to subsistence standards. This leads to an exodus of young people who seek more lucrative employment elsewhere and finally to the desertion of whole areas".[34] Reverend William E. Hart, the most prolific spokesman for the small wood producers, wrote on the theme of rural decay and the importance of redevelopment built on forest resources:

> Our two greatest resources are land and young people. In rural New Brunswick we are rapidly losing both. Farm land is being bought up by the lumber companies and thereby passing out of the hands of rural people. Too many young rural people are leaving the country, for they say, as things are now, there is nothing to keep them in the country. A well managed forest based rural economy would support a more prosperous rural community in many parts of the province.[35]

Over and over again, organizations pointed to the deplorable economic and social conditions in New Brunswick and contrasted the abundant forest wealth of the province with the poverty of rural people.

Protest against the paper industry was basic to the organization of small wood producers; however, there were regional differences in the extent to which groups blamed the mills for their problems. The Southern New Brunswick Pulpwood Producers Association, the largest and best-organized group in the province, directed restrained criticism toward the mills, while at the same time emphasizing the need and possibilities for co-operation. In the spring of 1962, for example, the association met with K.C. Irving, president of the Irving Paper Company, to "get acquainted" and discuss the problems of small wood producers with the openly sympathetic industrialist.[36] Producers on the Miramichi and the North Shore — marginal farming areas traditionally dependent on the forest industries — were less sanguine about the prospects for voluntary solutions with the paper industry. Walter Cameron of the Miramichi Federation of Agriculture pointed out that "it is evident that this system has failed at the expense of the many unorganized and socially insecure primary producers who are at the mercy of a comparatively few powerful

---

34 Miramichi Federation of Agriculture, brief submitted to Seheult, dir., *Primary Forest Products*, p. 2.

35 *Maritime Farmer*, 8 September 1965.

36 *Maritime Farmer*, 3 April 1962.

financial interests".[37] The most militant of the organizations was the Forge and Acadian Federation of Northern New Brunswick, whose brief insisted that the people of New Brunswick would not "tolerate the existence of a private industry which enriches itself at the expense of tar paper shacks, wasted minds and bodies, impoverished, badly educated children, despairing fathers, despondent mothers and ruined communities"; the federation concluded by calling for the "phased withdrawal of our renewable resources from foreign and domestic private control".[38] In a rural economy that was collapsing under the weight of a variety of different forces, the paper mill was the most — perhaps the only — visible symbol of oppression. From this perspective the passion with which some groups condemned the industry is more understandable.

In their briefs, each organization made positive recommendations for the alleviation of the problems of small producers. The influence of the regional co-operative ideology was particularly evident in the emphasis that nearly all of the groups put on practical education. It was generally agreed that a better understanding of proper woodlot management, with the aid of government and university extension services, would improve the value of small woodlots. The associations lobbied for tax incentives for tree farming and expansion of the extension programmes.[39] The *Maritime Farmer* began a column entitled "The Tree Farmer" in early 1964 that disseminated useful information from various forest service organizations. Better woodlot management, the argument ran, would lead to full utilization of forest resources and, therefore, less dependence on pulpwood. In their requests for forestry services and in a wide range of other demands, the agricultural societies and producer associations showed little hesitation in appealing to the government for assistance. Even the conservative Southern New Brunswick Pulpwood Producers Association expressed the view that "we should have the help of the government we elected to protect our interests".[40]

There was less agreement among the organizations in the early 1960s over the role of the government in solving the problem most responsible for the uprising of small producers: the price of wood. Most of the groups proposed long-term solutions that involved direct government intervention. The Miramichi Federation of Agriculture advocated that the provincial government establish a price structure for the industry, and a quota system by which each mill would be required to purchase

---

37 Miramichi Federation of Agriculture, brief submitted to Seheult, dir., *Primary Forest Products*, p. 1.

38 Forge and Acadian Federation of Northern New Brunswick, brief submitted to Seheult, dir., *Primary Forest Products*, p. 24.

39 See, for example New Brunswick Federation of Agriculture, brief submitted to Seheult, dir., *Primary Forest Products*.

40 Southern New Brunswick Pulpwood Producers Association, brief submitted to Seheult, dir., *Primary Forest Products*.

a stated amount of pulpwood from independent producers.[41] Using the developments in Quebec as a model, many of the organizations called for some type of compulsory marketing board. "To assume or even hope that the corporate 'robot' blindly seeking out maximum profit, will make an honest effort now, to root out and correct the real causes of the evil social conditions of this area would be naive indeed", remarked the Forge and Acadian Federation, bluntly pointing out the general lack of faith in the paper industry among producers. "We see no change in prospect without government action".[42] There were producers, mainly in the southern half of the province, who were reluctant to pursue state intervention. Some independent minded farmers were suspicious of agreements that were not purely voluntary, "being more in favour of the co-operative approach".[43] Reverend Hart — who, when he was not writing on the potential rewards of the forest, was railing against the evils of unemployment insurance and other forms of "creeping socialism" — was lukewarm to the idea of marketing boards with compulsory bargaining rights. His southern New Brunswick association advocated this strategy only as a last resort. The argument for voluntary co-operation was that it had been effective in other areas, such as the marketing of hogs.[44] As attempts at voluntary agreements with the mills met with industry resistance, the consensus for government action grew. By 1970 the New Brunswick Federation of Wood Producers, which by this time spoke for all of the producer associations, identified compulsory marketing boards as their top priority.

The reaction of the paper industry toward the sweeping changes demanded by the independent producers was less than enthusiastic. The Bathurst Power and Paper Company argued in 1963 that the "marketing problems of the primary producer would seem to be his responsibility". If small producers planned their cut and obtained a sales contract in advance, the company suggested, they would be assured of receiving the "top market price".[45] It was an interesting argument from a company whose minimum, maximum and average price had remained at $14 for the past six years (see Table II). The Irving Paper Company declared that it was "interested in the problems of small producers" and promised to "do all possible to co-operate with them".[46] In 1964 the company offered forestry management ser-

---

41 Miramichi Federation of Agriculture, brief submitted to Seheult, dir., *Primary Forest Products*.

42 Forge and Acadian Federation of Northern New Brunswick, brief submitted to Seheult, dir., *Primary Forest Products*, p. 4.

43 *Maritime Farmer*, 9 June 1963.

44 Southern New Brunswick Pulpwood Producers Association, brief submitted to Seheult, dir., *Primary Forest Products*, p. 13

45 Bathurst Power and Paper Company, brief submitted to Seheult, dir., *Primary Forest Products*, p. 18.

46 *Maritime Farmer*, 4 April 1964.

vices similar to those given by the Forest Extension Service. The only difference with the Irving programme was that those availing themselves of the services were asked to sign a contract that gave the company "right of first refusal" on the sale of any pulpwood by the woodlot owner.[47] There was unanimous agreement among the companies that compulsory marketing boards would disrupt the mythical "competitive market" for wood and jeopardize the competitive position of New Brunswick mills. The Fraser Company in Edmundston at first resisted and later "exerted a firm hand" in the formation of the Madawaska Forest Products Marketing Board.[48] New Brunswick International Paper, on the basis of their experience with compulsory marketing boards in Quebec, was able to assure the Seheult Commission that they would "not resolve the woodlot owners problems".[49]

In one of his first columns as editor of the *Maritime Farmer* in 1962, James Thompson commented that, "it will be a long hard road for the pulpwood producers in these Maritime provinces as the pulp and paper companies have had it all their way for such a long time. They will not be liable to change their methods of buying unless a determined and steadfast effort is launched by the farmers and woodlot owners for years to come".[50] As events unfolded this turned out to be a prophetic statement. Although the commission did make positive suggestions for enhancing the position of small pulpwood producers, including a recommendation that the government establish a minimum price for pulpwood, the Robichaud government failed to take any action on them. The report of the Seheult Commission sided with the paper industry in deeming compulsory marketing boards inappropriate for New Brunswick.

Despite the unwillingness of the New Brunswick government to take actions that would challenge power relationships in the pulpwood market, small wood producers did achieve some positive results during their first wave of organization in the early 1960s. The price of wood did rise in some areas — a response, some associations claimed, to the agitation among producers.[51] The Madawaska Forest Products Marketing Board began signing contracts with the Fraser Company in 1964, and while the company still determined the price paid for wood, producers in the county were at least assured a more steady market for their pulpwood. The suc-

---

47   *Maritime Farmer*, 18 February 1964.

48   Fowler, "History of Marketing Boards", p. 6.

49   New Brunswick International Paper Company, brief submitted to Seheult, dir., *Primary Forest Products*, p. 6.

50   *Maritime Farmer*, 6 February 1962.

51   Private Wood Producers Association of Southern New Brunswick, brief submitted to the New Brunswick Forest Resources Study, September 1972, in RS 176, Records of the New Brunswick Forest Resources Study, file 110.2, PANB.

cess of the Madawaska producers in fulfilling their contracts also disproved the industry argument that small producers were incapable of providing wood on an even and sustained basis.[52] The market crisis of the early 1960s joined together, for the first time, a wide variety of groups with similar goals, and an organizational base was established for furthering the interests of small pulpwood producers on a long-term basis. Many of the producer associations of the early 1960s would survive and act as the foundation for marketing boards in the 1970s.

During the mid-1960s, however, pulpwood prices increased with the recovery of the world paper market, and the agitation among producer groups became less persistent. With provincial funding, the New Brunswick Federation of Wood Producers, representing seven regional member associations, articulated the interests of independent wood producers at the provincial level. However, popular participation in the regional associations declined in the late 1960s. Some of the associations had become, as a Charlotte County organizer suggested, "organizations that exist on paper only, with little else besides a membership list and elected officers".[53] By 1970 the Madawaska Forest Products Marketing Board was the only marketing organization in the province, even though producers in other parts of the province were legally entitled to form such boards. A second marketing board was established in the late 1960s in the northeastern region of the province, but it collapsed after a short period when the mill with which it had made a contract raised pulpwood prices, prompting members to avoid selling through the board, in favour of direct sale to the mill at a higher price.[54] Such strategies on the part of the industry, the inaction of the New Brunswick government, and the inherent problem of keeping small producers involved under favourable economic conditions kept the movement in a holding pattern during the second half of the 1960s.

From the beginning the movement to organize small independent wood producers in the early 1960s directed much of its energy toward influencing government policy, but the Robichaud Liberals proved unwilling to take legislative action to enhance the market position of the independent producer. The Seheult Commission turned out to be what many producers had feared: a way for the government to deflect criticism. The Conservative government that came to power in 1970 proved no more responsive to the needs of the independent wood producers. Indeed, the Hatfield government only began to intervene in the pulpwood market after 1970 when the paper industry was suffering through another recession. Layoffs and the spectre of some mills closing down permanently sparked a growing feeling among New Brunswickers that the paper industry cared little for the social welfare of the province. Successive studies completed in the first few years of the decade, which were critical of the industry for failing to reinvest in New Brunswick mills and of the government for its forest development policy,

---

52 Fowler, "History of Marketing Boards", pp. 2-3.

53 *Saint-Croix Courier* (St. Stephen-Milltown), 17 October 1974.

54 Curtis, *Woodlot Owner Organizations*, p. 63

added to the growing agitation for reforms. The Hatfield government was thus faced with the challenge of legitimizing and/or altering the relationship between the state and the pulp and paper industry. Addressing the problems of small producers was an integral part of that process.

Aided by federal and provincial development policies, the changes in rural New Brunswick that began after the Second World War accelerated in the 1960s. The number of farms in the province decreased by 53 per cent in the decade, from 11,786 to 5,485; the disproportional 41 per cent decrease in farm area, from 2.2 to 1.3 million acres (891,000 to 526,500 ha), indicated the ongoing commercialization and mechanization of agriculture. Even more marked in this regard was the 94 per cent increase (597 to 1,160) in census farms reporting more than $10,000 annual income and, conversely, the 67 per cent decrease (8,685 to 2,864) in farms with incomes of less than $2,500.[55] Market forces were the primary factors in the continuing transformation of New Brunswick agriculture, but, government programmes, particularly those undertaken by the federal Agricultural Rehabilitation and Development Administration (ARDA), also facilitated the process. The compelling logic behind ARDA was to rationalize agricultural production by encouraging marginal producers to move off farms, and to aid those remaining on the land to expand production and specialize in single commodities.[56] State-sponsored rationalization of resource use also extended into the independent production of forest products. The recommendations of a 1965 ARDA report on northeastern New Brunswick, for example, called for "larger producing units" on freehold forest land and "the establishment of co-operating groups for purposes of bargaining, marketing and forest management".[57] Implementation of many recommendations of this ARDA report in the early 1970s, by a Department of Regional Economic Expansion (DREE) programme, would be instrumental in the formation of a pulpwood marketing system for the province. The negative effects of such rural development policies were that they promoted and legitimized the very processes that the organizations representing independent wood producers in the early 1960s sought to arrest: the deterioration of the small mixed-farming economy and consequent rural depopulation.

---

55 The figure 11,786 represents the unadjusted number of farms in the province. It is used here for comparison, because the census change in 1961 was carried over to 1971 (see note 1). Canada, DBS, *Census of Agriculture*, New Brunswick, vol. 4, pt. 1, Bull. 4.1-5, pp. 2.1-3.1.

56 See Jean-B. Lanctot, Chief, Rural Community Development, Agricultural Rehabilitation and Development Administration, "The ARDA Programmes on Community Development", (Ottawa, 1965); and J.A. Abramson, "Rural To Urban Adjustment", ARDA Research Report, no. RE 4 (Ottawa, 1968).

57 Lockwood Survey Corporation Ltd., "A Report on the Rural Development Pilot Research Region Northern New Brunswick", ARDA Project no. 4022 (Toronto, 1965), p. 20.

For the second time in ten years, the world paper markets went into a downward spiral in the 1970s. The natural advantages that Canadian mills enjoyed in helping them to survive earlier market problems — cheap wood and hydro power resources and state-of-the-art technology — had been diminished by the expansion of production into new regions, most notably the southern United States. Failure on the part of companies in Eastern Canada to reinvest in their mills and keep pace with changing technology made conditions particularly difficult for the region's pulp and paper manufacturers.[58] Some of the mills in New Brunswick, such as the huge International Paper newsprint mill in Dalhousie, had shut down completely by the end of 1971; all of the mills were, by this time, experiencing some cuts in production and layoffs.[59] The problems of the industry in New Brunswick were well documented in a government commissioned report that was prompted by the now obvious threat to the future of pulp and paper manufacturing in the province. The report of the Industrial Inquiry Commission on the Pulp and Paper Industry, made public in October of 1972, revealed that all of the mills in the province lost money in 1971 and only one had even a chance of turning a profit in 1972. Moreover, the report expressed grave doubts as to whether five of the 11 pulp and paper enterprises in New Brunswick could be viable even after the market recovered. Clarence D. Clark, a former Fraser Company executive, who wrote the report, estimated the cost of revitalizing the decrepit mills in the northern half of the province at between $80 and $130 million. Citing three major studies on the provincial forest industries in the previous 15 years — none of which had been acted upon — Clark characterized the forest management record of successive administrations as "deplorable", "characterized by cynical disregard and neglect". "The need today is not so much one of study", he concluded, "but of action".[60]

The problems of the paper mills did not go unnoticed by the tens of thousands of New Brunswickers in communities dependent on the industry. In response to layoffs and shut-downs in the area's resource-based industries, among which those in the pulp and paper industry were most dramatic, the New Brunswick Federation of Labour called for a "Day of Concern" to be held on 16 January 1972. The parade and rally at Bathurst College, attended by Premier Hatfield and crowds estimated at near 20,000, was marred by angry demonstrations and shouts from the largely francophone audience. This show of dissatisfaction with the economic conditions of the region, an integral part of the Acadian uprising of the early 1970s, was followed up in February by the occupation of the Unemployment Insurance office in Bathurst and other public demonstrations, one of which nearly erupted into a riot. English-

---

58 R.E. Tweeddale, Executive Director, *Report of the New Brunswick Forest Resources Study* (Fredericton, 1974).

59 *Northern Light* (Bathurst), 25 November 1970, 3 February 1971, 3 March 1971.

60 *Report of the Industrial Inquiry Commission on the Pulp and Paper Industry of New Brunswick* (Fredericton, 1972), Part I, p. 1; Part VII, p. 1.

language newspapers in the region began to worry about the "agents provocateur" and "revolutionary fervour" of people on the North Shore.[61]

As the most important manufacturing industry in the province, pulp and paper was a central focus of public dissatisfaction. "One often hears the question", commented one columnist, "shouldn't money have been invested in new machinery over the years so that these mills would not have become more and more obsolete?" "Many people are of the opinion", he continued, "that profits have been taken out and invested elsewhere. The result is that the future prosperity of our communities has not been ensured".[62] The growing consensus that improving the long-term prospects of the industry would require a massive infusion of government money met with calls for more public control over the actions of companies. At the annual meeting of the Newcastle Board of Trade in February 1972, L.H. Lorain, Canadian Director of the International Brotherhood of Pulp, Sulphite and Paper Mill Workers, called for a Crown corporation to be established in northern New Brunswick. "They [the companies] should have realized long ago that they had a responsibility to the community in which they operate", Lorain told the audience; he then went on to criticize the provincial government for failing to monitor and impose strict regulations on the industry.[63] Under the desperate economic conditions of the early 1970s, the always lingering undercurrent of hostility toward the pulp and paper industry — especially in Northern New Brunswick — surfaced in a widespread public discussion of social accountability.[64]

The call for government action became a rallying cry for small wood producers in the early 1970s, as the depressed conditions of the pulp and paper industry revitalized their efforts. It was in the northern counties of the province, so dependent on the forest economy, that small producers reacted most dramatically to the deteriorating conditions in the paper industry. Representing Gloucester and Restigouche counties, the North Shore Forestry Syndicate (NSFS), which in the late 1960s evolved with the aid of government funding from the Forge and Acadian Federation of Northern New Brunswick, emerged as a leading producer association in the province. When a provincial task force on social development travelled to Bathurst to meet with the NSFS in the fall of 1970, they were told that producers in the area were as tired of government commissions as they were of the lack of progressive legislation on their behalf. Speaking to the task force, NSFS president Michael Henry delivered a stern warning to the industry and the government:

---

61 *Moncton Times*, 17 January, 26 February 1972, cited in John Reid, "Sharpening the Skeptical Edge", in E.R. Forbes and D.A. Muise, *Atlantic Canada in Confederation* (forthcoming).

62 *Northern Light*, 8 December 1971.

63 *Evening Times Globe* (Saint John), 2 December 1972.

64 On the reservations of people in northern New Brunswick toward large scale pulp and paper development in the 1920s, see Parenteau, "The Woods Transformed".

The private woodlot owners of New Brunswick are still being exploited...the exploiters are the Provincial Government and the pulp and paper mills working together....Are you able to look at the misery and hardship and poverty in a land of plenty and not have a feeling of violence and revolt within you? How much longer in a land of plenty can there be poverty without provoking violence? How much longer will it be possible for Task Forces and Survey Teams and Consultants to visit the poor and make their reports to file them away until another survey is made or another task force visits or another group of consultants consult. I ask this question in all seriousness....How close are we to violence in our country?[65]

The need for state intervention in the forest industries was also becoming obvious to government and industry. At the time the Clark Commission was making its inquiry into the pulp and paper industry, a multi-million dollar, two-year, federal-provincial forest resources study of New Brunswick was already under way. Both commissions demonstrated the growing recognition in Eastern Canada that unprecedented long-term government participation was necessary in each phase of the process from tree planting to marketing, in order to revive and sustain the forest industries.[66] The integration of wood produced on small private woodlots into a comprehensive plan for full utilization of the forest resources of New Brunswick, which had been recommended to the government as far back as the mid-1950s, became part of the agenda for reform.[67]

There could be little doubt by this time that small independent producers suffered from their unequal relationship with the mills, and that government action was necessary if the market for privately produced wood was to be stabilized. These points were driven home by the recommendations of the Task Force on Social Development in 1971. "In the case of woodlot owners", the Task Force recommended that, "all necessary measures be taken to ensure that publicly owned resources, (that is Crown Land Leased to the pulp and paper companies) are not used as a weapon against the small producers in maintaining low prices for his product. This might be accomplished through introduction of legislation that would require the companies to purchase a fixed proportion of the wood from small, independent woodlot owners".[68] It was in this context that the Hatfield government appointed the New Brunswick Forest Products Commission (FPC).

---

65 *North Shore Leader* (Newcastle), 11 November 1970.

66 As early as 1971, there was talk in Quebec that the government was planning to end the Crown land lease system and replace it with a system that would allocate wood on the basis of need. Ultimately, this strategy was also recommended by the *Forest Resources Study* in 1974. See *Financial Post,* 4 December 1971; *Globe and Mail* (Toronto), 3 March 1971; and Tweeddale, *Forest Resources Study*, pp. 5, 205-6, 289.

67 Bates, dir., *Forest Development Commission.*

68 Report of the Task Force on Social Development (Fredericton, 1971), p. 3.

The commission was created under authority of the Forest Products Act (chapter 5, 1971) and Order-in-Council no. 71-527, dated 11 August 1971. The stated objective of the FPC was "to encourage and facilitate the achievement of expanding markets and equitable prices for both the producer and consumer of primary forest products".[69] As an advisory body to the Minister of Agriculture and Rural Development, it consisted of six members, two each representing the provincial government, the paper industry and the small producers. Reverend W.E. Hart and Claude Pelletier, secretary of the Madawaska Forest Products Marketing Board, were appointed to represent the producers. To determine the relationship between the cost of wood produced on company land and the price of wood paid to small producers, the commission visited small producers around the province during the last months of 1971 and throughout 1972. The response of small independent wood producers to the creation of the Forest Products Commission was uniformly optimistic. The feeling that the producers were on the verge of making tangible gains was reflected in the calls to action by activists such as Peter DeMarsh in the *Northern Light* and Bob Spurway in the *Maritime Farmer*.[70] More than 200 representatives of the Kent County Wood Producers Action Committee attended its first meeting in late February, and the late April meeting of the New Brunswick Federation of Wood Producers was reported to be the largest in its seven-year history, with two new regional associations from Kent and Northumberland counties seeking membership.[71]

The practical limitations of the Forest Products Commission, however, soon became clear to small producers in the province. It was merely an advisory board and, evidently, a slow acting one. Wood producers reacted with suspicion and hostility when they were informed that the commission planned to take six months to a year before they would make recommendations. The North Shore Forestry Syndicate came away from their early April meeting feeling that the role of the FPC was "simply to protect the government from the necessity of taking immediate action", and concluded that "we should waste no time dealing with such a slow acting body, but should approach government directly".[72] By the end of April, the sentiments expressed by North Shore producers seem to have become general. "Extreme disappointment" was expressed by many of those who attended the federation's annual meeting, where the commission was assessed as "just another study", "a sleeping pill", and "a shock absorber for the government".[73] A consensus for direct

69 New Brunswick Forest Products Commission, *First Progress Report of the New Brunswick Forest Products Commission* (Fredericton, 1971), p. 1

70 *Northern Light*, 24 November 1972, 19 January 1972; *Maritime Farmer*, 21 December 1971.

71 *Telegraph-Journal* (Saint John), 4 March 1972, 3 May 1972; *North Shore Leader* (Newcastle), 4 May 1972.

72 *Telegraph-Journal* (Saint John), 4 November 1972.

73 *Telegraph-Journal*, 3 May 1972; *Campbellton Graphic*, 20 May 1972.

political action had also emerged. The federation demanded and was granted a meeting with the provincial government, to take place on 3 May 1972.

At the May meeting between the cabinet and regional representatives of the federation, little was accomplished. However, the meeting did open a direct channel of communication with the Hatfield administration. In June the premier travelled to Bathurst to attend an information day for MLAs, set up by the NSFS and attended by more than 1,000 wood producers and their supporters. Woodlot owners, truckers and independent contractors outlined the problems they faced and repeated the now well-articulated arguments for state control of the pulpwood market, but Hatfield's response gave them little encouragement. The premier suggested that legislation to control prices "really isn't the answer" and added that taking Crown land rights from the companies would be too disruptive to the provincial economy.[74] The "information day" in Bathurst was part of an extensive province-wide campaign aimed at rallying public support and getting clear answers from New Brunswick politicians as to where they stood on the issue of regulating prices. The Union of Woodlot Owners of Southeastern New Brunswick, for example, called for the resignation of MLAs who would not state their position, and the North Shore Forestry Syndicate harassed candidates for a by-election in Gloucester County.[75] It was becoming increasingly clear to the Hatfield administration that the organization of producers had developed to a point that it would not simply go away if the administration dragged its feet or the market improved.

More substantive contact between representatives of the wood producers, the industry and the government began to take place during the late summer and fall of 1972, although little progress was made on the central issue of price determination. Minister of Agriculture and Rural Development J. Stewart Brooks became the point man for handling the pulpwood issue, as the Hatfield government began to assume a greater role as an arbitrator. Brooks met with a federation delegation in September and agreed to oversee negotiations between representatives of producers in northern New Brunswick and the six mills in the region. The understanding at the time was that these meetings would establish a foundation for provincial legislation.[76] When negotiations between the industry and independent producers broke down after only one meeting, the New Brunswick Federation of Wood Producers pressed the government for a definitive policy statement.[77] The response from Brooks on 24 November was a clear rejection of the principle of mandatory collective bargaining. Specifically, he stated, "I am opposed to price fixing by the government", and "to

---

74   *Telegraph-Journal*, 20 June 1972; *Northern Light*, 28 June 1972.

75   *Kings County Record* (Sussex) 6 July 1972; *North Shore Leader*, 6 July 1972; *Moncton Transcript* (Moncton) 12 September 1972; *L'Évangéline* (Moncton) 11 September 1972.

76   *Telegraph-Journal*, 16 September 1972.

77   N.B. Forest Products Commission, *Third Progress Report of the Forest Products Commission*, (Fredericton, 1972), pp. 2-3.

relate negotiations to the administration of Crown forest would, in my opinion, be inequitable and impractical". As an alternative to strict government regulations similar to those in Quebec, Brooks encouraged the producers to form marketing boards under the existing legislation: the Natural Products Control Act. He also pledged to make available the services of the Natural Products Control Board and the Forest Products Commission and to use his "personal influence to persuade buyers to negotiate".[78] The federation expressed "great disappointment" with the statements of Brooks, "having been under the impression that the Minister had agreed on the need for legislative action". Reiterating its long-standing position, the federation further stated that the Natural Products Control Act needed "more teeth" before it could be of any real benefit to independent producers.[79]

Thus, at the end of 1972, independent wood producers seemed no closer to their ultimate goal of mandatory collective bargaining for the price of pulpwood than they had been in the early 1960s. The reluctance of politicians in New Brunswick to enact progressive legislation on behalf of the private wood producers was indicative of the subservient mentality that had developed over the course of decades, and was reflected in the statements by Richard Hatfield and J. Stewart Brooks regarding the possibilities of using the Crown land leases to compel companies to negotiate with independent producers. The introduction to a brief submitted jointly by the pulp and paper companies of the province in the summer of 1972, to the Forest Products Commission, demonstrated the rhetoric and veiled threats that had long been effective in maintaining the powerful leverage large companies exerted over provincial forest policy. Noting the "progressive imposition of additional restraints which have consistently weakened the competitive position of the companies" and which "eventually will make it uneconomic to remain in existence", the brief warned the government that:

> The ultimate decision that the legislator must now make, is whether forest-based industry is needed, or even desirable. Do the existing and potential benefits derived from the industries outweigh the possible inconveniences and irritations which they may cause? And what alternative source of revenue is available to support the provincial economy if the source ceased to exist?
> The answer appears to be obvious.
> Any evaluation of New Brunswick's resources must acknowledge that the forest is the major source of existing and potential revenue. This implies that all provincial functions and activities are dependent upon it, to some extent.

---

78 The "open letter" from Brooks was eventually published in some of the province's newspapers. See, for example, *Telegraph-Journal,* 13 December 1972; *North Shore Leader,* 7 December 1972.

79 *Kings County Record,* 21 December 1972; *St. Croix Courier,* 28 December 1972; *L'Évangéline,* 30 November 1972.

It follows, therefore, that the products of the forest must be maintained in a competitive position, and this position must be improved continually, if the Province is to prosper.[80]

The habits of making a range of concessions to the paper industry for politically expedient development projects and depending heavily on the forest-based industries for provincial revenue had developed to such a degree that this statement hardly need have been made. Responding to the "considerable discussion" about "the adequacy of the price the woodlot owner receives", the brief stated bluntly that, "as the provincial industry in its present state cannot afford to support marginal, or inefficient operations, it would appear that the majority of woodlots would serve the provincial economy more effectively if they were absorbed by the province as Crown Land".[81]

The Forest Products Commission reacted negatively to the brief, noting that "prices substantially below the average cost of wood produced on company limits" paid to independent producers had little to do with the size or efficiency of their operations.[82] But the point had been effectively made: the paper industry would resist with all its power any changes in their relationship with small independent producers that would impose an added financial burden on the mills.

Despite the lack of progress toward collective bargaining rights, 1972 was a pivotal year for wood producers in the province. The message that was persistently delivered by the politicians, leaders of the movement, and the Forest Products Commission was that organization was a necessary precondition to substantive change. A great deal of organization did take place. The North Shore Forestry Syndicate, representing Gloucester and Restigouche counties, was helped by a federal grant of $45,000 obtained in August 1971, which they used to hire Peter DeMarsh as a full-time organizer.[83] DeMarsh was instrumental in constructing local councils of wood producers and forging links between the syndicate and other organizations in the region that were concerned with the crisis in the resource-based industries. The NSFS kept a high public profile through a column written by DeMarsh in the

---

80 "A Brief on Factors Effecting the Competitive Position of the Forest-Based Industries", to the New Brunswick Forest Products Commission and the New Brunswick Forest Resources Study, by Acadia Pulp and Paper Ltd., Consolidated-Bathurst Ltd., Fraser Companies Ltd., Fundy Forest Industries Ltd., MacMillan-Rothesay Ltd., Miramichi Timber Resources Ltd. and St. Anne-Nackawic Pulp and Paper Ltd., in RS 176, Records of the New Brunswick Forest Resources Study, 1972-4, file 960, p. 1, PANB.

81 "A Brief on Factors", RS 176, Records of the New Brunswick Forest Resources Study, 1972-4, file 960, p. 9, PANB.

82 N.B. Forest Products Commission to C.C. Landegger, 11 December 1972, in RS 176, Records of the New Brunswick Forest Resources Study, 1972-4, file 115, PANB.

83 *Northern Light,* 25 August 1971.

Northern Light and by continually releasing statements that were carried in northern New Brunswick newspapers. In April 1972 the NSFS, now 1,300 strong,
defiantly told the Forest Products Commission that producers on the North Shore
were determined not to accept less than $25.21 per cord of wood, the price paid by
the Dalhousie mill for wood coming from producers in Quebec.[84] The Union of
Woodlot Owners of Southeastern New Brunswick, which came together in May
1972, representing Kent and parts of Northumberland counties, attracted several
hundred members in just a few months.[85] The older organizations, such as the
Private Wood Producers Association of Southern New Brunswick, also added new
members to their roles.[86] Their president, W.E. Hart, having spent a good deal of
time in Sweden examining forest practices and policy, had not lost any of his passion for the cause. He also continued to serve as president of the New Brunswick
Federation of Wood Producers and on the Forest Products Commission. Canon
Hart's vision of a rural New Brunswick rebuilt on socially conscious use of the
forest resources was presented in "The Forests of New Brunswick for the People of
New Brunswick", a pamphlet written in 1972 that, at the same time, preached the
social gospel and scientific forest management.[87] By this time even Hart had
reached the conclusion that government intervention was necessary to prevent
paper companies from exploiting small producers.

At the end of January 1973, the Conservative government informed the New
Brunswick Federation of Wood Producers and the North Shore Forestry Syndicate
that they were planning to introduce an amendment to the Forest Products Act to
aid producers in their negotiations with the paper industry. There were, in all
likelihood, a number of reasons for the policy shift. Certainly the persistent pressure
of wood producers was a factor. They had also been able to persuade the Liberal
opposition to make progressive legislation for wood producers a high-profile issue.
Another determining factor may have been the industry's less than co-operative attitude. It was reflected in the lack of progress at the fall 1972 meetings with the
NSFS and in the brief sent to the Forest Products Commission, which, one government forester suggested, "did little to dispel the belief that they care nothing for
their social obligations".[88] Finally, and most important, the policy shift reflected the
forest management reform agenda that Premier Hatfield was to introduce at the

---

84   *Dalhousie News,* 20 April 1972.

85   *L'Évangéline,* 6 June 1972; *Telegraph-Journal,* 27 June 1972; *Kings County Record,*
     6 July 1972; *North Shore Leader,* 31 August 1972.

86   Private Wood Producers Association of Southern New Brunswick, brief submitted to
     the New Brunswick Forest Resources Study, September, 1972, in RS 176, Records
     of the New Brunswick Forest Resources Study, file 110.2, PANB.

87   W.E. Hart, "The Forests of New Brunswick for the People of New Brunswick,"
     typescript, January 1973, at Legislative Library of New Brunswick.

88   T.E. Sifton to R.E. Tweeddale, October 1972, RS 176, Records of the New
     Brunswick Forest Resources Study, file 960, PANB.

opening of the legislature in March. Specifically, the rationalization of production on private holdings, which could be better facilitated by marketing boards, fit into the government's express plan to "exercise more direct management control over the province's forest resources, including the allocation of the annual timber harvest to its best economic use".[89]

The message that the Hatfield administration delivered to independent producers in January was twofold and perfectly in keeping with their larger forest management scheme. J. Stewart Brooks informed the North Shore Forestry Syndicate that he was prepared to participate actively in the formation of a marketing board in northeastern New Brunswick. But the aid was dependent upon the condition that the NSFS prove to the minister that they had the support of a "strong majority" of producers in the region.[90] Neither the timing of the announcement nor the place the government chose to make its initiative were random. As part of the federal and provincial Forest Resources Study, the government was planning a "pilot project" for northeastern New Brunswick, which was to begin in the fall of 1973. The central point in the plan was for the provincial government to end the Crown land leases in the region and replace them with a system whereby cutting rights were dispensed on the basis of anticipated production. To promote full utilization of the forest resources, the project would also include the integration of raw materials from Crown and private lands. Because they would help to systematize the flow of pulpwood from private woodlots to the mills, marketing boards, from the perspective of the state, were an attractive proposition.[91]

The small producers of the province were, however, dissatisfied with the amendment to the Forest Products Act when it was introduced to the legislature in April. It was the first time that they had seen the exact wording, which sparked another round of condemnation. The key points of the one-sentence amendment were that if a Crown land holder was deemed to have "failed to negotiate in good faith with a producer association...for a contract of sale and purchase specifying, among its terms, price, quantities, delivery schedules and containing reasonable assurances with respect to future supplies on a regular basis, the Lieutenant Governor-in-Council may...reduce the allocation of wood from Crown Land to that consumer".[92] Small wood producers had two objections to the bill. First, there was no guarantee that the government would take action. After two years of experience, small wood

89 Speech from the Throne, 6 March 1973, *Synoptic Reports of the Proceedings of the Legislative Assembly of the Province of New Brunswick*, 1st session, p. 3.

90 *Telegraph-Journal*, 5 February 1973.

91 Public statements made after the introduction of the bill would seem to support this interpretation. "Outside the House," the *Telegraph-Journal* of 13 April 1973 reported, "Mr Horton said that the new change in the legislation would permit a better approach to be taken in the administration of Crown Land wood and provide a bargaining process for small woodlot owners".

92 "An Act to Amend the Forest Products Act," *New Brunswick Acts*, 1973, p. 216.

producers in the province had little confidence in the ability of the Forest Products Commission to administer the Forest Products Act, much less initiate punitive action against the mills. Ill-defined terms such as "in good faith" and "may" (with regards to taking action against companies), the producers argued, rendered the amendment meaningless for all practical purposes. The second objection to the bill was that it compelled producer associations to agree to delivery schedules, something that the groups felt should be part of the negotiations.[93]

Expressing the sense of betrayal among wood producers, Lawrence Vienneau of Free Grant, Gloucester County, remarked: "we expected a law for woodcutters but what has come out of the legislature is on the side of the companies".[94] In protest, an estimated 250 woodsmen marched on the provincial legislature, with chain saws buzzing, on 28 April. They made their demands, predominantly in French, in front of cabinet members, MLAs and a "massive contingent of RCMP and local police" who were there in response to rumours that some of the woodsmen might cut down the elm trees in front of the legislature. On a less dramatic note, the New Brunswick Federation of Wood Producers drafted a nine-point proposal to change the amendment in favour of giving producers "more power in negotiations with the companies".[95] The federation again asked that wood producers be given collective bargaining rights and that the negotiations be tied to the Crown land leasing system.

As producers throughout New Brunswick were reacting to the pending Forest Products Act amendment in April 1973, the task of organizing on the North Shore was coming to a head. With financial help from federal grants, the North Shore Forestry Syndicate had been building an organization based on local committees since 1969. The challenge to prove the support of a "strong majority" of producers in the region would provide a stern test for the organizers. Almost immediately the NSFS applied to the Forest Products Commission to hold a plebiscite among wood producers in Gloucester and Restigouche counties and the parish of Alnwick in Northumberland County. Under the guidelines of the FPC, independent truckers, wood producers and persons owning 25 acres (10 ha) or more of woodland, and not involved in the manufacture of wood products, were eligible to vote. To be successful, at least 50 per cent of the acres of private forest land in the area had to be represented, and a minimum of 75 per cent of those voting had to be in favour of the applicant organization.[96] In late March the FPC and the Natural Products Control Board moved in to prepare a marketing plan for the North Shore and supervise the plebiscite, which would take place from 23 to 29 April at 56 local polling

---

93 *Telegraph-Journal,* 13 April 1973, 23 April 1973; *Daily Gleaner,* 18 April 1973.

94 *Moncton Transcript,* 26 April 1973.

95 *L'Évangéline,* 28 April 1973; *Daily Gleaner,* 28 April 1973; *Telegraph-Journal,* 23 May 1973.

96 N.B. Forest Products Commission, *Fourth Progress Report of the New Brunswick Forest Products Commission* (Fredericton, 1973); Curtis, *Woodlot Owner Organizations,* pp. 68-70.

places. The plebiscite was a resounding vote of confidence for the syndicate: 98.6 per cent of the 2,461 woodlot owners who cast ballots voted in favour of the NSFS, and the turnout of eligible voters in at least 12 localities was more than 90 per cent. In addition, 1,400 pulp cutters voted, almost unanimously, for the syndicate.[97] Peter DeMarsh noted, with obvious satisfaction: "We have done our best to set up an organization run by its members and not some clique sitting in some office. We intend to do our best to make sure it stays that way".[98]

Even as NSFS members were savouring their achievement, they were aware that under the legislation proposed by the Conservative government, meaningful negotiations with the mills were far from assured. The plea of the NSFS and the Federation of Wood Producers was for the government to send the proposed legislation to the law amendments committee, to enable the producers at least to present their recommendations for strengthening the bill. Their request was refused. When the bill came up for debate on 1 June 1973 it was unchanged from April. In the divisive day-long debate, interrupted on several occasions by name-calling and accusations, the Liberals called for stronger measures on behalf of the independent producers. In one noteworthy exchange, George Horton, the newly appointed Minister of Agriculture and Rural Development, responded to the claim that the amendment did "not go far enough" by remarking: "Well, I think it does. I have discussed it thoroughly with all the pulp mills and they are quite prepared to negotiate in good faith".[99] The bill was passed without revision.

Although the Liberals spoke out on behalf of small producers, their arguments in fact reflected the traditional relationship between the state and the paper industry that was accepted by both parties. The line of argument used by Alan Graham, point man for the opposition, was revealing:

> if we are ever to bring in better legislation it should be this year when the market is improving. Next year may be too late. When the market is on its way down, the mills can always use the threat that if any more pressure is put on them they will close the mills and 600 or 800 people will be out of work, but this isn't the case this year.

To which Premier Hatfield replied:

> While it is true that all the mills in New Brunswick are benefitting this year from the increase in pulp and paper prices, the fact is that they are not into a heavy profit position at the moment. I think they are optimistic, but they are

---

97 N.B. Forest Products Commission, *Fourth Progress Report; Telegraph-Journal*, 13 April 1973, 23 April 1973; *Moncton Transcript*, 4 May 1973; Fowler, "History of Marketing Boards", p. 6.

98 *Moncton Transcript*, 4 May 1973

99 *Synoptic Reports*, 1973, 1st session, p. 2022.

not in a position where, as I think the honourable minister is trying to suggest, we can be as tough as we will be when we know that they are in a profitable position.[100]

It was this mentality — underscored by an acceptance of the limited power of the state to control forest capital, despite guardianship of more than half of the productive forest land of the province — that for so long had prevented the New Brunswick government from developing the forest resource base to its full potential and using the publicly owned forest to improve social and economic conditions for the tens of thousands of people dependent on it for their livelihood.

In more than one sense, the events of the spring of 1973 were a climax to the second wave of agitation among small wood producers in New Brunswick. The amendment to the Forest Products Act was a definitive statement that the government would not require the paper industry to enter into mandatory collective bargaining agreements for independently produced pulpwood. In this respect, the legislation upheld and legitimated the existing power relationships between wood producers, the forest industry and the provincial government. The aid of the Minister of Agriculture and Rural Development and the Forest Products Commission in setting up the marketing plan on the North Shore established the state in a permanent and central role in the promotion of a province-wide marketing system and in the ongoing negotiations between producers and the industry. Legislation passed in the late summer of 1973 vested the FPC with the responsibility of supervising negotiations and settling disputes between producers and the mills.[101] Thus, after 1973, the Forest Products Commission began to provide indispensable services to the small producer groups. On the one hand, these services helped producers in many ways, most notably in raising the price of pulpwood. On the other hand, the aid of the state increasingly confined the movement within bureaucratic structures that were defined by the limited vision of politicians in the province.

Marketing agreements between producer associations and mills took shape throughout New Brunswick during the remaining years of the 1970s, each following the pattern established in 1973. Starting with Northumberland County in 1974, the FPC supervised six more plebiscites during the decade, five of which were successful. By 1980, 80 per cent of the province was covered by marketing agreements. The ground rules and role of the FPC in the bargaining process was also refined, due in large part to another amendment to the Forest Products Act that more sharply defined the phrase "in good faith" as it pertained to negotiations. For its part, the industry continued to view producer associations as an unneeded imposition on their competitive position, but it was also recognized that they helped to

---

100 *Synoptic Reports*, 1973, 1st session, p. 2027.

101 Curtis, *Woodlot Owner Organizations*, p. 69; Fowler, "History of Marketing Boards",
    p. 4.

rationalize and stabilize the flow of wood from private sources.[102] The price paid for pulpwood increased substantially after 1973, but only slightly faster than the cost of living index. Even officers of the Federation of Wood Producers wondered to what extent marketing boards were responsible for the higher prices.[103] Speaking at a forest management conference in 1979, Lawrence McCrea, treasurer of the federation, remarked: "A more equitable government policy towards the marketing of privately produced wood would mean better prices. In Quebec, where the policy is more equitable wood prices are at least 20 per cent higher than in New Brunswick. This is due to politics, not economics".[104] It was a statement that may well have been made at the beginning of the producers' agitation in the early 1960s.

The pulpwood marketing system put in place in New Brunswick during the 1970s was the result of the pressure that wood producers exerted on reluctant politicians. As in other resource based industries in the Atlantic Region, the movement of wood producers took shape within the context of structural changes in the rural economy, most notably the growing market domination of large corporations and concentration of primary production in larger units.[105] Finally, it was the successive crises in the pulp and paper industry in the 1960s and 1970s that provided the impetus for widespread organization. The demands of wood producers that the government enhance their ability to conduct business with the mills on an equal basis were also not unique among independent producers in the region, and

---

102 New Brunswick Forest Products Association Inc., "An Industry Brief in Response to Current Government Forest Policy to the Minister of Natural Resources of the Province of New Brunswick", August 1976, at the New Brunswick Legislative Library.

103 New Brunswick Federation of Wood Producers, *Annual Report of the New Brunswick Federation of Wood Producers*, 1981, p. 1, at the New Brunswick Legislative Library.

104 Lawrence McCrea, "Forest Management on Small Woodlots in New Brunswick," in *Proceedings from a Conference on Forest Management in New Brunswick, Fredericton: Conservation Council of New Brunswick*, 29 September 1979 (Fredericton, 1979).

105 This is not to suggest some grand alliance of independent primary producers in the region, but to point out that the combination of structural economic change and crisis prompted similar reponses among producers in the region and that, in the absence of sufficient power and/or organization, these reponses were state-centred: see Wallace Clement, *The Struggle to Organize: Resistance in Canada's Fishery* (Toronto, 1986); Silver Donald Cameron, *The Education of Everett Richardson: The Nova Scotia Fishermen's Strike 1970-71* (Toronto, 1977); Gordon Inglis, *More Than Just a Union: The Story of the NFFAWU* (St. John's, 1985); Tom Murphy, "Potato Capitalism: McCain and Industrial Farming in New Brunswick", Darrell McLaughlin, "From Self-Reliance to Dependence to Struggle: Agribusiness and the Politics of Struggle in New Brunswick", Marie Burge, "The Political Education of Bud the Spud: Producers and Plebiscites on Prince Edward Island", in Gary Burrill and Ian McKay, eds., *People, Resources and Power: Critical Perspectives on Underdevelopment and Primary Industries in the Atlantic Region* (Fredericton, 1987).

reflected the expanding role of the state in, among other areas, resource-based industries. However, the partial resolution to the producer-industry conflict engineered by the New Brunswick government demonstrated the contradictory nature of state intervention. From the beginning the government provided much-needed technical and financial assistance and acted informally and then formally as an arbitrator with the industry. Underlying the valuable assistance of the government, however, was an unwillingness to significantly alter power relationships by using state control of the Crown lands as a lever to ensure bargaining "in good faith", and an active promotion, exemplified by the ARDA and, later, DREE programmes, of the structural processes against which independent wood producers were reacting.

Table I

Small Holdings:
Production of Pulpwood and Sawlogs by District

	District	1959-60	1960-61	1961-62	1962-63	Average
Pulpwood	1	52,200	54,100	61,900	24,000	48,000
(rough	2	37,900	27,000	16,300	4,200	21,400
cords)	3	49,600	77,400	96,300	47,300	67,600
	4	209,600	109,100	124,100	92,900	134,100
	5	42,300	40,500	39,000	15,200	34,200
Total						
		391,600	308,100	337,600	183,600	305,200
Sawlogs	1	1,500	3,400	500	500	1,500
(Mfbm)	2	3,000	2,500	5,300	1,600	3,100
	3	16,700	33,400	46,400	28,500	31,200
	4	17,300	13,700	16,600	9,900	14,400
	5	8,800	5,200	5,600	10,700	7,600
Total		47,300	58,200	74,400	51,200	57,800

Source: *Report of the Royal Commission on Primary Forest Products in New Brunswick* (Fredericton, 1964).

Table II

Bathurst Power and Paper Company, Purchased Farm Wood
New Brunswick, 1951-1962

Year	Minimum Price	Maximum Price	Average Price	Number of Cords
1951	$13.00	18.50	18.36	40,650
1952	18.50	19.50	19.28	18,994
1953	14.00	14.00	14.73	37,852
1954	14.00	14.00	14.00	39,241
1955	14.00	14.00	14.00	28,646
1956	16.00	16.00	16.00	41,695
1957	16.00	16.00	16.00	16,059
1958	14.00	14.00	14.00	34,489
1959	14.00	14.00	14.00	45,158
1960	14.00	14.00	14.00	50,091
1961	14.00	14.00	14.00	38,716
1962	14.00	14.00	14.00	30,360

Source: Bathurst Power and Paper Company, *Brief Submitted to Royal Commission on Primary Forest Products in New Brunswick*, 1964, Appendix II.

The Politics of Pulpwood Marketing in Nova Scotia, 1960-1985

Peter Clancy

For more than a generation, Nova Scotia small woodlot owners and producers have campaigned politically for a system of organized marketing.[1] A prolonged series of struggles eventually yielded a state-sanctioned marketing regime, though it fell far short of its sponsors' intentions. According to one recent report, it has "not resulted in a stable market-place for wood from private woodlots, nor what can be objectively considered a 'fair' price for that wood".[2] In a province where some 30,000 small holders own over half of the forested land, such a paradoxical outcome requires explanation. It certainly contrasts sharply with the situation in agriculture, where state-supported marketing won early acceptance. The case of Nova Scotia pulpwood is even more intriguing when compared with neighbouring jurisdictions in Eastern Canada, where private forest tenure is also common. David Curtis observed in 1988 that "there is a marked difference between the price of pulpwood in New Brunswick and Quebec where woodlot sector marketing groups have been functioning since the early 1960s, and Nova Scotia (Nova Scotia being lower)".[3]

This paper will examine the 25-year struggle over the terms of pulpwood marketing, a struggle that remains very much alive today. It will examine the interplay of economic forces and state institutions, the resulting marketing regime and the political capacities of the small woodlot owner and producer factions in forestry. In Nova Scotia, the pricing and supply of pulpwood has been one of the most contentious issues of modern forest policy. It pits the rural small-holder population against a leading industrial sector characterized by a dense network of political affiliations and a privileged place in the economic strategy of the provincial state. The breadth and direction of this conflict is also impressive. It has unfolded across several decades, entailed a complex web of production and exchange relations, and ranged across a wide terrain of state institutions.

This contemporary struggle dates from the late 1950s, with the efforts to organize small woodlot owners and producers in eastern Nova Scotia. In the first

---

1   The author gratefully acknowledges the financial support of the Centre for Research on the Future of Work, St. Francis Xavier University, Antigonish, Nova Scotia.

2   Bruce S. Curtis, *Toward an Effective Marketing Structure for Woodlot Owners in Nova Scotia*, for Nova Scotia Primary Forest Products Marketing Board (Halifax, 1988), p. 2.

3   Curtis, *Toward an Effective Marketing Structure*, p. 2.

instance it involved rejecting the prevailing "open" market, where individual suppliers faced industrial buyers and their networks of rural dealers and agents. In its place the woodlot owners sought a regulated marketing structure under state auspices. The owner-producers and the industrial buyers, though no monolithic blocs, were the main protagonists in this encounter.

They are linked by a "forest fibre chain", a network "typically characterized by key control points, representing economic actors with strong bargaining power vis-à-vis other elements in the chain".[4] Private forest tenures, rooted in the Nova Scotia practice of dispensing timber lands in fee simple title, dominate. By the time this system was discontinued in 1899, over 80 per cent of the province's forests had passed into private hands.[5] The private-land segment is highly stratified by size of holding. Today the large privately owned share (defined as landholdings in excess of 1,000 acres, or 405 ha) amounts to 21 per cent. The 30,000 small owners own 50,000 woodlots, which account for 52 per cent of forest land (with an average-sized holding of 115 acres, or 47 ha). The provincial Crown owns a further 24 per cent and the federal Crown three per cent.[6]

With control of almost three-quarters of the provincial forest, private owners have always played an important role in timber production. Until relatively recently, the leading product was sawlogs. Yet after record production during World War Two, the sawlog market began a protracted decline. In 1962 the absolute volume of pulpwood surpassed sawlogs for the first time, signalling the rise to dominance of the pulp and paper sector.

Though the manufacture of pulp began in 1875, three plants constructed during the 1920s (at Sheet Harbour, Hantsport and Liverpool) formed the core of the modern pulp and paper industry until 1962, when Nova Scotia Pulp Ltd. opened its mill near Port Hawkesbury (see Figure 1).[7] With the arrival of the latter, the domestic consumption of pulpwood more than doubled from 230,000 to 480,000 cords per year. Four years later, the opening of the Scott Maritimes pulp mill near Pictou had a similar impact, and the addition of a newsprint mill to the Stora complex

---

4   For an example of this approach, see Anthony Winson, "Researching the Food Processing-Farming Chain: The Case of Nova Scotia", *Canadian Review of Sociology and Anthropology*, 25, 4 (1988), p. 524.

5   For a detailed survey of Nova Scotia timber rights and ownership, see Ralph S. Johnson, *Forests of Nova Scotia* (Halifax, 1986), esp. chs. 23, 29.

6   Nova Scotia, Department of Lands and Forests, *Submission to the Royal Commission on Forestry* (Halifax, 1983).

7   The Port Hawkesbury mill underwent several changes of name: Nova Scotia Pulp Ltd., 1957; Nova Scotia Forest Industries Ltd., 1972; and Stora Forest Industries, 1985. Hereafter it will be referred to as Stora.

Figure 1

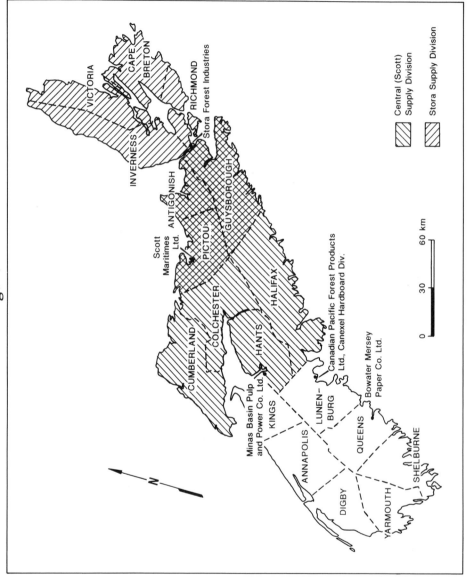

raised the total domestic consumption still further, to 935,000 cords in 1971.[8] The pulpwood export market declined from its interwar prominence, but still accounted for approximately 100,000 cords per year in 1960.[9]

Nova Scotia pulp and paper companies utilize private timberlands in two respects. Firms such as Bowater Mersey, Minas Basin and Scott have purchased extensive freehold tracts to build up their timber reserves. At the same time, most firms purchase significant volumes of privately produced pulpwood for immediate use, to minimize input costs and to extend the life of company-controlled stands. This commercial pulpwood market is typically structured so that for the woodlot owner, the "open market" for the sale of pulpwood is anything but classically competitive. Writing of Nova Scotia in the interwar period, R. McGregor Dawson described the primary market as "disorganized" insofar as "the pulpwood producer was completely at the mercy of the shipper of the pulpwood, whose own profit depended on the widest possible margin between the prices paid to the producers and the selling prices laid down by the foreign buyer".[10] The Restrictive Trades Practices Commission (RTPC) shed considerable light on pulpwood buying arrangements in Ontario and Quebec during the 1950s. It found that no "continuous market" existed in the conventional sense. Rather, supply contracts were signed at fixed prices early in the season. Each mill maintained a buying network consisting of "brokers", who tended to be self-financed businessmen delivering wood to the mills, and "dealers", who were part-time buyers (often local storekeepers) operating as the local extension of the broker network. The mills set target prices for supply contracts, and paid their agents by commission. R.J. MacSween described a similar relationship in Nova Scotia in the early 1960s. Private sales accounted for 80 per cent of the Nova Scotia market, compared with 25 per cent in Ontario and 30 per cent in Quebec.[11] In its final report, the RTPC concluded that:

> Notwithstanding the frequent breakdowns in the pricing arrangements, such arrangements were nevertheless effective in depressing the prices to farmers and other small producers below the levels such prices would have reached had the companies acted independently and competitively.[12]

---

8   Nova Scotia, Department of Lands and Forests, *Nova Scotia Producers and Production of Forest Products, 1971* (Halifax, 1972).

9   John S. Donaldson, *The Pulp Industry in Nova Scotia*, Department of Lands and Forests, Bulletin 27 (Halifax, 1961).

10 Nova Scotia, Royal Commission on Provincial Development and Rehabilitation, *Report on Forest Industries* (Halifax, 1944), p. 34.

11 Nova Scotia, Royal Commission on the Prices of Pulpwood and Other Forest Products, *Report* (Halifax, 1964).

12 Canada, Restrictive Trades Practices Commission, *Report Concerning the Purchase of Pulpwood in Certain Districts of Eastern Canada* (Ottawa, 1958), p. 4.

Not surprisingly, the issue of organized marketing had been raised in Nova Scotia as early as the 1920s. At that point the small-producer segment of woodland owners consisted primarily of farmers with woodlots attached to their lands, and the disputes arose principally between the farm producers and agents buying pulpwood for export purposes. For the next several decades, it was the Nova Scotia Federation of Agriculture that lobbied periodically for pulpwood to be added to the list of "orderly marketed" farm commodities. Significantly, this paralleled the policy dispositions of the provincial bureaucracy. Here, small woodlot interests were of greatest concern to the Department of Agriculture. In 1938 a Forestry Marketing Branch was established with the task of "organizing producers of wood products so that they could better protect themselves from the low prices that resulted from a disorganized marketing system".[13] One of the earliest projects of the one-person forest products bureau was to organize co-operative groups for some Guysborough County and Cape Breton producers, to facilitate their dealings with the pulpwood buyers. After the Second World War the branch director became Deputy Minister of Agriculture, though the forest products mandate was transfered to the Department of Lands and Forests, where it was promptly forgotten.[14]

When the issue of organized marketing was raised anew in 1960, it was in eastern Nova Scotia.[15] As part of a deal to secure a new pulp mill at Port Hawkesbury, the province had leased 1.3 million acres (520,000 ha) of Crown lands to Nova Scotia Pulp Ltd., a subsidiary of the Swedish forest giant Stora Kopparberg. The lease called for a very low stumpage rate of $1 per cord. This carried serious pricing and supply implications for small private pulpwood producers, who were the most significant source of wood. It raised the prospect that cheap Crown stumpage would set the ceiling for private stumpage sales and force down the roadside prices for privately cut pulpwood. Thus it triggered a campaign by some small woodlot owners, on farm and off, who acted "in anticipation of the unfair competitive situation that would develop as a result of the provincial government's decision to make available to NSFI [Stora] all Crown lands in eastern Nova Scotia on a lease basis".[16] This appraisal proved to be remarkably prescient. Subsequent events confirmed that the woodlot owners were battling the government's timber and industrial policies as much as they were battling the pulp and paper companies. In

13 N.S., *Report on Forest Industries*, p. 34.

14 F.W. Walsh, *We Fought for the Little Man* (Moncton, 1978).

15 Two outstanding contributions to the history of small woodlot politics in Nova Scotia are A.A. MacDonald, "Organization of Woodlot Owners for Market Power", presented at the University of Reading, 1986, and "Exploitation of the Private Owners of Forest Resources in Nova Scotia", presented at the St. Francis Xavier University Forest Conference, 1975.

16 A.A. MacDonald, "Planning and Control of Nova Scotia's Forest Industry", presented to the Nova Scotia Community Planning Conference (November, 1976), p. 7.

their initial approaches to Stora, the owners proposed to negotiate a formal supply relationship. The failure to reach a voluntary agreement led them to take a different tack.

The Eastern Wood Producers Association, led by Wendell Coldwell (a long-time activist in farm marketing), approached the provincial government to secure a pulpwood marketing board under the authority of the Natural Products Marketing Act. Enacted during the Depression years, this statute provided the enabling authority for the organized marketing of a variety of primary commodities, but did not include forest products.[17] To remedy this, the owners' group worked through the provincial Department of Agriculture and in 1962 secured the necessary legislative amendment.[18] By the terms of the act, cabinet consent was required to implement each new commodity scheme. However, when the woodlot owners sought consent for the forest products board, the government did not respond directly. Instead it announced a royal commission, with a mandate to investigate Nova Scotia pulpwood prices and marketing arrangements in a regional context. The commissioner, R.J. MacSween, had enjoyed a lengthy association with the Nova Scotia Marketing Board, the regulatory overseer of the various agricultural commodity boards.

The MacSween Commission found that while pulpwood prices across the Maritimes had run closely together since the war, the most striking fact was their low level. In nominal terms, the prices had languished for almost a decade at their 1954 level of approximately $15 per cord at roadside. Taking into account the costs of harvesting, the stumpage return to the private owner was almost negligible. According to MacSween, "the producer, at best, could not do better than earn sub-standard wages with little or nothing for stumpage or maintenance".[19] The report drew attention to the marketing boards already operating in Quebec and northwestern New Brunswick. Preliminary evidence suggested that "they [were] getting along satisfactorily" in their role as bargaining agents for their members. When it came to marketing structures, however, MacSween advocated the formation of a Swedish-inspired private woodlot organization. Representing over 125,000 private owners, the Swedish associations were a key force for conservation, through their commitment to selective cutting and other forest-management techniques. The commissioner advised the government of Nova Scotia to require that a well-established woodlot owner association be put in place *in advance* of any decision on marketing structures. MacSween argued that the organizing campaign would also serve as an educational forum on marketing practices. Furthermore, since a statutory marketing board would provide only a bargaining framework, the private

---

17 For a detailed discussion of the evolution of this act, see A.A. MacDonald, *Policy Formulation Process: Nova Scotia Dairy Marketing, 1933-1978* (Antigonish, 1980) ch. 4.

18 *Statutes of Nova Scotia* (Halifax, 1962), c. 40, p. 704

19 Nova Scotia, *Royal Commission on the Prices of Pulpwood and Other Forest Products* (Halifax, 1964), p. 22.

producers would need a separate vehicle to negotiate contracts with the pulpwood buyers.

In critical ways, the MacSween report shaped the future direction of the marketing struggle. It channelled the process of mobilizing small producers by closing off certain options while advancing others. The findings on low stumpage returns, unambiguous in themselves, were balanced against the narrow revenue margins of the pulp and paper companies, yielding the conclusion that there remained "little, and in some cases no margin, for an increase in the price of wood".[20] This alleged lack of redistributable surplus made the case for a policy standstill (the recommended interlude for woodlot owner organization and education) politically attractive, thereby obscuring what constituted a serious political setback for the woodlot activists. MacSween acknowledged the feasibility of small producer boards, though he favoured the advantages of the Swedish organizational infrastructure over either the Nova Scotia status quo or the arrangements in Quebec and New Brunswick. It was not clear from the report why a most sophisticated organizational infrastructure, the product of decades of Swedish experience, was a prerequisite to organized marketing in Nova Scotia. Neither did the report explain how the pulp and paper sector in other jurisdictions could absorb the higher prices attendant with organized marketing. It is clear that the woodlot activists were forced to yield to an agenda set by the pulp and paper industry, thereby experiencing their first serious defeat.

There remained the possibility of organizing the wide constituency of woodlot owners. Out of this came a 1966 application to the federal-provincial Agricultural and Rural Development Act (ARDA) programme. Submitted jointly by the Nova Scotia Federation of Agriculture, the eastern regional activists and the Extension Department of St. Francis Xavier University, it sought funding support for an organizing programme among provincial woodlot owners. A major thrust of the ARDA programme was to ameliorate rural poverty. In Nova Scotia it sponsored projects dealing with land consolidation on rural micro-lots, land reclamation and improvement, work force and leadership training, and research.[21] ARDA was thus a natural target, and an ally, for the woodlot activists. Covering a three-year period commencing in March 1967, the project was delivered by the St. Francis Xavier Extension Department, with the provincial Department of Lands and Forests as the administrative agency of record. The organizational campaign was built around the efforts of fieldworkers, animators who would contact prospective members and work with them through public meetings to establish formal groups at the county

---

20   N.S., *Royal Commission*, p. 30.

21   For a list of ARDA projects in Nova Scotia, see Canada, Department of Forestry and Rural Development, *ARDA Catalogue* (Ottawa, 1968). The general ARDA policy approach is discussed by L.E. Poetschke, "Regional Planning for Depressed Rural Areas: The Canadian Experience" (Ottawa, 1967).

level.[22] To encourage the widest possible membership base, the minimum size of a woodlot holding was set at a rather low 50 acres (20 ha).

Just over one year after the programme began, the first "province-wide" meeting was convened. Delegates attended from six local associations and adopted eight resolutions on a variety of forest policy questions. These included a call for the tripling of public funds for forest-stand improvement, the need for independent grading of Christmas trees, the prospect of establishing a purchasing system with Christmas tree buyers, the call for an official log rule in Nova Scotia ("to free owners from dependence on the buyer's scale"),[23] and the need for wider circulation of forest policy information to small woodlot owners. Given this strong beginning, the ARDA steering committee authorized a broadening of the programme to include the entire province. By the time of the second general meeting in January 1969, 12 county-level associations were involved. Here the delegates agreed to form a Nova Scotia Woodlot Owners Association (NSWOA), electing an executive and a board of directors.

Three specific objectives were set for the new association. It was to articulate the interests of woodlot owners on matters affecting the industry, to promote woodlot development policies for increased productivity and income, and "to promote the organized marketing of any forest product when its producers consider it necessary".[24] Just before the ARDA contract expired in 1970, the NSWOA held its first annual meeting. By this point only three counties (Kings, Shelburne and Yarmouth) remained to be organized. While situational factors inevitably shaped the pace and direction of associational growth, it is worthy of note that all three of these counties ranked among the lowest in proportion of wood produced within the province. The director of the organizing programme, Richard Lord, was candid in his appraisal of the strengths and limitations of the new structure:

> The viability of these [local] associations and the degree to which they will have accepted their responsibilities to their members is expected to vary. Some have been very active and have had the benefit of strong local leadership; others must be considered less successful. Several of the older associations have experienced a decline in membership. In part this may be attributed to the initial and somewhat naive expectation that the local associations might have some immediate and beneficial effect on such areas as the price of pulpwood. However in most cases local associations and their

---

22 This programme is outlined in greater detail in St. Francis Xavier University, Extension Department, "Research on the Organization and Education of Woodlot Owners" (Antigonish, 1966).

23 Press Release, 13 May 1968, Files of the Nova Scotia Woodlot Owners and Operators Association, Truro, Nova Scotia.

24 St. Francis Xavier University, Extension Department, "Report of the Contracting Agency" (Antigonish, 1970).

members have realized that little could be accomplished in any of the major areas of concern until a provincial body had been established and had had time to work out its general objectives and specific policies. The role of the local associations in developing policies on their own for local implementation and in seeking broader application of such policies by placing them before the provincial association has only rarely been realized...this remains as a major objective of the overall program which is yet to be achieved.[25]

This underlines the pivotal role that the pulpwood marketing question was assuming to the entire endeavour. From the outset, the association was concerned with a wide range of forest policy and woodlot management issues.[26] Yet it was the prospect of organized marketing that had underlaid the organizational drive, and it was from organized marketing that conservation and management activities would spring. For several years the NSWOA staff and executive were preoccupied with the issue.

The establishment of a province-wide association in just three years was a considerable achievement. Having met MacSween's threshold condition for renewing the marketing initiative, the NSWOA petitioned once again for an order under the Natural Products Marketing Act. A formal marketing proposal was prepared during 1970, in consultation with the Department of the Attorney-General. Once the Nova Scotia Marketing Board had given tentative approval, the NSWOA mounted a campaign to register owners across the province, in anticipation of the referendum that was required under the law. The provincial Minister of Agriculture, William Gillis, impressed on the association the importance of a high voter turnout if the initiative was to succeed.[27] With eligibility open to all woodlot owners, some 8,500 returned application-to-vote forms to the board.

At this point, the marketing question was again side-tracked, this time by considerations of industrial policy. The matter was referred for discussion to the Forestry Sector Committee of Nova Scotia's Voluntary Planning (VP) organization. Established in the early 1960s (and known until 1970 as Voluntary Economic Planning), it offered a consultative network linking organized business (and to a lesser degree labour) interests with the province. Initially charged with the design of a province-wide economic development plan, the VP evolved after 1970 into a series of sectoral advisory bodies with privileged access to the provincial bureaucracy.[28]

---

25 St. Francis Xavier University, "Report of the Contracting Agency".

26 Something of this scope is indicated by the list of working committees in 1969: Constitution and Finance; Forest Improvement Act; Forest Taxation; Pulpwood Marketing; Woodland Tenure and Consolidation; Sawlogs; and Christmas Trees.

27 Nova Scotia Woodlot Owners Association, Second Annual Meeting, *Report* (Truro, 1971).

28 For a history of Voluntary Economic Planning Board, see Anthony Lamport, *Common Ground* (Halifax, 1988), pp. 47-52.

As a member of the Forestry Sector Committee, the NSWOA proposed a motion endorsing

the *right* of pulpwood producers to join a marketing mechanism which will protect their interests...and furthermore, that the Government of Nova Scotia facilitate through newly enacted or amended legislation, the establishment of a pulpwood marketing mechanism which will protect the interests of Nova Scotia pulpwood producers and thus provide for bilateral and co-equal negotiations between buyers and sellers.[29]

Befitting its sectoral advisory role, the Forestry Sector Committee included representatives of the pulp and paper industry, the sawmilling industry and a variety of other forest-related associations. The opposition of the industrial buyers was already on record through the Nova Scotia Forest Products Association.[30] According to one observer, the association "actively opposed the plan and proposed a variety of delays, restraints and alternatives".[31]

A fortnight prior to the scheduled referendum, the Forestry Sector Committee defeated the NSWOA's resolution on the principle of organized marketing. The committee went on to discuss an alternative approach. This continued at a 29 April special meeting of the Forest Products Association, convened to formalize its position. While representatives of the Department of Lands and Forests and VP Board were in attendance, the secretary-manager of the NSWOA (an associate member of Forest Products Association) was refused permission to attend. While the sentiment clearly ran against the marketing plan, the most revealing intervention was by the Deputy Minister of Lands and Forests, who "assured the participants that his department would prepare legislation to have 'Forest Products' removed from the *Natural Products Marketing Act* and that legislation would be prepared for the establishment of a Forestry Commission"[32] (recommended by the Forest Products Association as a substitute for the Marketing Plan). The Forestry Sector Committee convened again on 6 May 1970, when it recommended that the planned vote be cancelled, that eligibility for any future vote be limited to owners of more than 200 acres (81 ha), and that forest products be removed from the Natural Products

---

29 MacDonald, "Planning and Control", p. 9.

30 The Forest Products Association was established in 1934 "by a group of dedicated lumbermen". Duncan K. MacLellan, *A Study of Selected New Brunswick, Nova Scotia, Regional and National Forestry Sector Interest Groups* (Halifax, 1986), p. 48. While it was open to all segments of the industry, the leading roles were assumed by sawmill sector personnel, with the increasing presence of the pulp and paper sector after 1965. The political positions advanced by the FPA were more complex than an index of its leaders suggests.

31 M.J.L. Kirby, "The Nova Scotia Pulpwood Marketing Board Case" (Halifax, 1979), p. 6.

32 MacDonald, "Planning and Control", p. 11.

Marketing Act. The final proposal called for the establishment of a "Forestry Commission". Consisting of buyers, producers, consumers and other interested persons, it was offered as a substitute for the proposed marketing plan.[33] On 14 May the umbrella VP Board met to consider the competing proposals. The NSWOA marketing plan was put to a vote, and was carried by a margin of one. However, the matter was not allowed to rest. After further discussion, it was decided to disqualify the two provincial government representatives on the VP Board. When the question was put again, the marketing plan was defeated by one vote. Following this, the resolutions from the Forestry Sector Committee were brought forward. They were adopted as the official VP Board position, and were conveyed subsequently to the government.

On the advice of the Nova Scotia Marketing Board, the NSWOA decided to alter its plan. Voting was now restricted to owners possessing at least 50 acres (20 ha). This compromised the initial registration campaign (open to all woodlot owners) and necessitated a reregistration, this time undertaken by the board. The effect of the delays and procedural changes was compounded by an administrative error at the board, by which new applications to vote were distributed less than a week before the mailing deadline. In the end, only 4,857 owners qualified (slightly more than half of the original registrants).

Despite the pressure from the Forest Products Association and the VP Board, premier Gerald Regan was unwilling to interfere with the scheduled referendum. However, he did indicate to VP officials, at a 1 June meeting, "that an affirmative vote on the plan would not commit the Government to implementing the plan, and that the provincial government would consult with VP before any final plan was implemented".[34] Of the 3,483 ballots tallied in the July vote, 86 per cent were cast in favour.

In August 1970 the government informed the NSWOA that the Marketing Board would not be authorized to accept the plan. Instead, the various forest organizations were directed to seek an agreement along the lines of the "commission" concept. Faced with a continuing deadlock, the government appointed a conciliation committee chaired by a lawyer, Ian MacKeigan. This brought together three representatives of the NSWOA and three from the Forest Products Association. Finding no grounds for a workable consensus, MacKeigan submitted a report in January 1972, which led directly to a legislative settlement. He proposed the establishment of a Pulpwood Marketing Board by separate statute, with powers to

33 The commission would consist of a commissioner and board to serve as advisors to the Minister of Lands and Forests and to "act as conciliator between various segments of the forest industry and between private and public interests". Nova Scotia Forest Products Association, "Proposal for the Formation of a Forestry Commission", (Truro, 1971), p. 5. It would function, on a more select basis, in the same manner as the Forestry Sector Committee.

34 MacDonald, "Planning and Control", p. 9.

register and license all producers, buyers, dealers and traders, and to require reports on their pulpwood transactions. The board would also certify any association seeking to act as a bargaining agent.

The government was not long in responding, and its draft bill was significant both for its inclusions and its omissions. The minister frankly conceded that it was "a bill that the government was not too anxious to introduce".[35] In effect, Bill 134 perpetuated the tensions which MacKeigan had acknowledged, thereby perpetuating the political confrontation between the small woodlot owners and the pulp and paper industry. In the interim, the government proposed, in the words of Lands and Forests Minister Comeau, "a compromise, an attempt to reconcile two irreconcilable positions".[36] The government's only hope was that a flexible, quasi-independent agency might broker the differences in such a way as to contain the tension. Thus the bill aimed to establish

> a neutral marketing board, to give it adequate authority within broad limits and to leave it to double up and modify a marketing system for pulpwood that the need and interests of the industry may dictate from time to time. If the bill seems to avoid details and to establish powers that are permissive rather than mandatory, this is by design.[37]

For the first time there would be an element of direct state regulation of the pulpwood-buying sector. Bill 134 gave the Pulpwood Marketing Board the power to register and license all producers, buyers and bargaining agents. It could also collect information on prices and volumes, and levy charges on pulpwood transactions to help finance the work of the board and of recognized bargaining agents. But the essence of its marketing role lay in administering a framework of collective bargaining between producing and buying interests. It held the power of official recognition, through certification, of bargaining agents of both producers and buyers. Once recognized, these agents enjoyed exclusive rights to bargain for their designated memberships. The board could also facilitate the bargaining process for recognized associations. Where contract talks were not joined, either party could apply for a declaration of "bargaining situation". Once issued, this obliged both sides to commence negotiations within 20 days. Should no agreement be reached after a month of bargaining, the board could be approached for a declaration of "deadlock". Thereafter, either party could apply for mediation, in which the board had the power to investigate the dispute and issue a report recommending terms of settlement. Notably absent were any provisions for compulsory arbitration, which could bring such deadlocks to a definitive conclusion. Finally, the board offered an avenue of appeal on disputes over compliance with existing agreements, with

---

35 Nova Scotia, House of Assembly, *Debates*, 4 May 1972, p. 2331.

36 N.S., *Debates*, 4 May 1972, p. 2332.

37 N.S., *Debates*, 4 May 1972, pp. 2331-2.

powers to dismiss, or to order compliance. All in all, this type of market regulation fell somewhere between a natural products marketing board and a labour relations board. Clearly the former was preferred by the NSWOA, offering as it did a confirmed framework for negotiating commodity prices, within an operational paradigm built upon decades of experience in the poultry, hogs, tobacco, wool and dairy sectors.[38]

Both the Pulpwood Marketing Act and the board began life with few friends. The NSWOA felt that it left much to be desired, and what was more, it imposed costly delays when time was of the essence.[39] With each passing year, more small properties were being sold, cut over or abandoned as timber resources.[40] The Forest Products Association was also critical of the act. The association's president, R.R. Murray, described the marketing plan as "the biggest waste of time and energy that I have ever encountered". He saw it as a bid "for the immediate gain by a few who wish to control our industry, in which they have a limited investment and no concern for the future".[41] To contain such "marginal" elements, the Forest Products Association pressed for a higher minimum acreage qualification (200 acres, or 81 ha) for producer status. The effect would be to exclude thousands of small holders, including many from the activist core of the early woodlot owner associations. It also fit with a programme of mechanized, capitalized logging on increasingly large-scale properties, a strategy in which small landowners and occasional producers had little place.

The passage of the Pulpwood Marketing Act marked more of a starting point than a finish. Henceforth, the contending interests in the pulpwood market would have to work *within* this framework. In this, its institutional biases would play a critical role. The decision to create a marketing system *de novo* bore both political opportunities and liabilities. Set beside agricultural marketing or labour relations, the Pulpwood Marketing Board was neither fish nor fowl. Both the legislative foundation and the administrative structure began from scratch, unable to borrow or benefit from either stream of practical experience in procedural design, economic analysis or judicial interpretation. Even the demands of administrative organization imposed a heavy brake on a political process that had been surging ahead in the years 1969-72. Five months elapsed before the appointment of board members in October 1972. Then, somewhat surprisingly, the cabinet set the term of the initial

---

38 For details of marketing arrangements in the province, see Nova Scotia, Department of Agriculture, *1974 Directory Agriculture* (Halifax, 1974).

39 G. Higgins, "President's Report", Nova Scotia Woodlot Owners and Operators Association, 4th Annual Meeting, *Report* (Truro, 1973).

40 Richard Lord, "Forest Management Situation on Small Private Holdings", Paper presented to the Nova Scotia Section, Canadian Institute of Forestry (September 1977), pp. 3-4.

41 Nova Scotia Forest Products Association, 38th Annual Meeting, *Report* (Truro, 1972), p. 5. The president was also the woodlands manager for Scott Maritimes Ltd.

appointments at just one year. In addition, adversarial dynamics were inserted directly into the board. Three members (including the chairman and vice-chairman) were appointed "at large" by the cabinet, while the NSWOA and Forest Products Association proposed one member each. The board began meeting at the end of 1972, and devoted its initial efforts to "studying the Act to define the powers of the board, in developing operations, procedures, regulations and systems for collecting market information".[42]

This preparatory phase was neither perfunctory nor brief. Both the lack of precedents and the broad grant of enabling authority posed challenges. The vice-chairman, Edwin Elliott, frankly admitted to the NSWOA that "he accepted personal responsibility for urging the Board to go slow until it was sure it had developed effective policies".[43] He pointed to the difficulties experienced earlier by the Apple Marketing Board and the Dairy Commission.

At the same time, the NSWOA was intent on forcing the pace. In January 1973, it was the first group to apply to the Pulpwood Marketing Board for certification as a bargaining agent for all primary pulpwood producers in the province. A competing application followed from the Forest Products Association, seeking to bargain for that portion of its members (sawmillers, logging contractors and large woodland owners) producing pulpwood. After clarification meetings with both parties, the board convened three days of public hearings in July 1973. Here the NSWOA argued that the presence of major pulp buyers within the Forest Products Association rendered it unsuitable as a bargaining organization. The association countered that its members produced 73 per cent of all pulpwood in Nova Scotia.[44] The two proposals reflected a segmentation of the pulpwood market, between the small farm and non-industrial woodlot owners and the larger scale, mechanized producers.

The dual applications posed major choices for the board, as it discovered first hand the depth of contradiction between the two organizations. Neither application was without ambiguity. The NSWOA's blanket claim far exceeded its membership base, though it had won a ringing endorsement in the only popular consultation to date. On the other hand, the Forest Products Association was clearly compromised on this issue, given that both its membership and leadership mixed harvesting and processing. This was most evident in the position of Hollis Routledge. As both the Woodlands Manager for Stora, and the Forest Products Association representative on the board, his outlook was far more that of an industrial user than a pulpwood producer.

It took seven months for the certification rulings to be announced. In February 1974, the NSWOA was certified as a bargaining agent. This decision was carried by

---

42 "Pulpwood Marketing Committee Report", Nova Scotia Forest Products Association, 39th Annual Meeting, *Report* (Truro, 1973), p. 38.

43 Nova Scotia Woodlot Owners Association, 5th Annual Meeting, *Report* (Truro, 1974).

44 "Executive Director's Report", Nova Scotia Forest Products Association, 40th Annual Meeting, *Report* (Truro, 1974)

a three to one vote at the board. A week later the Forest Products Association's bid was denied by the same margin. Immediately the woodlot owners applied for the declaration of a bargaining situation with Stora. A negotiating committee had been struck from the membership in the seven eastern counties, long the bedrock of the organization. The two sides held an initial meeting on 6 May 1974, which ended in deadlock. According to the NSWOA, "the Company refused to acknowledge our right to represent all producers and nothing came of this meeting, and the Company refused any further meetings".[45] Two weeks later, the board declared that a bargaining situation existed. Certainly this was a victory for the woodlot owners. But now the weakness of the act served the interests of the industry.

Stora reacted in July 1974 by launching a court action seeking to quash both the certification and the declaration. In October, the Trial Division of the Nova Scotia Supreme Court upheld the certification but quashed the declaration of a bargaining situation. Stora announced its intention to appeal the former, while the board joined the proceedings with a cross-appeal of the latter part. This deepening litigation shifted the marketing conflict to a new plane. For virtually a year, the negotiating process was frozen. Indeed the NSWOA was relegated to the margins while Stora and the Pulpwood Marketing Board squared off in the courts.

The pulp and paper industry's case was aided through the intervention of the provincial Department of Lands and Forests. For some time, the NSWOA had argued that senior administrative officials in the department had compromised themselves by displays of open partiality toward the pulp and paper interests. Thomas Smith, then president of the NSWOA, charged that the deputy minister, R.H. Burgess, had promoted the removal of forest products from the Natural Products Marketing Act back in 1971, during the first marketing campaign. This was viewed as "a direct attempt to wreck the NSWOA".[46]

As the marketing issue ran its course, this sense of bias on the part of senior Department of Lands and Forests officials spilled over onto other matters. In 1970 the department's Extension Division was disbanded, and the six extension foresters whose job it was to work with small woodlot owners were re-assigned. When the NSWOA called for the creation of a private lands directorate within the department, officials responded by defending the value of existing programmes and rejecting the concept as unnecessary.[47] Yet when all was said and done, provincial officials

---

45   "Pulpwood Marketing Advisory Committee Report", Nova Scotia Woodlot Owners Association, 6th Annual Meeting, *Report* (Truro, 1975), p. 22

46   "President's Report", Nova Scotia Woodlot Owners Association, 3rd Annual Meeting, *Report* (Truro, 1972). Smith took pains to dissociate the minister from this project. Mr. Comeau, it was felt, "gives every indication of being in full agreement of [*sic*] a Producers Pulpwood Marketing Board." His failure to prevail over the bureaucracy was attributed to inexperience.

47   A Private Lands Division was established some 15 years after the NSWOA first raised the issue.

knew very little about woods activities on Nova Scotia's small private woodlands. Periodically the department enlisted the federal Forestry Service to conduct or finance baseline studies, but no coherent policy framework had been developed.[48] In contrast to this, the relationship between senior officials and the Forest Products Association was characterized by co-operation and trust. The most significant example was the Gas Tax Access Road programme established in 1967. The association pointed out that forest operators paid gasoline tax in fuelling their off-road vehicles, without the rebates available to farmers. It then persuaded the Department of Lands and Forests to create a new programme of financial assistance for logging access roads, delivered by the association and with eligibility restricted to its members.[49] This prompted many woodlot owners to join the Forest Products Association, if only for a few years, in order to qualify for the grants. By contrast, the NSWOA failed in its efforts to be designated the delivery agent for the ARDA programme of forest improvement grants and services on private lands.[50] No doubt this sort of experience influenced Kingsley Brown Jr., the NSWOA representative on the board, when in 1975 he described the deputy minister as "counselling and advising the Forest Products Association in their opposition to the efforts of the Woodlot Owners Association".[51] To the woodlot owners, there may have been little surprise in 1979 when Donald Eldridge, then executive director of the Forest Products Association, was appointed Deputy Minister of Lands and Forests.

By any account, the Supreme Court judgement of June 1975 (the "MacKeigan decision") stands as a watershed event in the struggle over pulpwood marketing. Led by the now Chief Justice Ian MacKeigan, the court found against the Pulpwood Marketing Board on both questions.[52] Grave procedural flaws were found in the board's procedures, and the requirement of substantial levels of producer consent

---

48 See R.M. Nacker, M.R.C. Massie, K.L. Runyon and J.V. Stewart, *Small Private Woodlands in Nova Scotia* (Ottawa, 1972), and Peter MacQuarrie, *A Survey of Private Woodland Owners in Nova Scotia* (Halifax, 1981).

49 Statement by E.D. Haliburton, Minister of Lands and Forests, 21 April 1967, MG 1, vol. 2861, no. 4, Public Archives of Nova Scotia. By 1975-6 this programme dispensed $650,000. Nova Scotia, *Supplement to the Public Accounts* (Halifax, 1976), pp. 52-3.

50 The failure of this bid took on added importance after 1976, when the first of a series of Forest Sector Sub-Agreements was signed under the Canada-Nova Scotia Development Agreement. These programmes dramatically expanded the scope of private land forestry services. They also led to the creation of an entirely new level of management vehicles in the form of the Group Ventures, which brought small woodlot owners together for forest management work.

51 Nova Scotia Woodlot Owners and Operators Association, 6th Annual Meeting, *Report* (Truro, 1975), p. 9.

52 N.S. Forest Industries v. N.S. Pulpwood Marketing Board, 12, Nova Scotia *Reports* (2d) 1975, pp. 91-148

necessitated greater precision in delineating producer groups in the future. By quashing the recognition of the NSWOA as bargaining agent, the ruling effectively set the issue back a full three years, to the origins of the act.

By necessity, the ruling triggered a massive review of the statute, together with the procedures and standards of board decisions. One key legislative amendment served to fundamentally re-orient the private producer constituency. The definition of pulpwood production, which originally embraced wood "standing or severed from the stump",[53] was changed to include only the commodity "at the time it is cut and prepared from trees for sale".[54] As a result, woodlot owners who sold their timber for stumpage, thereby enabling the contracting party to cut and haul the pulpwood to roadside for sale, were no longer a part of the regulated marketing transaction. The effect was to exclude from the producer group a significant part of the woodlot-owning public. At the same time, the amendment enhanced the importance of the logging contractor who purchased stumpage from the woodlot owner. This cleavage between the NSWOA membership and the small producer marketing group membership would widen over time until the tension could no longer be contained.

The NSWOA renewed its efforts in August 1976, applying for recognition as a bargaining agent for eastern county producers supplying Stora. At public hearings in October, the association presented 206 pledges of support, some of which were challenged by the company. In the end, the NSWOA was left with support of those providing 41 per cent of the privately produced wood to Stora. For its part, the Forest Products Association argued that its member suppliers neither desired, nor could be adequately served by, another bargaining agent. Early in 1977 the board released its decision, rejecting the NSWOA application on the basis of insufficient membership strength.

As part of its response, the board set out standards and practices to guide all future certification cases. Applications would have to be specified by geographical region, be sponsored by bodies separate from the existing associations, and be directed by negotiating committees chosen openly by the direct producers. To facilitate the process of consulting with the producers during organizing campaigns, the board announced that it would release lists of pulpwood producers supplying licensed buyers, and that it would directly conduct the formal votes.

The Pulpwood Marketing Board's decision in February 1977 made abundantly clear that the NSWOA's long-standing goal of bargaining for all Nova Scotia pulpwood producers would never be realized in that form. At a time when the estimated number of private woodland owners ran from 25,000 to 30,000, the association could hardly claim even one-tenth of them as members. In most years, the NSWOA's paid-up membership stood between 900 and 1,600. In the face of

---

53   *Statutes of Nova Scotia* (Halifax, 1972), c. 15, p. 194.

54   *Statutes of Nova Scotia* (Halifax, 1976), c. 42, p. 229.

this, there was every possibility that all future applications would be contested, and certifications challenged, by rival organizations.

The NSWOA was forced to rethink its organizational and tactical approach. Three years of setbacks, running from the MacKeigan decision to the statutory amendments to the 1977 certification ruling, dictated certain adjustments. Already the organization had changed its name to formally embrace woodlot "operators" (i.e. logging contractors). During 1977, the Nova Scotia Woodlot Owners and Operators Association (NSWOOA) altered its constitution. While membership remained open to all private owners of more than 50 acres (20 ha), it was broadened to include anyone who met the statutory definition of "producer" (an owner of pulpwood when prepared for sale). This ensured that the association's terms of membership included all classes of private wood suppliers. Moreover, at a time when the regulatory regime was deepening the divide between woodlot "owners" and woodlot "producers", the association was attempting to preserve a base among the contractor segment, particularly the small- to medium-sized independent loggers. It is significant that Donald MacLeod, the NSWOOA president in 1976-9, was the first commercial operator to head the group.[55] At the same time, however, political and economic differences between woodlot owners and contractors were widening. With the organizing campaign deadlocked, and pulpwood prices remaining low, Richard Lord observed in 1977 that

> the more progressive woods-oriented individuals generally find it more advantageous to neglect their own holdings and to seek employment on company-operated land, or to turn to private contracting, purchasing stumpage from other owners.[56]

Secondly, the NSWOOA was forced to reconsider another issue: its status as a bargaining agent. There were essentially two alternatives. The association could foster independent producer groups completely outside its structure, or it could establish "producer divisions" within by "allowing these divisions autonomy with respect to bargaining but under the umbrella of the broad, province wide organization".[57] Once it settled on the latter option, the association mounted yet another campaign. It asked the board for a list of Stora's eastern county producers (now an essential tool of organizing). In August 1977 the board agreed to release the lists of pulpwood producers over the previous three years. Stora promptly sought a court order to prevent the list's release. In early November Stora's application was dismissed "on the grounds that the Board's decision to release the lists was a policy

---

55 MacDonald, "Review of Woodlot Owners' History" (mimeo, 1976).

56 Richard Lord, "Forest Management Situation on Private Holdings", Paper presented to the Annual Meeting, Nova Scotia Section, Canadian Institute of Forestry (September 1977), p. 4.

57 Nova Scotia Woodlot Owners and Operators Association, 9th Annual Meeting, *Report* (Truro, 1978), p. 5.

decision made in the exercise of the Board's administrative discretion, involving no wrong principle of law and as such was not reviewable in court".[58] Once again the company appealed this ruling to the Appeal Division of the Nova Scotia Supreme Court. Here the original ruling was upheld, thereby clearing the way for the list's release. However, the judicial cycle had once again consumed the better part of an organizing year, thus postponing the new pledge campaign until the latter half of 1978.

In March of 1979, the first organizational meeting was convened in Port Hawkesbury, to establish the Stora Suppliers Division of the NSWOOA. A month later the division applied for certification as the sole bargaining agent for the private suppliers to the company. After public hearings in July (which found almost 85 per cent of the eligible suppliers in support), the board approved the application. With certification settled, the negotiating process could begin. In September 1979 the Suppliers Division sought a declaration of a bargaining situation, which the board granted in December. Immediately in the new year, Hollis Routledge, the Forest Products Association nominee to the board, resigned this position in order to assist his employer in the negotiations, which began forthwith. Nine negotiating sessions yielded an agreement. Ratified in March 1980, the contract covered delivery of most of Stora's private wood purchases (140,000 cords) for a period of 18 months, with an immediate price increase of $4 per cord.[59]

No sooner was the ink dry when the NSWOOA launched a second organizing campaign. This was aimed at the private pulpwood suppliers to Scott Maritimes Ltd., the prime outlet for producers in central Nova Scotia. By contrast to the Stora experience, several competing applications were made in this case.[60] One of these came from the Wood Products Manufacturers Association (WPMA), whose membership consisted of some 20 medium- to large-sized sawmill companies (each processing over 1.5 million boardfeet of lumber per year), which sold pulpwood and woodchips to Scott. Many of its principals were also leading figures of the sawmill sector in the Forest Products Association. Indeed, the latter had anticipated such a development as far back as 1975, when it encouraged its sawmill segment to form their own bargaining group.[61] By the spring of 1981 a third application was also before the board. It was sponsored by the North Nova Forest Owners Co-

---

58 Nova Scotia Forest Products Association, 44th Annual Meeting, *Report* (Truro, 1978), p. 8.

59 *Forest Times*, 2,3 (May 1980), p. 1. The second contract, running from August 1981 to July 1982, brought a further increase of $4.50 per cord and an increase in contract volume to 176,000 cords.

60 *Forest Times*, 3,2 (March 1981), p. 1.

61 Resolution No. 3, Nova Scotia Forest Products Association, 41st Annual Meeting, *Report* (Truro, 1975), p. 36.

operative (NNFO), a group venture based in Cumberland County.[62] While the first two applications covered separate segments, there was a limited overlap between the much smaller North Nova group and the NSWOOA, whose efforts to negotiate a common front came to nought.

The NSWOOA campaign followed the pattern pioneered in the eastern counties. The Scott Supply Committee invited all producers to sign pledges of support, and by early 1981 over 70 per cent of the 1,100 private suppliers were involved. The application covered all Scott suppliers in the eight mainland counties (from Kings and Lunenburg moving east, and excluding the WPMA sawmillers). After public hearings in June, the board announced in August that WPMA and the NSWOOA were approved while the NNFO was denied. In November, R.R. Murray, the Woodlands Manager for Scott Maritimes, resigned as the Forest Products Association member of the board, in order to participate in the bargaining. Murray was replaced on the board by Leif Holt, the Woodlands Manager of Bowater Mersey Paper Company, and the only company yet to be challenged.

In mid-December the Suppliers Division applied for a declaration of bargaining situation, which the board granted on 31 January 1982. Although ten meetings were held over the following two months, no agreement emerged. The Scott Suppliers Division then applied for a declaration of deadlock, which was quickly granted. A request for mediation (the first ever under the act) led the board to hold several sessions during the summer of 1982, while in August the Wood Producers also applied for their own declaration of deadlock. In the fall, a draft agreement was struck on the first contract between the Suppliers Division and the company. This brought a $3 per cord price increase, and a delivery quota of 62,000 cords.[63] However the culmination of this drive was anything but normal, interupted as it was by a nine-month strike at the Scott mill.[64] Production was not restored until June 1983, with wood deliveries only resuming in July. Thus it was in the context of reduced mill purchases, financially pressed contractors, and severe acrimony between woods and mill labour forces that the Scott Suppliers Division came to life.[65]

---

62 Group Ventures constituted a new level of "group management ventures to overcome the fragmentation and scale problem and to ensure more efficient and cost-effective management of these small holdings". "Canada-Nova Scotia Subsidiary Agreement on Forestry" (Ottawa, 1977), Section E.1(d).

63 The contract set $39 per cord for softwood pulpwood and $36 per cord for hardwood. *Forest Times*, 5,2 (June 1983), p. 1. This does not capture the full impact of the organizing campaign, however, since Scott had already raised its softwood price in the midst of negotiations (May 1982) from $30 to $36, matching the Stora price.

64 See Sheri King, "The Scott Paper Strike, 1982", in C.H.J. Gilson, ed., *Strikes in Nova Scotia, 1970-1985* (Hantsport, 1986), pp. 114-28.

65 *Forest Times*, 5,2 (June 1983), p. 1.

By 1983, the marketing campaign had reached something of a high-water mark. Bargaining units had been certified and financed, and contracts covered the supply of private pulpwood, in two of the three major catchment areas of Nova Scotia. Although 20 years had passed since the way was cleared for a forest products marketing regime, the momentum appeared finally to belong to the woodlot owners association. With its paid-up membership expanding, the NSWOOA was at last starting to fulfil its commitment to transform the terms of market transactions. Yet events of the next few years would indicate that the marketing issue was far from resolved. In due course criticism would be raised, not only toward the particular scheme then in place, but also toward the very principle of organized marketing.

Now that the board was actually certifying supplier groups, and the corporate sector had become less litigious, some practical limitations of the regulatory scheme were more evident. The woodlot and supplier groups revived the call for binding arbitration to speed the process of contract settlement. The board was also taken to task for dragging its feet. For example, in 1981 the WPMA applied for certification to represent the sawmill suppliers to the Bowater Mersey Paper Co. in western Nova Scotia. Over the time between the application and the board's public hearing, Bowater made a direct appeal to these sawmillers to withdraw from the WPMA application:

> Over the years we have been able to maintain an open and flexible relationship....The Company believes that this relationship which has served us so well in the past should continue into the future. It cannot do so if the [WPMA] is registered as the bargaining agent for the sawmills that sell pulpwood to Bowater Mersey.[66]

Over three years elapsed before the application was considered in June 1984, by which point significant attrition had occurred among the owners.[67] The combination of product dependence and political intimidation had broken the application.[68]

On a more general level, the 1984 Report of the Royal Commission on Forestry questioned the foundation of the marketing regime. It argued for a management strategy based on the concept of conservancy (intensive forest management to in-

---

66   Leif Holt to Sawmillers, Wood Products Manufacturers Association of Nova Scotia, "Submission to the Nova Scotia Royal Commission on Forestry" (Halifax, 1983), Appendix.

67   While only a minority of sawmillers supported the application (11 of 35), they accounted for three-quarters of the pulpwood sold by sawmills to Mersey. "Sawmillers Apply to Bargain with Bowater", *Forest Times,* 6,3 (June 1984), p. 1.

68   In this context, it is not surprising that the NSWOOA was even less successful. In 1981 the Lunenburg County Group called a meeting of Mersey suppliers in the Bridgewater area, which drew a poor attendance. The matter was deferred "until the producers show more interest". Nova Scotia Woodlot Owners and Operators Association, 1981 Annual Meeting, *Report* (Truro, 1981).

crease future yields). Yet the price mechanism did not figure as a significant management variable. After duly noting the negligible return to private forest land in the prevailing market, the report concluded that conditions of oversupply precluded any improvement. Echoing MacSween's thinking two decades earlier, it declared that "the attainment of a better price must necessarily await improved quality, stronger markets, and a more even balance between potential supply from the forest and requirements for raw material".[69] Since this was not forecast to occur before the turn of the century, the effect was to marginalize the small private producers in both the market and the policy process. They could sell their product without return, or hold it in green storage for a generation. The report did not directly discuss the existing marketing regime, although the Pulpwood Marketing Board was described in passing as an obstacle to the fulfilment of the Lands and Forests mandate. Accordingly, the commission recommended legislative amendments to restrict the board's role to one of registering bargaining agents. In the more distant future even these last vestiges could be eliminated, since the commission observed that:

> Eventually it ought to be possible to eliminate government direction and support, allowing free competitive market conditions to prevail, as demands approach an equality with supply, or exceed potential supply.[70]

Perhaps of even greater significance was a set of centrifugal pressures at work in the NSWOOA, and in the producer constituency more generally. After 1979, the organizational dynamics of the NSWOOA were being transformed. Undeniably, the creation of the two new Suppliers Divisions brought a new economic importance to the organization. Yet as virtually autonomous business wings, the divisions threatened to overshadow or even eclipse the workings of the parent association. Given the autonomy provisions stipulated by the board, the very success of the marketing drive sowed the seeds of tension within the NSWOOA. The Suppliers Divisions qualified for funding through the compulsory levy which the board collected on all privately sold pulpwood. At the initial rate of $.50 per cord, this enabled the Stora Division to operate in its first year with a budget more than twice the size of the NSWOOA. Similarly, the division's membership of some 1,300 rivalled the dues-paying membership of the parent association. By contrast, the association continued to limp along financially, lacking the revenue to mount new programmes. The largest single source was the grant (fixed at about $40,000 per year) for which the NSWOOA applied each year to the Department of Lands and Forests. No permanent (much less expanded) sources of finance had been secured over the association's lifespan.

---

69 Nova Scotia, Royal Commission on Forestry, *Report* (Halifax, 1984), p. 40.

70 N.S., Royal Commission on Forestry, *Report*, p. 74.

It was not long before political leadership followed financial capacity in shifting from the parent to the Supplier Divisions. In 1984 the Stora Suppliers Division severed its ties completely. Reconstituted as the Eastern Nova Scotia Landowners and Forest Fibre Producers Association, it assumed the certification as the Stora bargaining agent, virtually displacing the NSWOOA in the eastern part of the province.[71] The Forest Fibre Association also challenged the NSWOOA as a provincial voice for small woodlot owners and producers. By 1985, the woodlot constituency was more fragmented organizationally than ever before. A final source of cleavage became evident at this time, as some of the larger logging contractors began to openly challenge the new marketing groups. In 1986 a number of contractors asked the Pulpwood Marketing Board to decertify the Scott Suppliers Division, on the grounds that, "The NSWOOA's quota allocation rules are incompatible with the aspirations of producers who want to increase production or who had not sold pulpwood to Scott in the past".[72]

An understanding of the political outcomes traced above must acknowledge two levels of analysis. One involves the shifting alignments of economic forces within the forest sector, which condition the possibilities of political alliance and conflict on an issue such as marketing. The other concerns the patterns of political representation which these forces can secure within the provincial state.

The first point recalls the paradox noted at the outset, of a majority small landowner bloc, collectively holding a dominant block of assets, but unable to secure the political leverage commensurate with its ownership position. Part of the answer stems from the diversity masked by the label "private woodlot owners", and from the changing orders of magnitude among the segments within the bloc. Until the 1960s, the leadership and prospective membership of the woodlot organizations came from the non-industrial woodlot owner, initially farm-based but widening into a rural small-holder coalition. During this period most owners were also "operators", cutting accessible and high-quality wood from their own woodlots and selling at riverside, railside or roadside. Galvanized by the prospect of low-cost competition, as the pulp and paper industry extended its reach into the forest, these owners looked to the state for support in formalizing a group marketing regime in the 1960s. Given the heavy prior commitments by the Department of Lands and Forests, in the form of concessionary Crown stumpage, the prospects for success depended heavily on the breadth of the coalition and the degree of unity which it could maintain. The 1970 marketing plebiscite and the later votes of support for the supplier divisions suggest that majorities could be maintained at critical moments.

---

71 *Forest Times*, 6,3 (June 1984), and "New Group Certified", *Forest Times*, 6,4 (August 1984), p. 4.

72 "Decision Due This Fall on Decertification Bid", *Forest Times*, 8,4 (August 1986), p. 3. Scott had been cultivating a special relationship with its large volume contractors even before the appearance of the Supply Division, when it offered a $2 per cord premium to producers whose annual deliveries exceeded 2,000 cords.

It is evident that the small woodlot owners achieved their most effective representation through the provincial Department of Agriculture, and other agencies with rural development mandates. These institutional ties were rooted as far back as the 1930s, forged on issues such as orderly marketing and pulpwood producer co-operatives. The alignment remained effective up until the passage of the 1972 Marketing Act. While this failed to establish a "strong" marketing regime, it did ensure that the small producer organizing efforts were not entirely dismissed in the antagonistic climate of the day. However, the nature of the new regulatory treaty, installed by a separate (i.e. non-agricultural) statute, and under the policy umbrella of the Department of Lands and Forests, excluded Agriculture from a future role, thereby narrowing and isolating the small woodlot forces within the state.

Similarly, the federal-provincial ARDA programme had proved instrumental to the initial success in organizing the Woodlot Owners Association. This important secondary channel of representation was likewise engaged in a contest of competing policy paradigms, in this case concerning regional economic development. Ultimately, ARDA's rural renewal mandate was submerged by the industrial growth pole model, which was embraced by federal and provincial agencies alike. The terms of this debate offer a striking parallel to the forest policy case.[73]

At the same time, a number of distinctions lay dormant within the bloc, but were triggered by the struggle, such as the status of woodlot owner vis-à-vis the producer or operator, the woodlot operator vis-à-vis the commercial contractor, and the spatial variations defined by regional geography and markets. To be sure, these distinctions were already well established in the woods industry. But over the generation of struggle for an organized marketing structure, the continuing regime of low prices and private buying networks exerted its own influence. Most particularly, the proportions and the balance among woods industry segments changed dramatically. The older generation of woodlot owner-operators was not being replaced, small properties were sold and clearcut for one-shot profits, and the total share of small woodlot production in the pulpwood market fell from 60 per cent in 1969 to less than 40 per cent by 1982.[74]

The antidote was to build unity through issues of shared interest. For the NSWOA the marketing issue led all others, eventually becoming the association's raison d'être. While it strained to keep its membership base open to all woodlot owners, the trajectory of the marketing dispute dictated basic compromises and adjustments. This took place in an intensely adversarial atmosphere, where the opponents of organized marketing, and of the NSWOA, adroitly manipulated the

---

73 For detailed discussions of this story, see T. Brewis, *Regional Economic Policies in Canada* (Toronto, 1968), or Anthony Careless, *Initiative and Response* (Montreal, 1977).

74 Richard Lord, "An Analysis of the Private Forestry Sector", Submission to the Royal Commission on Forestry (April 1983), pp. 7-14.

emerging schisms. The Department of Lands and Forests proved indifferent to the NSWOA as a potential vehicle for organizing the small woodlot constituency.

It was the pattern of representation embodied in Lands and Forests that emerged hegemonic. This department combined several roles: custodian of Crown lands, catalyst for forest improvement and management, and liaison with sectoral interest groups. There seems little doubt that on the pulpwood marketing issue the department served from an early date as an advocate for the secondary processors. From the beginning, massive tracts of Crown lands had been committed on concessionary terms to underpin the Stora and Scott projects. Subsequently, the department accorded little legitimacy to arguments for increased private land stumpage rates. Both in ideological outlook and practical intervention, it defended the interests of corporate forestry, consistent with the Forest Products Association. In this the Department of Lands and Forests served as an agent of subordination of small woodlot owners.

At the point where departmental advocacy left off, the Voluntary Planning apparatus took up the representational role for industry interests. During the critical years when the regulatory treaty was being debated and then fashioned, the Forestry Sector Committee (backed by the VP Board) provided a forum where established organizations could maximize their influence. Since the marketing issue arose at the very moment when VP was straining to redefine its role and establish its value as a consultative mechanism for business, the pulpwood marketing issue became a critical test case.

Despite such impediments, the NSWOA was an emerging political force by the early 1970s, with county-level organizations in most parts of the province. The woodlot owners were too potent to be ignored but insufficiently strong to carry the day. Ultimately, the cabinet could not deny some form of regulatory regime, so what followed in 1972 was an untenable hybrid. Once the board became operational, the same antagonistic interests continued the battle from within. The board itself became a conflict-wracked site of representation. Rianne Mahon has remarked on the particular capacities of regulatory agents, given their insulation from partisan and bureaucratic politics, to adjudicate the fine terms of business disputes.[75] Though far from a model of technical efficiency, the Pulpwood Marketing Board served this function in several respects. It provided the formal relations of organized bargaining, but little of the expected bargaining leverage. Indeed the terms of the regulatory regime allowed a particularly intense and sustained guerilla resistance. The pulp companies and their association first utilized the certification procedures, and then challenged their validity through extensive litigation, in an effort to slow or halt the organizing process. While the principle of state-supported marketing was never denied, the board's rulings diffused the claims of the woodlot owners and

---

75 Rianne Mahon, "Regulatory Agencies: Captive Agents or Hegemonic Apparatuses", *Studies in Political Economy*, 1 (Spring 1979).

even redefined the basis of small producer rights in directions contrary to the movement's intent.

Integral to the conflicts of the 1972-85 period was the implicit acquiescence of the Department of Lands and Forests. After declaring their views bluntly during the formative policy period, senior officials did little to remedy an evidently flawed design, at either formal or informal levels. David Curtis' 1988 observation is redolent with significance to the past:

> The provincial government has a variety of ways to influence industry's behaviour, including gentle persuasion. The government should let the industry know that it does not want its legitimate initiatives continually dragged through the courts, and that it wants the industry to deal...with the new marketing agencies in a professional and businesslike manner.[76]

Given the NSWOA's limited political leverage, and the entrenched pattern of representation within the province, another strategic option involved striking alliances across the forest sector. Here the forest fibre product flows proved critical. As suppliers of sawlogs and purchasers of wood chips, the pulp and paper mills could directly affect the viability of the sawmill sector. Such transactions underlay the political coalition that was formalized in the Forest Products Association. These fibre flows (and the threat of their interruption) were of sufficient magnitude to rule out an alternative alliance between small woodlot owners and sawmillers, based on a shared interest in wider access to Crown lands and competitive bidding for Crown stumpage. Similarly, the open challenges from the larger logging contractors, as they were drawn increasingly into the orbit of the mills, precluded an alliance of producers small and large. Such wider alignments would have been indispensable for the woodlot owners to prevail decisively on the pulpwood marketing question. As it was, the woodlot groups became increasingly isolated, while the goal of market power proved ever more elusive.

---

76 David Curtis, *Toward an Effective Marketing Structure for Woodlot Owners in Nova Scotia,* Report to the Nova Scotia Primary Forest Products Marketing Board (Halifax, 1988), p. 71.

The Political Economy of
Nova Scotia's Forest Improvement Act,
1962-1986

Glyn Bissix and L. Anders Sandberg

This paper examines the political and economic forces shaping forest legislation in Nova Scotia, focusing on the Forest Improvement Act (FIA) from 1962 to 1986.[1] The FIA was based on Swedish forest legislation, where forest management is mandatory by statute on private as well as public lands. Such legislation was introduced in Sweden in the early 20th century. Since then the Swedish legislation has become more demanding but nevertheless accepted over the years.[2] In Nova Scotia, by contrast, the FIA has had a checkered and controversial history. It took ten years to proclaim, it was never enforced, and in 1986 it was rescinded. A recent study has attributed the FIA's rescission to the political and economic power of the transnational pulp companies, their special treatment by government, their domination in the pulpwood market and the concomitant weakness of small woodlot owners.[3] This paper provides a more detailed account of the dominance exerted by the powerful pulp and paper companies in industry organizations, professional groups and the state bureaucracy, and their influence on a weak and dependent province in the rise and fall of the FIA.

Our point of departure is that forest practices are not merely a function of legislative, institutional and technological innovations, but also varying political, economic and ideological pressures.[4] Several powerful interest groups exert such

---

1   In addition to secondary sources, this study utilized approximately 40 semi-structured interviews with key actors in the forest management sector. These actors included ministers, deputy ministers, senior administrators, foresters of the Department of Lands and Forests, woodlands managers and senior administrators from the three transnational pulp and paper companies in Nova Scotia, as well as sawmillers, forest contractors, small woodlot owners and their representatives and various members of Provincial and District Forest Practices Improvement Boards. Representatives from the federal government and wildlife and recreation organizations were also interviewed.

2   Per Stjernquist, *Laws in the Forests* (Lund, 1973)

3   L. Anders Sandberg, "Swedish Forestry Legislation in Nova Scotia: The Rise and Fall of the Forest Improvement Act, 1965-1986", in D. Day, ed., *Geographical Perspectives on the Maritime Provinces* (Halifax, 1988), pp. 184-96. In spite of their political weakness, small woodlot owners hold over 50 per cent of the forest lands in Nova Scotia.

4   Bruce Mitchell, *Geography and Resource Analysis* (London, 1979), p. 6; R. Mayntz, "The Conditions of Effective Public Policy: A New Challenge for Policy Analysis", *Policy and Politics*, 11, 2 (1983), pp. 123-43.

pressures. Three important, though not homogeneous, groups can be identified in Nova Scotia. There is the powerful pulp and paper industry lobby, composed of major industrialists and their foresters who hold a "technocentric" view of forest management, favouring clearcutting, chemical treatments, heavy mechanization and the planting of even-aged monocultures.[5] Their actions are generally driven by firm-based profitability and economic efficiency, and justified because they support present standards of living.[6] The technocentric view emerged in the 1960s and has since held an increasingly dominant position in Nova Scotia. The FIA posed a challenge, which was in the end effectively subordinated.

The pulp and paper industry lobby should be contrasted with the "soft" industrialist/forest-management school, which rejects the technocentric approach in favour of selective cutting, natural regeneration, and at least some species and age diversity.[7] In the Nova Scotia context, this group has occupied an important but declining position since the 1960s. Advocates have included a rapidly disappearing generation of professional foresters from the pulp and paper industry and the Department of Lands and Forests (DLF), as well as lay foresters from the sawmill and small woodlot owner sectors, and various non-government groups, such as wildlife and recreational groups. The board charged with administering the FIA adopted a "soft" industrial stand.

The final group of importance on the Nova Scotia forest scene comprises the environmentalists who harbour "ecocentric" beliefs.[8] They advocate a balanced and integrated approach to forest management, often providing ardent oppostion to in-

---

5   T. O'Riordan, *Environmentalism* (London, 1981), pp. 3-17.

6   Peat, Marwick and Partners, *Factors Limiting Investment in Forest Management: Final Report* (Ottawa, 1981), p. 39; J. O'Neill, "Maritimers Aren't Stupid", *Pith and Periderm* (January 1979), p. 49.

7   Selective cutting involves removing only mature, old, and dead trees from the forest. This gives seedlings and young trees more light and space to grow. Gordon Robertson, "A Conservationist's View of the Case Against Even-Age Management", *Forest Industries*, 97, 12 (November 1970), pp. 54-5. Several prominent members of the Nova Scotia forest industry community embraced this point of view in the 1960s and 1970s. Some of the more important were Dr. W. Creighton, Deputy Minister of Lands and Forests, 1949-69; Ralph Johnson, Chief Forester for Bowater Mersey, 1934-65; Murray Prest, a long-time critic of the pulp and paper companies in Nova Scotia, should be mentioned among sawmillers, see Harry Thurston, "Prest's Last Stand: Keeping Kafka and the Bureaucrats out of the Acadian Forest", *Harrowsmith*, 30 (August/September 1983), pp. 22-31; Walter Webber, who worked for the DLF in the 1940s, claims "clear cut was a dirty word, and we marked the merchantable trees to be removed on any area [of Crown lands] that was being put up for tender", Nova Scotia Section, Canadian Institute of Forestry, Report of the 36th Annual Meeting, 1989, p. 41.

8   O'Riordan, *Environmentalism*, p. 1.

secticide and herbicide spraying, monoculture and heavy mechanization.[9] The position of the environmentalists toward the FIA has been supportive, though critical of some select forest practices.

Our objective is to explore the role of the provincial government in mediating between these competing interests in the context of the FIA. A fundamental tenet of our argument is that provincial forest management policy, or the conception and initial shaping of the FIA, was subordinated to the grander provincial scheme of attracting and maintaining transnational pulp and paper industry investment in the late 1950s and 1960s. This argument is consistent with O'Riordan's concept of a policy hierarchy, where one economic growth strategy is favoured above, or even at the expense of, broader economic and environmental concerns.[10] It is also consistent with the concept of a "client state", with a long-standing history of attracting foreign capital for provincial economic development.[11] We will argue that the FIA was conceived by the pulp and paper companies and the government to cope with projected wood scarcities for the growing pulp and paper industry, primarily by mobilizing the pulpwood resources of small woodlot owners, at that time the major suppliers of pulpwood. In time, however, the FIA came to threaten the new technocentric forest management techniques (such as clearcutting) employed by the transnational pulp and paper companies and their contractors on large and small freeholds and Crown leases. As wood scarcities abated, the pulp and paper industry mounted an opposition campaign against the FIA. Several technocentric factions, embodied in the government, the pulp and paper industry, and the provincial foresters' association, began to lobby for the rescission of the FIA, an objective achieved in 1986.

There were two versions of the FIA. The first contained provisions for mandatory registration of wood producers and buyers and green belts along provincial highways. This version, enacted in 1962, was expanded in 1965 but never proclaimed. The second version provided for the establishment of District Forest Practices Improvement Boards (DFPIBs), and, through an amendment in 1968, a Provincial Forest Practices Improvement Board (PFPIB). The boards were composed of a large array of forest interests, including the pulp and paper and sawmill industries, foresters, small woodlot owners, wildlife groups and government. The function of the boards was, through consultation and education, to formulate and enforce certain rules pertaining to the timing and methods of harvesting and managing the woodlands of the province. The green belt provisions were expanded to include designated rivers and lakefronts.

---

9   G. Peabody, *Forestry* (Halifax, 1984); see also the contributions in Gary Burrill and Ian McKay, eds., *People, Resources, and Power* (Fredericton, 1987).

10   O'Riordan, *Environmentalism*, p. 26.

11   L. Anders Sandberg, "Forest Policy in Nova Scotia: The Big Lease, Cape Breton Island, 1899-1960", *Acadiensis*, XX, 2 (Spring 1991), pp. 105-28, also in this volume.

The FIA was partially proclaimed in 1968. Nine district boards were established from 1968 to 1970, and a provincial board in 1969; their activities were frustrated by the withholding of proclamation of the crucial harvesting and management sections of the act, and by 1972 the terms of their appointments expired. In 1973 a newly expanded PFPIB was appointed and in 1976 the full act was proclaimed. This was followed by a new period of frustration. In 1980 the PFPIB published a manual of good forest practices to serve as a guideline for the district boards, and in 1981 two district boards were appointed. The enforcement of the green belt provisions on two designated rivers was started in 1982 but then failed. In 1984 the chairman of the PFPIB took a leave of absence, which in effect made the board inoperable, and in 1986 the FIA was rescinded.

The first priority of the Nova Scotia government in the mid-1950s was industrial development. In November 1956, the Conservative administration of Robert Stanfield took office with an election promise to deal with high unemployment and slow industrial development.[12] The mainstays of the Nova Scotia economy in the past, the steel and coal industries, experienced serious problems with little relief in sight, and the pulp and paper industry was touted as a new opportunity for development.[13] The industrial development strategy was one of industrialization by invitation, and among the invited guests were new transnational pulp and paper companies. The completion of the Canso Causeway in 1955, linking Cape Breton Island with mainland Nova Scotia, was an integral part of the development programme.[14] At the time, the province harboured but one large pulp and paper complex, the newsprint mill operated by Bowater Mersey in Liverpool. This mill was established in the late 1920s by I.W. Killam of Montreal after several government concessions had been granted, especially with respect to power development.[15] In contrast to many other pulp and paper companies at the time, Bowater Mersey possessed considerable freehold lands for its wood supply, and also purchased pulpwood from small woodlot owners throughout Nova Scotia.

---

12 Wilfrid Creighton, *Forestkeeping: A History of the Department of Lands and Forests in Nova Scotia, 1926-1969* (Halifax, 1988), p. 102.

13 Arthur D. Little Consultants, Nova Scotia, Department of Trade and Industry, *Industrial Development in Nova Scotia* (Halifax, 1956).

14 The location of a pulp mill at the Canso Causeway was particularly important to the government. One official later stated that "We worked tooth and nail to get them [Stora] to come in and set up a kraft process to handle that poor quality material we had up there (Cape Breton)". Interview with R.H. Burgess, Deputy Minister of Lands and Forests, 1967-77, 1987.

15 Sandberg, "The Big Lease". The Mersey Paper Company was acquired by the British Bowater Corporation in 1956. From 1956 to 1968, the Nova Scotia branch was known as the Bowaters Mersey Paper Company. Since then, the name has been the Bowater Mersey Paper Company. We will refer to the company as Bowater Mersey. Ralph Johnson, *Forests of Nova Scotia* (Halifax, 1986), pp. 272-5.

The government had one crucial bargaining chip in the quest for new pulp mills in the 1950s. The key attraction was the substantial Crown lands (24 per cent of the forest area) that could be licensed to the transnationals.[16] There was also some potential to tap federal government funds. The province possessed a labour surplus, a stagnating sawlog sector, a supply of cheap pulpwood from a politically weak small woodlot owner sector, and, compared with more isolated parts of Canada, a good transportation network. The previous Liberal government had failed to attract a major pulp and paper company. In 1956 it came near but failed to close a deal with Scott Paper, a transnational corporation based in Philadelphia.[17] Scott Paper, however, having just built a new pulp mill in British Columbia, was still intent on building a pulp mill in Nova Scotia, declaring it was merely postponing construction for ten years.[18] Negotiations with other companies yielded even less. As a result, the provincial government was subjected to hard bargaining from prospective pulp companies.

The vulnerability of the provincial government in soliciting foreign transnationals is well illustrated in the coming of the Swedish pulp and paper company Stora Kopparberg AB (Stora) to Nova Scotia in the late 1950s, and Scott Paper in 1965. In the case of Stora, the government failed to check the credentials of its alleged negotiators; it provided extensive Crown leases, totalling 1,283,948 acres (520,000 ha) (increased by 197,530 acres, or 80,000 ha, in 1969), for the same stumpage rates charged Bowater Mersey in the late 1920s; it awarded subsidies and grants in all phases of the construction of the mill; and it flaunted the opposition to Stora by the sawmill sector and Bowater Mersey.[19] Scott Maritimes enjoyed tax holidays on its pulp mill site and extensive freeholds. The company received a Crown lease of some of the finest stands of timber in Nova Scotia, 230,000 acres (93,150 ha) in eastern Halifax County. The provincial government also promised to pick up the

---

16 In order to make these lands available, the so-called Big Lease, held by the Oxford Paper Company, of Rumford, Maine, had to be repurchased by the government at great public expense. See Sandberg, "The Big Lease".

17 Creighton, *Forestkeeping*, pp. 101-2.

18 There was good reason to believe the company's claims at the time. Scott Paper acquired the extensive Nova Scotia holdings of the Hollingsworth and Whitney Pulp and Paper Company of Maine in the mid-1950s. Creighton, *Forestkeeping*, pp. 101-2.

19 Dietrich Soyez, "Stora Lured Abroad? A Nova Scotia Case Study in Industrial Decision-Making and Persistence", *The Operational Geographer,* 16 (September 1988), pp. 11-14; Sandberg, "The Big Lease". Bowater Mersey found it more difficult generally to influence provincial forest policy after the coming of Stora. Interviews with Johnson, 1987, and E.D. Haliburton, Minister of Lands and Forests, 1959-68, 1987.

expense for treating the effluent produced daily at the pulp mill.[20] The federal government contributed $5 million and a five-year income tax holiday.[21]

An integral part of the use of Crown leases to attract pulp and paper companies to the province was the manipulation of forest inventories. One precondition for the establishment of new pulp mills was documentation that the Nova Scotia forest could support additional pulp mills.[22] Senior civil servants in the DLF were reluctant to give such assurances. In support, they referred to the wood scarcities forecasted in a recently published forest inventory.[23] Bowater Mersey, fearing competition, supported the position of "forest scarcity".[24] As a result there were powerful forces arguing that Nova Scotia's forests could not sustain a second, let alone a third, major pulp mill. The provincial government, however, turned scarcity into plenty. Premier Stanfield instructed Lands and Forests Minister Haliburton to "get those people of yours 'thick as sweat' down to the [Hotel] Nova Scotian and lock em up until they come up with an answer".[25] G.I. (Ike) Smith, the Minister of Trade and Commerce, played an important part in the meeting. According to Haliburton, it was Smith, a lawyer by profession, who forced the departmental personnel to concede that there was enough wood to support a second pulp mill. The revised forest inventories were subsequently dubbed G.I. Smith's "new forest", pointing to the strong government bias in favour of pulp industry development.[26] The Department of Trade and Commerce clearly prevailed over Lands and Forests.

In 1964, on the eve of the establishment of the Scott Paper pulp mill at Abercrombie in Pictou County, a similar revision of forest inventories was made.

---

20 The clean-up, however, has been seriously neglected over the last 20 years. See, for example, *Evening News*, 29 November 1991.

21 Thurston, "Prest's Last Stand", p. 27.

22 Interview with Haliburton, 1987; E.D. Haliburton, *My Years with Stanfield* (Windsor, 1972), pp. 18-9.

23 Interviews with Creighton, 1987, and L.S. Hawboldt, Director of Extension, DLF, 1951-70, 1987; L.S. Hawboldt and R.M. Bulmer, *The Forest Resources of Nova Scotia* (Halifax, 1958).

24 Burgess complained that Ralph Johnson, the chief forester for Bowater Mersey, "preached that you're going to ruin the province bringing another company in, we're going to be out of wood". Interview with Burgess, 1987.

25 Interview with Haliburton, 1987. Haliburton, *My Years with Stanfield*, p. 18.

26 Wilfrid Creighton did not participate in this meeting. This seems unusual as he was the senior manager of DLF and a highly respected forester. He was, however, a strong opponent of unbridled pulp processing growth. Perhaps it was not strange that Haliburton could not recall whether Creighton was left out on purpose or simply did not want to come. Creighton claims he was was not invited. Interviews with Creighton and Haliburton, 1987.

The DLF "re-examined" its records and increased the allowable annual cut from 1,375 thousand to 2,400 thousand rough cords, an increase of about 74 per cent.[27] Then, in 1969, when Stora expanded its sulphite mill from 135,000 to 175,000 tons per year, installed a 160,000 ton newsprint facility, and concluded a new management agreement, covering an extra 200,000 acres (81,000 ha) of Crown lands, the annual allowable cut was increased from 12 to 25 cubic feet per acres per year.[28]

Projected forest scarcities, revised inventories and increased allowable cuts heightened the concern for forest management. The Minister of Lands and Forests put it well: "there's general agreement that with the new demands in our forest industry as a consequence of the establishment of a large new pulp mill in Pictou (Scott Maritimes), and the expansion and modernization of many saw mills, that a more positive policy towards planning and safe-guarding future supplies must be adopted, otherwise the future of our forest industry is bleak".[29] It was in the context of major pulp and paper industry development, projected forest scarcities and inflated forest inventories that a major debate emerged with respect to provincial forest legislation in the late 1950s. Up to this point, forest legislation in Nova Scotia was subordinated to production and exploitation imperatives.[30] Forest degradation and wood scarcities were overcome by new technologies that allowed the use of more diverse tree species in previously inaccessible areas.[31]

The Small Tree Act (STA) was enacted in 1942 and revised in 1946 to deal with the unprecedented demand and indiscriminate cuts of sawlogs during the Second World War. It was only enforced on a limited scale from 1947 to 1962. The STA provided a diameter restriction of ten inches on the felling of three targeted species: hemlock, pine and spruce. The act provided some protection from widespread and indiscriminate clearcutting (and thus helped to preserve sawlogs otherwise destined for the pulp mills) and some educational value by pairing government foresters and woodlot owners together in the woods, but its overall effect was limited.[32] From a

27   "Plan for the Forestry Sector" (June 1966), Voluntary Economic Planning, Nova Scotia Voluntary Planning Board, RG 55, series VP, vol. 4, no. 22, p. 17, Public Archives of Nova Scotia [PANS].

28   Hans Akesson, "The Nova Scotia Pulp Limited Story: Forest Management for the Revitalization of the Eastern Nova Scotia Forests, Nova Scotia Pulp Limited, and the Nova Scotia Economy", Paper presented to the Standing Forest Management Committee, Canadian Institute of Forestry [CIF], 63rd Annual Meeting, Victoria, 1971.

29   Nova Scotia, *Debates,* 22 February 1965, p. 527.

30   Sandberg, "The Big Lease".

31   F.B. Goldsmith, "An Evaluation of a Forest Resource - A Case Study from Nova Scotia", *Journal of Environmental Management,* 10 (1980), pp. 83-100.

32   L.S. Hawboldt, "Forestry in Nova Scotia", *Canadian Geographic Journal* (August 1955), pp. 5, 14. Hawboldt felt the act "altered the course of forestry in the Province...[and] despite its many problems...the indirect results and benefits have

forest management point of view, however, the diameter cutting limit of the STA was considered "one of the least effective of silvicultural methods", since it did not allow thinning and removal of dense older forests, except by ministerial permit.[33] The act failed to give instructions to forest management on Cape Breton Island, whose major species, the balsam fir, was not covered in the act.[34] The STA applied only to lumbering operations producing more than 50,000 board feet measure or its equivalent per year.[35] This stipulation exempted most private forest lands from the legislation.[36] Some government foresters felt the act lacked sufficient teeth to guarantee proper administration. They also felt public interest and enthusiasm were lacking, while they themselves lacked enthusiasm in enforcing the act due to the policing aspects.[37] Perhaps these shortfalls could still have been overcome. Many foresters never applied the diameter limit strictly but adjusted it to local conditions.[38] Some claimed increased clearcutting was more the result of patchy implementation than any inherent practical weakness in the enforcement of the act. The most influential foresters, Deputy Minister Creighton and some prominent sawmillers, still supported the STA.

The technical shortfalls of the STA, the projected scarcities in the forest supply and the prospects of two large pulp mills establishing operations in Nova Scotia

been tremendous". Others recognized the benefits of the act but were more critical. Interview with Burgess, 1987; Creighton, *Forestkeeping,* pp. 74-5; "The Small Tree Act", Johnson Papers, MG 1, vol. 2862, no. 21, PANS.

33 "The Small Tree Act", Johnson Papers, MG 1, vol. 2862, no. 21, PANS; The same applied to forests affected by storms. Hurricane Edna in 1954, for example, made the STA irrelevant for many regions in Nova Scotia. Interview with Dave Dwyer, 1987; Creighton, *Forestkeeping,* p. 90.

34 The exclusion of the balsam fir made good sense. The balsam grows in dense stands, matures and dies quickly, and, when thinned, is prone to blowdowns. The balsam is best clearcut (although views differ on the size of the cuts) and used for pulpwood. Interview with W.I. Creighton, Deputy Minister of Lands and Forests, 1949-69, 1987.

35 *Statutes of Nova Scotia,* c. 6, 1942.

36 In 1958, for example, it was estimated that from 1952 to 1957, only 362,752 acres (146,752 ha) or 4.2 per cent of the total of 8,695,000 acres (3,521,475 ha) of private lands were examined under the act by provincial foresters. Of the 362,752 acres (146,752 ha) examined, cutting to a diameter limit was restricted to 11.6 per cent, or 42,000 acres (17,010 ha). Clearcuts were allowed on 56.6 per cent, or 205,000 acres (83,025 ha). On the remaining 115,350 acres (46,717 ha) examined under the act, cutting was voluntarily limited to trees of not less than the ten-inch minimum diameter limit. "The Small Tree Act", Johnson Papers, MG 1, vol. 2862, no. 21, PANS.

37 "The Small Tree Act", Johnson Papers, MG 1, vol. 2862, no. 21, PANS.

38 Hawboldt, "Forestry in Nova Scotia", pp. 5, 14.

called for a major change in provincial forest legislation. The change was spear-headed by the Nova Scotia Section of the Canadian Institute of Forestry (CIF), representing professional foresters in the province. In February 1959 it unani-mously passed a resolution asking the provincial government to replace the STA. This resolution subsequently received unanimous support from the Nova Scotia Forest Products Association and the Nova Scotia Resource Council.[39] Ralph Johnson, the chief forester of Bowater Mersey, as chairman of the Nova Scotia Sec-tion of the CIF, led the foresters' attempt to introduce legislation concerning the practice of forest cutting of a minimal nature, worked out in collaboration with woodlot owners, "to assure adequate regeneration and the maintenance of growing stock of desirable species". Minimal forest legislation on private lands, he felt, was considered necessary "to prevent extensive devastation of...remaining forest resour-ces".[40] Opinion on the shape of the new legislation was, however, divided. Some members argued that cutting regulations had to be preceded by the establishment of demonstration areas, and that regulations were too onerous for small woodlot owners because of the poor market and price for wood products.[41]

The 1962 FIA was careful and tentative in the extreme. The act, emanating ex-clusively from the DLF, contained but two provisions, and these were never proclaimed.[42] One provision was mandatory licencing for wood producers, some-thing the department thought necessary in order to obtain the information "essential to the over-all management of our forest resources".[43] The second provision, the mandatory maintenance of green belts along major highways, favoured by Deputy Minister Creighton, was included to promote the tourist trade and the establishment of provincial parks and picnic sites along the highways. Park development entailed both political and financial pay-offs for the government and the Department of Lands and Forests, at a time when most Crown lands had been leased for harvesting and management to Stora and Scott Maritimes.[44]

---

39   Johnson, *Forests of Nova Scotia*, p. 300. The same organizations called for a Royal Commission on Forestry to investigate the forest situation in the province and the prospects of new forest legislation. This never materialized.

40   "Memorandum to Members of the Nova Scotia Section of the CIF: Proposed Forest Legislation for Nova Scotia", MG 1, vol. 2862, no. 21, PANS.

41   "Memorandum", MG 1, vol. 2862, no. 21, PANS. The necessity of demonstration areas was a concern shared by many North American foresters. See, for example, K.G. Fensom, *Expanding Forestry Horizons: A History of the Canadian Institute of Forestry, 1908-1969* (Pointe Claire, 1972), p. 20.

42   *Statutes of Nova Scotia*, 1962, c. 5, p. 238.

43   Nova Scotia, *Debates*, 9 April 1962, p. 1361.

44   Creighton claimed the green belt provision was his only input into the FIA. By 1959, the federal government offered financial assistance for camping and picnic parks along the Trans-Canada Highway, and the DLF established a Parks Division. The parks programme soon "proved so popular that every MLA was clamouring for a

Outside government, the opposition to the 1962 version of the FIA was nearly u-nanimous. Members of the legislature felt the green belt provisions were too dictatorial, interfering with the property rights of the landowner. Ralph Johnson advocated its repeal, claiming "there is nothing in the Act which provides for forest improvement" and branding the green belt provision "grossly unfair...[since] it practically confiscates the strip along highways, which is the most accessible and hence the most valuable forest land".[45] Jan Weslien, Stora's chief forester, felt the green belts may be good for fire control and beautification but useless for forest management.[46] He also felt that the reporting of every commercial forest operation "may be a good thing", but he failed to see how it would improve forest management.[47] In light of such criticism, the government felt ambivalent about the act. Haliburton conceded already in 1962 that the green belt section "was drafted too vigorously".[48] The act was never proclaimed. Instead the newly formed Forestry Section of Voluntary Economic Planning and the Nova Scotia Section of the CIF continued to negotiate revisions and additions to the FIA.

There can be little doubt that Swedish forest legislation had a major impact on the drafting of a revised FIA. A provincial royal commission on pulpwood prices, the MacSween Commission, recommended a study of Swedish forest organizations as a model for Nova Scotia.[49] The vision of Stora's chief forester, Jan Weslien (also chairman of the legislative committee of the Nova Scotia Section of the CIF), corresponded well with the final version as enacted in 1965.[50] At its core was the concept of District Forest Practices Improvement Boards, decision-making forums with representation from foresters, small woodlot owners, municipalities, owners of woodlands of a thousand acres or more and members at large. These were charged

---

park in his constituency, whether along the Trans-Canada or not". Interview with Creighton, 1989. Creighton, *Forestkeeping,* pp. 110-2.

45 "Forest Legislation in Nova Scotia", MG 1, vol. 2862, no. 21, PANS.

46 Weslien, mockingly, suggested a change in name to the Forest Fire Control Act or Land Beautification Act or Please Tourists Act. Jan Weslien, "The Forest Improvement Act as Compared with European Legislation", Paper presented at the Tenth Annual Meeting, Nova Scotia Section, CIF, 17 September 1964.

47 Weslien, "The Forest Improvement Act".

48 Nova Scotia, *Debates,* 9 April 1962, p. 1367.

49 Nova Scotia, *Report of the Royal Commission on Prices of Pulpwood and Forest Products* (Halifax, 1964).

50 Interview with Jan Weslien, 1989; Weslien, "The Forest Improvement Act"; Sandberg, "Swedish Forest Legislation in Nova Scotia"; *Statutes of Nova Scotia,* 1965, c. 7, p. 39.

with working with the DLF to do everything to encourage better forest management practices through education, persuasion and the enforcement of the FIA.[51]

The district boards were absolutely crucial to the act. The boards' guidelines were based on the principles of citizen involvement and the belief that "most citizens will accept the judgement and advice of their peers over the judgement and advice of government".[52] The Minister of Lands and Forests at the time was of the same opinion: "If these boards really can get the support and the approval, if they acquire the prestige, and can direct the forest operations as they do in Sweden, then the success of this bill will be assured".[53] The intended duties of the district boards were contained in Sections 9, 10, 11 and 12. Section 9 stipulated that no immature trees were to be cut unless permission was first given by the district boards. Section 10 stated that all commercial harvesting operations had to be conducted in accordance with practices recommended by the districts boards. Section 11 prescribed commercial forest operators to "use every effort to harvest all possible saleable wood of commercial value"; the extent of saleable wood was to be determined by the district boards, which also had the powers to request operators to harvest "saleable wood". Section 12 stipulated that green belts be maintained along highways and the banks of rivers or lakes "designated" by the district boards.[54]

The factors promoting mandatory forest legislation were not inspired solely by Sweden. Stora, along with Bowater Mersey and Scott Maritimes, were highly dependent on wood supplied by small woodlot owners. In the mid-1960s it was estimated that 75 per cent of all pulpwood supplies delivered at the combined mills originated from small woodlots.[55] Stora, however, had little success in fostering forest management among small woodlot owners.[56] It was thus not strange that the province turned to Swedish forest legislation, a proven success, to mobilize the pulpwood resources of small woodlot owners. The Minister of Lands and Forests put it well: "it is in the area of the small woodlot holdings where management is so essential, and these are the holdings that are near the highways, the most valuable

---

51 Sandberg, "Swedish Forestry Legislation in Nova Scotia".

52 Hugh Fairn, "Address to the Canadian Institute of Forestry", 26 September 1980, p. 6, RG 81, vol. 2, file 4, PANS.

53 Nova Scotia, *Debates*, 22 February 1965, p. 544.

54 Nova Scotia, *Debates*, 22 February 1965, p. 544.

55 RG 55, series VP, vol. 3, no. 14, PANS.

56 One measure employed was the distribution of forest management plans and manuals on good forest practices. The company expected the woodlot owners to send back copies of their management plans but this seldom happened. We are indebted to Dietrich Soyez for providing us with a copy of this manual.

land, the most potentially productive woodlots we have are these small woodlot holdings".[57]

With the strict cutting regulations proposed in Sections 9, 10, 11 and 12 of the FIA, the government was clearly prepared to override private property rights in mobilizing small woodlot owners to manage their forests in support of the pulp and paper mills. Such property rights were an ideological bastion in the Nova Scotia political economy, where private foreign capital was, and remains, such an integral part of the province's development agenda. They were also an important part of the ideology of laissez-faire and of non-state interference in the affairs of property owners. Such sentiments were referred to in the defeat of Bill 151, which proposed to embargo pulpwood exports from private lands in the 1920s. The STA was also subjected to criticism from a small but influential group of woodland owners and contractors who regarded the act as a socialist measure that interfered with a land-owner's property rights.[58] Such concerns were suddenly secondary to the pulp and paper industry agenda. Haliburton stated that the government was "nearly unani-mous — they are unanimous — as to the need, although they may differ as to some of the details". He was also adamant about the act being "no more drastic or dic-tatorial than the Small Tree Act...except that it carries the further requirements of replanting and licensing".[59] During the hearings of the law amendments committee in March 1965, Haliburton had to listen to "three hours of criticism". Officials from the Nova Scotia Forest Products Association and Bowater Mersey's Ralph Johnson charged the act was "dictatorial and coercive", "reduced the owner's rights to private property without compensation", and "spell[ed] death to local saw mills, woodlot owners, sportsmen and personal freedom". One sawmiller characterized the Nova Scotia lumberman as an "independent...who resented anything that restricted his personal right to run his business and control his property".[60]

Another set of criticisms focused on the bias of the FIA, favouring the pulp and paper companies at the expense of other producers. The FIA was at the time believed to affect only private lands, exclude the Crown land leases allocated to the pulp and paper companies, steer forest management in the direction of serving the

---

57 The province was less concerned with the Crown land leases and company freeholds which were managed according to plans approved by the DLF or, "on the whole...managed by professional foresters". Nova Scotia, *Debates,* 22 February 1965, p. 544-5.

58 See, for example, John S. Cameron to Angus L. MacDonald, 28 June 1952, MG 2, vol. 970, file 25, PANS; Nova Scotia Section, CIF, Report of the 36th Annual Meet-ing, 1989, pp. 41-3; Richard Lord, "Forest Management Situation on Private Holdings", p. 5, Paper presented to the Nova Scotia Section, CIF, 1977, MG 1, vol. 2862, no. 10, PANS.

59 Nova Scotia, *Debates,* 22 February 1965, p. 527.

60 *Chronicle Herald,* 3 March 1965.

pulp sector, and cut off or limit traditional supplies of sawlogs.[61] This was a thorn in the side of Stora, which complained that sawmillers "persisted in beating around the so-called monopolies and low stumpage acquired from the Government by Nova Scotia Pulp Limited [a predecessor of Stora]".[62]

The minister, however, paid little heed to such criticisms by referring to the FIA as "primarily an educational thing". He also minimized the complaints of saw-millers and small woodlot owners, claiming the forest industry's trade organization, the Nova Scotia Forest Products Association, "are the most difficult people in the world to get together".[63] He also had the support of the Forestry Section of Volun-tary Economic Planning, which paid some heed to the property rights of woodlot owners, but nevertheless argued that the "ownership of forest lands entails an obligation of responsibility for keeping land productive and from becoming a public nuisance".[64] It was ironic that the alleged coercive nature of the STA and the 1962 version of the FIA — which affected, or were to affect, a relatively small number of woodland owners and contractors — was enough to take the acts out the statutes, while the 1965 FIA, with even more stringent regulations applicable to all private woodlands, was now defended and promoted by the government. This can only be explained by the newly discovered concern for the long-term fibre supply. The pulp industry development agenda was clearly a first priority, particularly at a time when the pulp companies were highly dependent on pulpwood from the small woodlot sector. The rhetoric of the premier was stern: "we are either serious about making the most of our forests or we're not...I think if we are serious we have to carry through, and encourage our people to follow certain practices that will mean a great deal to our province in the future".[65]

---

61 *Chronicle Herald*, 3 March 1965. Clarence Porter, past president of the Forest Products Association, expressed some of these concerns in the following: "The saw-mill industry and its workers and private woodlot owners, might well ask where, if [the FIA] became law, they would get their sawlogs? Would they be forced to sell their forest yield to a favoured few [the pulp companies]? Would they be required to pay taxes on their land for an unspecified time, or sell the yield at a price arranged by a few companies in the province [the pulp companies] irrespective of world market value?"; see also Voluntary Economic Planning, "Plan for the Forestry Sec-tor", p. 18.

62 "Manufacturing and Woodlands Reports", March 1965, Stora Archives, Falun, Sweden.

63 *Chronicle Herald,* 3 March 1965. Sawmillers still exerted considerable influence over this organization. Murray Prest, prominent sawmiller and critic of the pulp companies' Crown leases, served as president in the late 1960s.

64 Nova Scotia, Voluntary Economic Planning, "Submission of Forestry Section to Nova Scotia Voluntary Planning Board" (Halifax, 1964), p. 61, RG 55, series VP, vol. 3, no. 14, PANS.

65 Nova Scotia, *Debates*, 22 February 1965, pp. 536-7.

Parallel to the concern of boosting production and management on small private wooodlands, the province also had to respond to mounting demands for the technocentric forest management regime. One important ingredient of this regime was clearcutting. Already in the late 1950s, the STA was under pressure from landowners who wanted to practice extensive clearcutting.[66] The Minister of Lands and Forests complained that the requests for clearcutting had become a heavy bureaucratic burden in light of the expansion of the pulp and paper industry.[67] He also conceded that approvals were given in the large majority of cases.[68] The records also show that the limited enforcement of the STA stopped completely in 1962. In 1965, Bowater Mersey, long under pressure to adopt clearcutting from corporate headquarters, resorted to clearcutting entirely after the retirement of its chief forester, Ralph Johnson, an advocate of shelterwood cutting.[69] As of 1966, Scott Maritimes confined most of its harvesting practices to clearcutting.[70]

The practice of clearcutting was an integral part of the technocentric ideas of forest management advocated by Stora.[71] One central feature of Stora's new plans was the clearcutting of mature and over-mature stands as well as so-called "sylvan junk", degraded and commercially non-valuable forests, before planting and tend-

---

66 Interview with Johnson, 1987. Some soft industrialists and environmentalists contend that the FIA was "window-dressing" brought in merely to get rid of the STA. Thurston, "Prest's Last Stand", p. 27. Don Eldridge, former woodlands manager for the Eddy Lumber Company and Deputy Minister of Lands and Forests, 1979-86, suggests that it was more crucial to get rid of the STA than to introduce the FIA: "had they left the Small Tree Act in place, it would probably have been better than the Forest Improvement Act but it would appear that two pulp companies were coming on stream and they were going to have to cut small trees". Interview with Don Eldridge, 1987. Eldridge's statement may well be correct, but we have not encountered any hard evidence to suggest that the FIA was adopted to get clear of the STA.

67 Nova Scotia, *Debates,* 9 April 1962, p. 1361.

68 Nova Scotia, *Debates,* 9 April 1962, p. 1362.

69 Interviews with Burgess and Johnson, 1987. Johnson's successor, Leif Holt, indicated that his company opposed the 1965 FIA from its inception even though they had an active part in the development of the proposed FIA legislation in 1962. Interview with Leif Holt, 1987.

70 Johnson, *Forests of Nova Scotia,* p. 292.

71 At least some evidence suggests that Stora did not expect much from the FIA. Jan Weslien had doubts about the success of the FIA. Interview with Weslien, 1989. Stora's woodlands manager in 1965, A.H. Andersson, wrote Swedish headquarters that the FIA "could possibly die a natural death as happened to the STA and other acts presented for better Forest Management and Conservation"; "Manufacturing and Woodlands Reports", March 1965, Stora Archives, Falun, Sweden.

ing more desirable species.[72] The increased level of mechanization that was part of the new technocentric management regime also promoted clearcutting: "Increasing mechanization may well result in a trend to complete removal of the stand [clear-cutting] followed by immediate planting or seeding".[73] The Forest Products Association therefore recommended that the FIA "be sufficiently flexible so as to allow this as an acceptable forest practice".[74] The majority of foresters supported clearcutting, the Nova Scotia Section of the CIF resolving in 1973 to carry out a public relations campaign with government and industry on the "merits of silviculture clear cutting systems".[75]

Government support for the FIA was initially hesitant. No doubt, the criticisms voiced before the law amendments committee was of concern. Although the Minister of Lands and Forests extolled the virtues of the FIA, and all but the most crucial sections were proclaimed, the main thrust of the act remained unproclaimed.[76] A grace period of ten years was stipulated in order to work out practical solutions to the formulation and enforcement of the new regulations, as well as to resolve the system of forest taxation. The establishment of a first DFPIB in Colchester County led to nine district boards by 1970, but then gave way to frustration as the board's recommendations were not subject to enforcement.[77]

In the late 1960s and early 1970s, technocentric harvesting and management methods increased among the pulp and paper companies and a growing dependent group of company contractors. The DLF was profoundly influenced by this trend.[78]

72 "Manufacturing and Woodlands Reports", March 1965, p. 17, Stora Archives, Falun, Sweden. Haliburton felt the question of what constituted a mature forest was one of the major issues of contention within the Department of Lands and Forests during the formative stages of the 1965 FIA. Interview with Haliburton, 1987.

73 "Nova Scotia Forest Products Association Brief on the Forest Improvement Act, ch. 7, 1967, Statutes of Nova Scotia", mimeo (January 1967), p. 4, MG 1, vol. 2862, no. 21, PANS.

74 "Forest Products Association Brief", p. 4, MG 1, vol. 2862, no. 21, PANS

75 "CIF, Nova Scotia Section: Historical Facts", handwritten document in possession of the Secretary of the Nova Scotia Section of the CIF.

76 E.D. Haliburton, *A Look at the Forest Improvement Act* (Halifax, 1966); the sections proclaimed were the registration of operators and buyers, the appointment of forest improvement practices boards and the Timber Loans Board. *Chronicle Herald*, 29 September 1965, p. 3.

77 *Chronicle Herald*, December 1965, p. 7; Sandberg, "Swedish Forestry Legislation in Nova Scotia", p. 182; interviews with Creighton and Burgess, 1987.

78 In interviews with several key actors associated with the Department of Lands and Forests, reference was made in various forms to a process of "pulp culturization". E.D. Haliburton, the Minister of Lands and Forests during the introduction of the FIA, was perhaps the most explicit. Others alluded to pressure to adopt this professional ideology while others clearly owed their professional advancement to such

This corresponded to international trends but was also paralleled by a generational change within the department. Many of the foresters of the "soft industrial school" who had entered the Forestry School as Second World War veterans and had occupied senior departmental positions in the 1960s and early 1970s, retired and provided room for a new group of pulpwood forest managers, more receptive to the relatively new technocentric position of forest management advocated by the pulp and paper companies. Company and even DLF foresters, with virtually all Crown lands leased to the pulp and paper companies, in effect became, despite rhetoric to the contrary, employees and servants of the pulp companies.

Small woodlot owners were marginalized in the drive toward efficiency in the forest economy of the 1970s. Although organized in an aggressive small woodlot owner organization, they received low prices and had no assured market for their pulpwood, which discouraged any form of forest management. In 1970 the understaffed and under-budgeted Extension Division of the DLF was disbanded in a reorganization of the department.[79] The provincial government proved unwilling to support effective pulpwood marketing legislation, in spite of repeated calls for such action.[80] The development of the new forest on the freeholds and Crown leases of the pulp and paper companies threatened small woodlot owners' share of the pulpwood market.[81] From 1967 to 1973, pulpwood coming from small woodlots declined from 64 to 36 per cent of total production.[82] Small woodlot owners also felt victimized by the provincial government programme of accelerated government purchases of private forest lands in 1974, feeling the department's record in the

views. By the 1970s the prevailing ideology was dominated by a "pulp culture" which at times was in conflict with explicit government positions and with growing environmentalist sympathies within the province. The development of Stora's "New Forest", based on clearcutting and the regeneration of "suitable species", was also sanctioned by the government. Stora's stumpage rates on Crown lands increased from $1 to $2.75 per cord. This increase was refunded to Stora when the company presented proof of silvicultural expenditures. Akesson, "The Nova Scotia Pulp Limited Story"; for a critical view of the "New Forest", see Julia McMahon, "The New Forest in Nova Scotia", in Burrill and McKay, *People, Resources, and Power,* pp. 99-105.

79 Richard Lord, "Forest Management Situation on Private Holdings", p. 6. Paper presented to the Nova Scotia Section, CIF, 1977, MG 1, vol. 2862, no. 10, PANS.

80 One statement in 1972 provides an illustration: "The present government by denying the Nova Scotia Woodlot Owners a producers' Marketing Board clearly indicates that the rights of the owners are not recognized", MG 1, vol. 2862, no. 11, PANS. For a fuller story, see Peter Clancy, "The Politics of Pulpwood Marketing in Nova Scotia, 1960-1985", in this volume.

81 Julia McMahon, "The New Forest in Nova Scotia"; Thurston, "Prest's Last Stand".

82 John Smith, "The Acquisition of Forest Reserves" (Department of Lands and Forests, Halifax, 1975), p. 7.

management of Crown lands to be one of a "public inheritance devastated and wasted".[83] The salvage operations of spruce budworm-infected wood on Stora's leases on the Cape Breton Highlands, which killed six million cords of balsam fir in the mid-1970s, were also resented: "it salvaged the Queen's woodlot at public expense...while the private woodlot owners' woodlot...received no consideration whatsoever".[84] The lack of provisions to empower the woodlot owner segment resulted in considerable bitterness on the part of woodlot owners toward government planning in general.[85]

It was in this general climate that George Snow, the Progressive Conservative Minister of Lands and Forests from 1968 to 1969, reactivated the FIA by sponsoring an amendment to create a Provincial Forest Practices Improvement Board (PFPIB).[86] The PFPIB consisted of six members: the Minister of Lands and Forests or one of his appointees as chairman (in this case Snow), and one member each from the Nova Scotia Voluntary Planning Board (as the Voluntary Economic Planning Board was renamed in 1970), the sawmill industry, the pulp and paper industry, the small woodlot owners, and the Nova Scotia Section of the CIF. Snow built considerable momentum with meetings of the provincial and district board

---

83   MG 1, vol. 2862, no. 11, PANS. The land acquisition programme had started in the late 1930s and by the mid-1970s, the government owned approximately 25 per cent of all forest lands. In the long term, the goal was to raise that share to 50 per cent. In the short term, the government hoped to raise the Crown lands from 20 to 25 per cent in western Nova Scotia because, at the time, the province "could not guarantee a continued supply of wood to a potential wood product industry". *Chronicle Herald,* 20 June 1974

84   Royal Commission of Forestry, Transcripts of Hearings, Nova Scotia Woodlot Owners and Operators Association Submission, RG 44, vol. 158A, no. 1, pp. 32-3. PANS.

85   While woodlot owners lobbied for and supported the FIA, they were at the same time suspicious of the general principles of government intervention and planning. In 1972, for example, the Forestry Sector Committee of Voluntary Planning endorsed the FIA along with the principle of a broader provincial plan "that the benefits deriving from the land are basically a public inheritance and that government must strive to develop a system of public and private stewardship that protects the long-term public welfare and the rights of the owner". The small woodlot owner representative, however, dissented, pointing to the past injustices suffered by his constituency. Thomas Smith, Nova Scotia Woodlot Owners Association, "A Proposal for Land Use and Management, Comments", p. 2, MG 1, vol. 2862, no. 11, PANS.

86   The duties of the PFPIB were to prepare a manual of good forest practices and to prescribe, advise and make recommendations concerning cutting practices and reforestation procedures in the province. However, it was Snow's opinion that these recommendations, coupled with the sections on harvesting and replanting already in the FIA, should serve as regulations. Interview with George Snow, Minister of Lands and Forests, 1968-9, 1987.

chairmen, but progress was slow and the Conservative government was defeated in the provincial election of 1970.

The PFPIB and district boards continued to operate under the new Liberal administration and the new Lands and Forests Minister Benoit Comeau, but in September 1971 the various boards were informed by Deputy Minister Burgess that no further meetings would be held at the expiry of the last board appointments (the last expiry date was 6 February 1972).[87] Some boards protested, feeling the FIA "is the one tool that can bring about better forest conservation if fully implemented".[88] The Minister of DLF advised that the cabinet "will be studying this matter in the near future".[89] The matter received a positive response. The re-institution of the PFPIB created a widespread and positive interest in making the FIA work. In 1971 the provision of green belts along major paved highways was proclaimed, although the board never "strictly adhered" to the provisions, feeling that "this particular part of the Act is of lesser importance".[90] In 1972 amendments allowed a member of the Nova Scotia Wildlife Federation to sit on the board, and the whole province was declared a forest district subject to the advice and regulations worked out by the PFPIB.[91]

At this stage, the FIA retained credibility with the pulp and paper companies as well as with the organizations that were later to take explicitly pro-industry stands, the Nova Scotia Forest Products Association and the Nova Scotia Section of the CIF. In 1971 the province's foresters "suggested that the full weight and resources of Government, Industry and woodland owners be channelled towards making this Act work". The section also proposed that a fund be established to assist landowners to carry out silviculture on their land. Industry was to contribute 25 cents per cord through a voluntary tax matched by the provincial government. Small woodlot owners were to contribute one-third of the cost in labour or money. The silvicultural programme, the brief suggested, "could be administered by the Forest Practices Improvement Boards".[92] In 1973 the province's foresters resolved to censor the provincial government because the FIA was not fully proclaimed.[93] In 1974

87 R.H. Burgess to Secretaries of Boards, 1 September 1971, RG 81, vol. 3, no. 20, PANS.

88 G.D. Dwyer, secretary and technical advisor to Halifax and Hants County DFPIBs, to Benoit Comeau, 26 May 1971, RG 81, vol. 3, no. 20, PANS.

89 Comeau to G.D. Dwyer, 1 June 1971, RG 81, vol. 3, no. 20, PANS.

90 Nova Scotia, Provincial Forest Practices Improvement Board, "Submission to Royal Commission on Forestry" (April 1983), p. 22.

91 Nova Scotia, "Submission to Royal Commission on Forestry".

92 "A Forest Policy for Nova Scotia", a brief submitted to the Nova Scotia Government by the Nova Scotia Section, CIF (1971), PANS.

93 "CIF, Nova Scotia Section: Historical Facts", handwritten document in possession of the Secretary of the Nova Scotia Section of the CIF.

the section's Standing Committee on the FIA accused the government of procrastination for not appointing district boards.[94]

Liberal Lands and Forests Minister DeLory appointed a new PFPIB in 1973, with Elmer Bragg, a prominent sawmiller and Liberal supporter, as chairman. Bragg died in 1974 and was replaced by Hugh Fairn, the representative of the Forestry Sector Committee of the Nova Scotia Voluntary Planning Board, in 1975. Fairn was not an expert on forestry but had a keen interest in wildlife. The PFPIB became a strong forum for the soft industrialist position under Fairn, who received support from the "official" wildlife, sawmill and small woodlot owner representatives on the board.[95] The board members were clearly sensitive to the growing public concern for the environment and the view that the forest be treated not only as an industrial installation, but also as a source of aesthetics, conservation, recreation, wildlife and culture.

Then, in 1976, the FIA was proclaimed in full. No doubt, the environmental and soft industrial lobbies exerted some pressure in favour of proclamation.[96] The Liberal government was also more sensitive to the electoral support from these lobbies. Yet, their influence was not sufficient to grant the FIA and the PFPIB legitimacy in the provincial context. Instead, it was the massive infusion of federal

---

94   Nova Scotia Section, CIF, Reports of the 18th and 19th Annual Meetings, 1973 and 1974.

95   Interview with Hugh Fairn, Chairman of PFPIB, 1975-84, 18 February 1986. The members were Lyndon Gray, Executive Director from the DLF; Murray Prest, sawmiller; Leif Holt, pulp and paper industry; Thomas McPhee, small woodlot owner; Don Eldridge, Nova Scotia Section, CIF; and Gordon Alguire, the Nova Scotia Wildlife Federation. The new board was charged with determining "the most appropriate ways and means of educating both land owners and the general public in better forest practices", using the FIA. *Chronicle Herald,* 17 November 1973.

96   The budworm spray issue in 1975 and 1976 provides one example of the strong position of the soft industrialists and the environmentalists at the time. In 1975, the Liberal government gave permission to Stora to spray an insecticide (Fenitrothion) on its budworm-infested forests, but then reversed its position in light of opposition from environmental groups, the general public, the Integrated Forest Management Committee of Voluntary Planning, and the PFPIB. The decision not to spray was not, however, a reflection of a major shift from a technocentric to an environmental stand. One of the key facts to sway the cabinet was that the infestation was so high that even an extensive spray program would have left enough budworm to "leisurely eat the remaining forests". The use of chemical insecticides was replaced by the *Bacillus thuringiensis* [Bt] bacteria, a biological weapon more expensive but allegedly less harmful to the environment. Bt spraying was sanctioned by the PFPIB and Voluntary Planning, but the government still proceeded with utmost care. The Minister of Lands and Forests at the time, George Henley, claimed: "the spray program was a brand new program and of course they (the Cabinet) were all terrified that they were going to get into the ill will of the public and they wondered if there was any need for spraying, you were sort of being cross examined by the Cabinet and by everybody opposed to forest development". Interviews with Vince MacLean and George Henley, Ministers

funds for forest management that forced proclamation of the FIA in 1976.[97] The letters of agreement forming the basis of the Nova Scotia-Canada Forestry Agreement, concluded in 1977, were conditional upon the full implementation of the FIA within 18 months.[98] In spite of the proclamation, however, financial support for the PFPIB was not forthcoming. Before the first federal-provincial agreement, the solicitation of funds by the PFPIB to enforce the green belt sections of the act had been turned down repeatedly. In 1974 the board asked cabinet for $500,000 for a year-round project of road improvement, but was turned down.[99] In 1975 the board requested a more modest $140,000 to hire the staff necessary for the proclamation of the FIA.[100] But the board was informed that no staff would be available in 1975-6, "and possibly not in 1976-7, since the Provincial Treasury Board reports a cut-back in financing".[101]

When the federal-provincial agreement was passed and the FIA proclaimed, funds were still not forthcoming to the PFPIB. Instead, the monies under the agreement were assigned to a new Directorate of Forest Management, Private Lands, under the DLF. The five-year agreement provided $25.6 million for the programme and $4.3 million for its administration. Slim Johnson, an industry forester, headed the directorate and supervised over 30 foresters and forest technicians throughout the province.[102]

The technocentric and soft management factions were now represented by two competing public bodies. The board structure of the FIA soon became the major

of Lands and Forests, 1976-8 and 1979-83, respectively, 1987; Anthony Lamport, *Common Ground: 25 Years of Voluntary Planning* (Halifax, 1988), pp. 107-15; Dietrich Soyez, "Scandinavian Silviculture in Canada: Entry and Performance Barriers", *The Canadian Geographer*, 32,2 (Summer 1988), pp. 133-40.

97 Federal-provincial funds supported forest inventory work and forest improvements as early as 1952. In 1962, a project was undertaken to cut woods roads, clean the sides of public roads and conduct thinning and cleaning in young stands. Again, in a similar programme in 1966, the highway from Louisbourg to Sydney was cleaned primarily as a make-work and tourism-development project. It also included, however, stand thinning around Mabou, Cape Breton, and improvements on Crown lands, such as the development of access roads, stand improvement, forest inventory and reforestation. Creighton, *Forestkeeping*, pp. 122, 128.

98 Nova Scotia, The Provincial Forest Practices Improvement Board, "Submission to Royal Commission on Forestry" (April 1983), p. 23 and Appendix "E".

99 G.E. Dix, Division of Administration, to G.R. Maybee, Co-ordinator of Operations, 13 September 1974, RG 81, vol. 13, no. 8, PANS.

100 *Chronicle Herald,* 11 December 1975.

101 Minutes of 9th 1975 Meeting, 7 August 1975, RG 81, vol. 13, no. 8, PANS.

102 Press releases, 28 June and 21 July 1977, RG 81, vol. 8, no. 5, PANS.

focus of attack by the technocentric factions. One set of actions sought to bring the duties of the PFPIB under the mandate of the DLF and to incorporate the FIA into the Lands and Forests Act.[103] It was alleged that the district boards, charged with enforcement of the FIA, were unnecessary as they would duplicate work of the DLF. The services of the executive officer of the PFPIB, a forester assigned by the DLF, were eroded and eventually withdrawn. At one point, the executive officer worked one day a week for the PFPIB, and the remainder of the week for the new Private Lands of the DLF, charged with dispersing the monies of the federal-provincial agreement.[104] The roles of the executive officer were thus split along contradictory and competing lines.[105]

The administration of the federal-provincial agreements by the DLF provided the technocentric factions with a decided advantage. DLF officials expressed optimism about the future of forest management in the province and argued that "a very comprehensive agreement is now in force in the form of a Subsidiary Agreement with DREE and new staff has been added to implement the Agreements".[106] DLF officials also felt that the guidelines of the FIA could be adopted by Private Lands, making the district boards redundant: "there is every reason to think that scope will be provided for guidelines provided under the FIA and that the personnel engaged for private land management can use the provisions of the Act in their work activities".[107]

The Nova Scotia Section of the CIF joined in the attack. Some members perceived the PFPIB and the district boards as ill-equipped generalists' forums. The section was lobbying hard to get a professional registry for foresters. The federal-

---

103 Nova Scotia Section, CIF, Report of the 22nd Annual Meeting, 1977, p. 15.

104 Nova Scotia Section, CIF, Report of the 22nd Annual Meeting, 1977, p. 15.

105 This may have reflected a process of co-option. The Executive Officer, David Dwyer, being a employee of DLF, was answerable to the Department: "the Executive Officer must be responsible to a Superior in the Department as is every one else in Lands and Forests and this cannot be the Board". Nova Scotia Section, CIF, Report of the 22nd Annual Meeting, 1977, p. 17. Once separated from the PFPIB, Dwyer was soon charged with launching the Group Ventures Programme, a co-operative forest management programme sponsored by the federal-provincial agreement. This programme, in spite of its many shortfalls, faced staunch opposition from the pulp and paper industry and factions within the DLF. The realization of the programme was a significant political achievement, and was based on Dwyer's conviction that the FIA would never be implemented. Even the Group Ventures Programme was later thwarted, which led to Dwyer's early retirement. Interview with Dave Dwyer, 1989. It remains to be seen if the Group Ventures can formulate alternative new forest management regimes and improved economic conditions for small woodlot owners.

106 Nova Scotia Section, CIF, Report of the 22nd Annual Meeting, 1977, p. 14.

107 Nova Scotia Section, CIF, Report of the 22nd Annual Meeting, 1977, p. 14.

provincial agreements, in turn, constituted an opportunity for the profession to draw up management plans for the woodlot owners operating under the federal-provincial agreements. The district boards, with their citizen participation, provided a serious threat to such an arrangement.[108] Yet the section was not unanimous in its opposition to the FIA. The most verbal opponents were prominent pulp and paper industry representatives and DLF officials who, in 1980, formed a committee to "look into" the FIA. The committee sent out a questionnaire to the membership and presented a report at the fall meeting in 1980. Based on the report, the committee presented, and the members passed, a resolution that the FIA be rescinded and that the goals of the FIA be placed in a revised Lands and Forests Act.

There was, however, concern expressed before the resolution was passed. The majority was slim, with many abstentions. Before the vote, many felt "that the report and its recommendations be looked at more closely before any stand is taken by this Section on any of the recommendations".[109] The response on the questionnaire was poor, 29 out of 92, prompting the PFPIB chairman to suggest that "this might be acceptable in a survey for some brand of soap, but not in a survey of professionals".[110] The membership of the section was heavily biased in favour of the DLF, with 30 members, and the pulp and paper industry, with 24 members. These groups may very well have biased the results as the board structure of the FIA was the provision criticized most heavily. In other respects, the respondents favoured the objectives and most of the guidelines. A large majority, 84 per cent, were in favour of enforceable regulations.[111] It was thus not unusual, given the cost and threat that the district boards constituted to the DLF and the forester profession, that the provincial board was stalled in completing the system. The DLF felt it more important for the board to develop, as stipulated in the act, a manual of good forest management. The manual was intended as a "bible" for the district boards, but proved difficult to produce, and delayed the appointment of district boards until 1981.[112]

Not surprisingly, when the PFPIB published its "manual of good forest practices" in 1980, the split widened between the soft industrialists and the technocentrists.[113] The manual, as Fairn later wrote, reflected the philosophy of the board, that a "healthy naturally-regenerated forest is part and parcel of the Forest

108 It was not strange, then, that the Nova Scotia Section of the CIF and the pulp and paper companies attacked the professional credentials of the other members of the PFPIB. See RG 81, vol. 1, files 6 and 15, PANS.

109 Nova Scotia Section, CIF, Report of the 24th Annual Meeting, 1980, p. 21.

110 Fairn, "Address to the CIF", p. 2.

111 Fairn, "Address to the CIF", p. 2.

112 Nova Scotia Section, CIF, Report of the 22nd Annual Meeting, 1977, p. 14.

113 Nova Scotia, Provincial Forest Practices Improvement Board, *The Trees Around Us* (Halifax, 1980).

Improvement Act".[114] It was thus opposed to the forest management agenda set by the pulp and paper industry. Stora made this very clear: "Recently, methods such as strip, patch, selection and shelterwood cutting have become popular methods of harvesting so as to promote natural regeneration. NSFI [Stora] does not anticipate any use of these methods because clear cutting followed by artificial regeneration where necessary is judged to be the most efficient method for our situation".[115]

In spite of opposition, the PFPIB remained an important political force in the forestry debate. When the Nova Scotia Section of the CIF sent a delegation to the Minister of Lands and Forests to propose the abandonment of the FIA in 1981, the minister reportedly responded that the FIA was popular, produced votes, and would stay.[116] In April 1981 the PFPIB secured regular meetings with a cabinet committee separate from the DLF, to ensure that positive action was taken toward the implementation of the FIA.[117] In the same year, the Minister of Lands and Forests appointed two new DFPIBs, one in the Eastern District (Pictou, Antigonish and Guysborough) and the other in the North-Central District (Cumberland and Colchester). The first year of operation was to constitute a "learning experience".[118]

Then, in 1981, the green belt sections along rivers were invoked and subject to enforcement. Two river systems were designated, the East and West rivers at Sheet Harbour, and the Stewiacke River. But enforcement, with government support, did not come easy. In spite of intense lobbying on the part of the PFPIB chairman, support from the federal Department of Fisheries and Oceans, favourable public hearings with concerned local citizens, and pressure from the local MLA, it took two years to designate the East and West rivers in May 1983.[119] The designation of the Stewiacke River, however, proved impossible due to vocal protests from affected landowners and the local Conservative MLA, Colin Stewart.[120]

---

114 Fairn to Gordon Waters, 1 December 1982, RG 81, vol. 1, file 17, PANS.

115 "NSFI Forest Management Policy and Guidelines", mimeo, 1981, RG 81, vol. 1, file 13, PANS.

116 "CIF, NS Section: Historical Facts", handwritten document in possession of the secretary of the Nova Scotia Section of the CIF.

117 "Annual Report to the Governor-in-Council by the Provincial Forest Practices Improvement Board, 1982-3", RG 81, vol. 3, file 4, PANS.

118 *Forest Times*, 3, 4 (August 1981), p. 1.

119 For more detail, see RG 81, vol. 2, files 16-18 and vol. 3, file 7, PANS.

120 The opposition of Stewart was in spite of his position against clearcutting and the resulting siltation of the whole Stewiacke River system. See "Annual Report to the Governor-in-Council by the Provincial Forest Practices Improvement Board, 1982-1983", Appendix III, RG 81, vol. 3, file 4, PANS. Fairn believed Stewart was part of a "deliberate plan to stop our work on the very river in Nova Scotia which most surely needs greenbelt protection". Fairn to Streatch, 22 February 1984, RG 81, vol. 3, file 4, PANS.

The herbicide controversies of the early 1980s added to the tenuous position of the PFPIB and the lack of support for the FIA. In 1982, Stora announced a major programme of aerial spraying of the herbicides Esteron 600 and Esteron 3-3E (containing the substances 2,4-D and 2,4,5-T), designed to combat the extensive competition from hardwood species in young softwood plantations.[121] Massive protests, with broad local and international support, followed and resulted in a court battle between Stora and a group of local environmentalists.[122] The latter lost their suit on appeal in the Supreme Court of Nova Scotia in 1983. The PFPIB was not a major player in the controversy but nevertheless opposed the scheme, favouring the use of chemical weed control "in forest nurseries and plantations only".[123] The board thus lost legitimacy, and was criticized by the technocentric position for its lack of a stand on "forest protection".

In May 1982, during a time of conflict and controversy, the government announced a Royal Commission Inquiry to defuse some of the attacks from the environmental and soft technology factions.[124] The hearings that followed revealed nothing new.[125] On the one hand, positions were presented in favour of the technocentric forest management agenda, as articulated by the pulp and paper companies, the DLF, the Nova Scotia Section of the CIF, and the various contractors, truckers and suppliers dependent on the pulp mills. On the other hand, the environmental and soft technology factions, and the marginal participants, small woodlot owners and forest workers in the pulp and paper industry, opposed and criticized the pulp and paper industry agenda. The FIA received widespread and unanimous support from these groups, including the Forest Section, Land Resources Co-ordinating Committee and the Integrated Forest Management Committee of Voluntary Planning, the Nova Scotia Wildlife Federation, the Nova Scotia Woodlot Owners and Operators Association, the Nova Scotia Salmon Association and the

---

121 Dietrich Soyez, "The Internationalization of Environmental Conflict: The Herbicide Issue in Nova Scotia's Forest and its Links with Sweden", in Jørn Carlsen and Bengt Streijffert, eds., *Canada and the Nordic Countries* (Lund, 1988); Soyez, "Scandinavian Silviculture in Canada", pp. 137-8.

122 Soyez, "The Internationalization of Environmental Conflict".

123 PFPIB, "Submission to the Royal Commission on Forestry", p. 27.

124 George Henley, then Minister of Lands and Forests, was quite candid about the reasons for the Royal Commission. Although the public was told that the enquiry was to make an in-depth analysis of the forest industry in general, Henley said the real reasons were "what it is, is an exercise in self survival isn't it? and if you can get something going that will carry the heat for you, you'll always go and do that...Royal Commissions really are a way of getting out from under the heat for a while". Interview with George Henley, Minister of Lands and Forests, 1987.

125 Transcripts and written submissions to the hearings are contained in RG 44, vols. 158a-160, PANS.

Group Ventures.[126] The province was clearly walking a tightrope, trying to respond to the public approval of the FIA and the demands of the PFPIB while at the same time accommodating the protests of the technocentric factions within and outside government. The Minister of Lands and Forests tried to resolve the contradiction by an unsuccessful attempt to take over the chairmanship of the PFPIB as well as by appointing representatives to the board who were openly hostile to the act.[127]

On 23 November 1982, the Minister of Lands and Forests appointed Laurie Ledgewick — a representative of the sawmill segment, which was openly opposed to the FIA — to replace long-standing member Murray Prest.[128] But Prest was still maintained on the board as a consultant until Management Board instructed Fairn that such expenses were not legitimate. Two other members were particularly critical and outspoken. L.G. Howard of Scott Maritimes, the representative of the Nova Scotia Section of the CIF appointed on 8 March 1983, openly criticized the green belts, feeling they benefited fishing more than forestry.[129] Howard, together with partner Vincent Clark of Scott Maritimes, the pulp and paper industry representative, also led the criticism against the PFPIB's position on herbicide spraying. When Fairn called for Howard's resignation for misrepresenting the board, Howard disagreed, referring to the stand of the Nova Scotia Section of the CIF on the FIA and arguing that his comments fell under the mandate of the act by "contributing to education".[130] Howard and Clark were joined by Hugh Ross of Stora, representing large landowners on the North Central DFPIB. Ross also spoke out against the FIA as an employee of Stora and a spokesman of the Forest Management Committee of the Nova Scotia Forest Products Association.

In February 1984, Fairn poured out his frustration in a long personal letter to Ken Streatch, the Minister of Lands and Forests: "Time and time again we have

---

126 See, for example, resolutions and letters of support in RG 81, vol. 13, no. 10, PANS.

127 Fairn to Hon. Ken Streatch, 22 February 1984, RG 81, vol. 3, file 4, PANS; "CIF, NS Section: Historical Facts", handwritten document in possession of the Secretary of the Nova Scotia Section of the CIF.

128 Order-in-Council, 23 November 1982, RG 81, vol. 13, no. 8, PANS. Ledgewick was nominated by the Nova Scotia Forest Products Association. It had been the practice, as a courtesy, to let the Forest Products Association nominate the sawmill and pulp and paper industry representatives to the PFPIB. The association, however, had reversed its support of the FIA in 1982, and, therefore, Fairn and Prest felt, had disqualified itself to make such recommendations. The association's change in position on the FIA corresponded with the pulp and paper industry members taking control of the organization, which had previously been controlled by the sawmill segment. Fairn to George Henley, 29 July 1982 and Prest to Lorne Etter, 17 June 1982, RG 81, vol. 13, no. 10, PANS.

129 Order-in-Council, 8 March 1983, RG 81, vol. 13, no. 10, PANS.

130 L.G. Howard to Hugh Fairn, 14 February 1984; L.G. Howard to Members of the Provincial and District Boards, 14 February 1984, RG 81, vol. 3, PANS.

been encouraged to 'get on with the Act', to quote the Premier, only to find roadblocks, procrastination and outright sabotage, to set the Board and its work back again".[131] He also complained bitterly about the appointment of board members who "'would do everything within their power' to be disruptive of the Act and the work of their fellow Board members".[132] Fairn's frustration eventually led to a leave of absence from the board in April 1984 (construed as a resignation by the press), in order to let the Minister of Lands and Forests, Ken Streatch, on record as supportive of the FIA, "move ahead" with the act.[133] Streatch, however, never "moved ahead" but waited for the results of the Royal Commission on Forestry.[134] When the Royal Commission Report was released in 1984, it fulfilled the bulk of the demands of the pulp and paper industry factions and recommended rescission of the FIA.

During the time the government considered the Royal Commission Report, the FIA remained in suspension. The pulp and paper industry factions continued their attack on the FIA. The Nova Scotia Section of the CIF called for a new act which would recognize "the supremacy of traditional private property rights with respect to forestry matters".[135] The foresters also called for wide ministerial powers, the reduction of powers of the Pulpwood Marketing Act, and the repeal of the FIA "in its entirety".[136] The section felt the federal-provincial agreements "had been successful and deserved applause", but urged the government to provide more extension services.[137] Such services, the section claimed, must include public input,

---

131 Fairn to Hon. Ken Streatch, 22 February 1984, RG 81, vol. 3, file 4, PANS; RG 44, vol. 158a, no. 5 and vol. 159, no. 1, PANS.

132 Fairn to Hon. Ken Streatch, 22 February 1984, RG 81, vol. 3, file 4, PANS.

133 Fairn to Hon. Ken Streatch, 2 April 1984, RG 81, vol. 1, file 17, PANS. For Streatch's support of the FIA, see Streatch to A. Tobin, Nova Scotia Wildlife Federation, 20 March 1984, RG 81, vol. 3, file 4, PANS.

134 *Chronicle Herald,* 25 February 1985.

135 Nova Scotia Section, CIF, "Submission to the Legislative Steering Committee on Forestry" (April 1986), p. 2. Their submission listed two legitimate traditional exceptions: the protection of public resources such as water and game and the elimination of public risk from infestation or fire. One deduces from these comments that a small woodlot owner can be forced to spray for the budworm, but cannot be told to harvest and tend the forest to reduce the risk of a budworm infestation in the first place. The ideological aversion to regulatory legislation was latent throughout the period. In 1975, for example, a DLF brief characterized "legislated management and production requirements as politically unacceptable...[it] has a negative connotation and is seemingly incompatible with our private enterprise economy". Smith, "The Acquisition of Forest Reserves", p. 14.

136 Nova Scotia Section, CIF, "Submission", p. 2.

137 Nova Scotia Section, CIF, "Submission", p. 45.

but "the government must rely heavily on groups directly involved in forestry to shape the basic policy".[138] The foresters' arguments carried the day in the end. In 1986 the FIA was repealed and replaced by a new act entitled "An Act to Encourage the Development and Management of Forest Land". In contrast to the FIA, the new act was voluntary, complemented by financial incentives, and, most crucially, administered by the DLF.[139]

The history of the Nova Scotia Forest Improvement Act from 1962 to 1986 is one of paradoxes and logical consistencies. The pulp and paper industry development agenda set by the provincial government in the late 1950s and 1960s, and its associated politics, clearly shaped and conditioned the fate of the act. The ultimate political hegemony of the pulp and paper industry factions, though not unchallenged, is expressed in all development stages of the FIA. Initially, the FIA was intended to cope with the inadequacies of the STA, as well as with future wood shortages for the pulp and paper industry, by encouraging forest management on small woodlots, the primary source of pulpwood in the 1960s. The mandatory provisions of the FIA, and their infringements on private property rights, were down-played in favour of the common good of the province.

As the pulp and paper companies increased their Crown leases and freeholds, intensified "technocentric" management on their own lands, increased the level of mechanization of woods harvesting, and encouraged the growth of a dependent group of harvest contractors, their support of the FIA diminished. The Provincial Forest Practices Improvement Board, charged with the administration and enforcement of the FIA, became a forum for the soft technology and environmental factions (sawmillers, wildlife interests, small woodlot owners and environmentalists), which questioned the hegemony and favourable treatment of the pulp and paper companies. The provision of district forest practices improvement boards, with citizen participation, threatened the professional status of the province's foresters. The record of the PFPIB and the district boards of the late 1960s and 1970s suggests that they were well received in their communities but were clearly a threat to established interests. They not only recommended good forest practices, but also politicized the forest policy field, showing concern over the sawlog supply, questioning the price of pulpwood and the terms of the Stora and Scott Crown leases. The PFPIB recommendation not to spray during the budworm infestations of the mid-1970s was a policy already formulated by district boards in the late 1960s and early 1970s. In both instances, the boards recommended that funds saved by not spraying be directed to assist small woodlot owners.[140] Another stand advocated by the boards, and supported by legal opinion, was that the FIA apply to *all* forest

---

138 Nova Scotia Section, CIF, "Submission", p. 47.

139 Sandberg, "Swedish Forestry Legislation in Nova Scotia", p. 185.

140 Forest Practices Improvement Board, Kings County District, RG 81, vol. 7, no. 10; Combined Meeting of Provincial Board and County Chairmen, 27 January 1970, RG 81, vol. 3, no. 15, PANS.

lands, private as well as Crown leases, a point clearly not favoured by the DLF and the pulp and paper companies.[141]

The first federal-provincial forest agreement in 1977, tied to the proclamation of the FIA, gave the PFPIB political legitimacy to continue its work but little financial support. The publication of a forest manual for good forest management by the PFPIB in 1980, the formation of two district boards in 1981, and the attempts at enforcing green belts along designated rivers yielded little progress. Instead, the Directorate of Forest Management, Private Lands, was established within the DLF to administer the funds of the federal-provincial agreements. On the whole, the chairman of the PFPIB noted in 1984: "It has been like pulling teeth to get the least bit of progress".[142]

The technocentric opposition directed at the PFPIB, and toward the FIA in general, was formidable. One critique centred on the alleged duplication of services provided by the district boards and DLF's Private Lands directorate: the district boards, through local citizen input, were aimed at replacing, rather than duplicating, a government bureaucracy that enjoyed little trust in rural Nova Scotia. As one of the commissioners at the Royal Commission on Forestry stated: "I think it could be argued, and some people have argued, that by decentralizing the bureaucracy and getting it down to the local level that it might in fact remove a lot of bureaucracy".[143] Another spurious claim against the FIA was that the federal-provincial forest agreements operated successfully. In reality, they were (and remain) costly (and therefore tenuous) and limited to a small portion of woodlot owners. Yet, they benefit the pulp mills, as they do not address the status quo of power in the forest industry.[144] Many small woodlot owners consider them a mere subsidy for the pulp and paper industry. Small wonder that the share of pulpwood supplied by small woodlot owners increased in the 1980s. In 1987 small woodlot owners harvested more than 50 per cent of the province's pulpwood for the first time since 1970.[145]

A final questionable claim against the FIA was its violation of property rights. No property rights are absolute, as evidenced by the challenge of woodlot owners' "rights" when the FIA was first introduced in the 1960s. Moreover, mandatory

---

141 PFPIB, 2 September 1969, RG 81, vol. 3, no. 15; Staff Meeting on FIA, 7 January 1974, and Minutes of the 9th 1974 Meeting of the PFPIB, 13 September 1974, p. 2, RG 81, vol. 13, no. 6, PANS.

142 Fairn to Hon. Ken Streatch, 22 February 1984, RG 81, vol. 3, file 4, PANS.

143 Transcripts of the Royal Commission on Forestry, 1984, RG 44, vol. 159, no. 2, p. 99, PANS. This point was sadly ignored in the final report.

144 Sandberg, "Swedish Forestry Legislation in Nova Scotia", pp. 192-3.

145 From 1970 to 1979, the small private holdings produced an average of 40 per cent of all pulpwood in the province. From 1980 to 1989, this share increased to 49 per cent. Nova Scotia, Department of Lands and Forests, data files, Forest Resources, Planning and Mensuration, Truro, Nova Scotia.

forest legislation may very well be accepted socially and politically by small wood-lot owners, if only public input is allowed, and they are assured a fair share of the wood market and a fair price for their wood.[146]

The pulp industry arguments prevailed in the demise of the Forest Improvement Act. The reasons are many. One refers to the inability of the soft technology and environmentalist factions, as well as the marginal participants in the forest industry, to form a cohesive coalition. Environmentalists remained isolated from the FIA, many categorically opposed the use of pesticides and herbicides and, moreover, criticized the forest manual published by the PFPIB in 1980.[147] There was also a general neglect of linking the success of forest management to improvements in the price and market structure of the forest industry. The Forestry Sector Committee of Voluntary Planning, for example, which supported the FIA, opposed the development of a marketing structure for small woodlot owners.[148] Another reason refers to the ideological shift in the foresters' profession toward technocentrism and the pulp and paper industry. No doubt, there was dissent within the foresters' ranks, but the pulp and paper industry position prevailed. Foresters were threatened by the district board structures and had much to gain from the administration of the federal-provincial agreements. Many of the company foresters were something more than professionals; they were also employees pressured to toe the line of their employers.

A final reason for the failure of the FIA is related to the political and economic clout of the pulp and paper industry. In the beginning years of the FIA, the industry factions envisaged the PFPIB and the district boards as vehicles to promote wood production and management on small woodlots. When the PFPIB became a forum for the soft industrial position, the industry factions first stayed on the boards as a "damage control" measure.[149] In time, the industry factions on the PFPIB openly criticized the FIA and the policy initiatives of the PFPIB, and the Nova Scotia Section of the Canadian Institute of Forestry urged its members to nominate "industry oriented persons" to the PFPIB and take major topics directly to the minister (not through the board), otherwise they would get "watered down".[150] At this point, the pulp and paper industry had asserted its dominance in the woods harvesting sector.

---

146 This is clearly the case in Sweden. See Stjernquist, *Laws in the Forest*, and Sandberg, "Swedish Forestry Legislation in Nova Scotia".

147 Two reviews, from an environmentalist perspective, argued that the manual promoted monoculture in favour of the forest industry, RG 81, vol. 2, file 25, PANS.

148 Clancy, "The Politics of Pulpwood Marketing".

149 Interviewees intimated that their role on the PFPIB was to contain environmentalist initiatives rather than to facilitate the implementation of the FIA. On those rare occasions when consensus was reached on the board, it often resulted in later retractions by the transnational corporations.

150 Nova Scotia Section, CIF, Report of the 21st Annual Meeting, 1976.

The supply of pulpwood exceeded the demand, with no organized marketing mechanism in place to stabilize the situation.[151] Sawmillers depended on the pulp companies' freeholds and Crown leases for sawlogs; they also depended on the pulp mills as a market for wood chips. Sawmillers' vulnerability was further increased by the fact that Bowater Mersey and Scott Maritimes operated two of the largest sawmills in the province.[152] Forest harvesting contractors and truckers, many heavily in debt, depended on the pulp mills for contracts. It was not strange that the criticisms of the FIA found many receptive ears, and that by 1986, the FIA was no more.

---

151 Clancy, " The Politics of Pulpwood Marketing".

152 For an eloquent and convincing statement of the pulp and paper companies' domination of the sawmilling sector, see "Wood Products Manufacturers' Association Submission to the Royal Commission on Forestry 1984", pp. 90ff, RG44, vol. 158b, no. 3, PANS.

Symptom or Solution?
The Nova Scotia Land Holdings Disclosure Act of 1969

Kell Antoft

In Nova Scotia, the private ownership of more than two-thirds of the total provincial forest acreage is a key determinant of how the resource is exploited. Crown lands can readily be made subject to public management policies, but the extension of such policies to private woodlots is no simple matter. The individual or corporate owner may have a variety of objectives for his or her piece of resource property. Some owners may be content with their woodlot as a source of lumber and firewood for family use, some look to a yearly cropping of pulpwood to supplement farm income, others may place their priority on Christmas tree production, while still others hold the land in reserve for recreation, for resale speculation, or for eventual development through subdivision.

During the postwar decades, successive Nova Scotia governments sought to put in place incentive programmes that would help to attract investment in the forestry sector. The relatively modest proportion of lands in public ownership made it essential that private owners be enlisted in the overall campaign to establish new pulp, paper and other forest-related industrial enterprises. Examples that best illustrate the results of the campaign include the Stora Kopparberg mill at Port Hawkesbury, the Scott Maritimes paper mill at Abercrombie in Pictou County, and the hardboard plant at East River in Lunenburg County.

But securing the participation of individual owners is fraught with complications. During the last half of the 1960s, such complications were compounded by indications that sizeable portions of Nova Scotia land were being acquired by purchasers resident outside the province. Questions inevitably arose about who these "non-resident" newcomers were, and what land-use changes, if any, might result from their property acquisitions.[1] There were no easy answers, since there was no readily available information on their identity, home addresses, or even locations for their Nova Scotia holdings. From within the Conservative administration of G.I. Smith arose a legislative initiative to seek information that could shed some light on these questions. The story of this initiative offers interesting insights into the political culture of Nova Scotia.

---

1   In this paper, I use a simple definition of "non-resident" as anyone whose principal residence is not within the province. Where the paper makes reference to a Nova Scotia resident who owns land elsewhere than together with a principal residence, the distinction will be made clear.

On 25 April 1969, the lieutenant-governor of Nova Scotia assented to "An Act to Provide for the Disclosure of Land Holdings by Non-Residents and Certain Corporations". This paper will review the legislation's provisions, how the legislation came into being, its strengths and weaknesses, the attempts to encourage compliance and the eventual abandonment of effective enforcement. Finally, questions will be posed to illustrate the need for the type of information that the act sought to provide. Such a review may shed light on Nova Scotia attitudes towards the acquisition of real estate by non-residents, and may underline some unsolved problems of absentee ownership.

In the late 1960s, "non-resident land ownership" of Nova Scotia shoreland, farm and forest properties became the subject of earnest and often heated debate. On the one hand, alarm was voiced by planners, environmentalists, conservationists and Canadian nationalists at indications that large acreages of both resource and scenic Nova Scotia were being purchased by eager buyers from outside the province, particularly from the United States. On the other hand, the developing market for land considered marginal was welcomed as a boon by the rural owners whose livelihoods had previously offered little prospect of improvement. The old homestead — unpainted, drafty and decaying — had unexpectedly become a nest-egg, a promise of security and comfort in old age.

Nova Scotia thus became a valued object in the continent-wide hunger for land. Indeed, the evidence of this modern "back to the land" movement was emerging everywhere. This land hunger radiated outwards from the cities of North America, bringing weekend land buyers into the rural hinterlands in droves, crowding the tax sales of rural municipalities, filling the corridors of land registry and assessment offices and fuelling the growth of real estate enterprises specializing in recreational land transactions. As prices responded to demand, the search fanned ever outwards. The geographical proximity to, as well as historical connections between, New England and the Maritime Provinces made it inevitable that the search would soon reach our shores.

Nova Scotia in particular felt the pressure of this land market strongly in the late 1960s and early 1970s. The press and broadcast media noted with unease that something fundamental seemed to be happening to rural Nova Scotia, and voices were heard to suggest that "something ought to be done" about it. Initially, the debate centred on specific instances where ocean frontage, in passing into the hands of non-Nova Scotians, had been closed off to public access. In some cases, as with Risser's Beach in Lunenburg County, the new owners "from away" attempted to bar beach access to local inhabitants, for whom the concept of trespassing had little meaning. In other instances, the revelation that public beaches were being lost at an alarming rate to out-of-province buyers aroused concern for the tourism industry. An important document in this process of awareness was the 1967 Agricultural and Rural Development Act (ARDA) study on Cape Breton Island authored by Redpath and Raymond.[2] Non-resident land ownership had not been specifically included in the terms of reference for this study, but the topic emerged as a major interest of the investigators. The relevance of this as a factor in the development of tourism was set forth bluntly:

> Aside from Baddeck and the summer cottage colonies near Sydney on East Bay, the traveller is left with the impression that tourism has made few inroads in this magnificent setting. While this may be quite true in a commercial sense, it is quite false in terms of land resource. Property maps compiled for 539 miles of the Bras d'Or shoreline in 1967 indicate that 188 miles (34.5 per cent) are controlled by non-residents who own some 59,435 acres [24,071 ha] of land in lots of more than five acres.[3]

But the unease was not limited to shoreline or tourism. Anxiety was also being voiced over the alienation of agricultural and forestry lands. In the proceedings of sector committees of Voluntary Economic Planning (VEP) — which in 1970 became Voluntary Planning — a government-private sector organization, the escalation of land costs and the transfer of ownership of formerly productive property to non-resident ownership appeared as frequent and prominent topics.

This public discussion aroused a growing demand for more comprehensive information on the extent of absentee ownership in the province. Such data were sparse, or at best difficult to retrieve. In response to this obvious need, the provincial government of the day introduced a bill entitled the Land Holdings Disclosure Act (LHDA). The first version of this proposed legislation required non-resident owners of property to file a disclosure statement with a provincial registrar describing their holdings, how they were acquired and their intended uses.[4] The stated purpose of the bill was simply to provide data not readily retrievable from deed registry offices. The bill thus envisaged a relatively simple procedure for gathering and tabulating information on the extent and location of lands owned by non-residents of Nova Scotia.

The debate on the bill during its passage through the legislative process illustrates the underlying caution that has characterized both the Liberal and Progressive Conservative parties in struggling with the question of absentee ownership. The Tory government disclaimed any suggestion of interference with the free market for land, pleading that awareness of the situation was all that was intended.

---

2   Kenneth Redpath and Charles Raymond, "Tourist Development: Western Cumberland County and Southern Cape Breton Island" (Truro, 1967).

3   Redpath and Raymond, "Tourist Development", p. 28.

4   For the purposes of the Land Holdings Disclosure Act, a non-resident was defined to mean an individual who is not a permanent resident of Nova Scotia.

The Minister of Lands and Forests, George Snow, set forth this view during the debate:

> this legislation does not interfere with the right of any person, including non-residents and aliens, or with the right of corporations,...to freely dispose of and acquire land within the Province.
>
> * * *
>
> We feel that it is desirable to be able to keep track of the lands owned by non-residents, so that if it should ever reach the stage where the public interest might suffer, appropriate action may be taken.

The Liberals opposed even this modest objective, arguing that the bill was an invasion of the traditional right of privacy enjoyed by property owners in Nova Scotia. The leader of the opposition, Gerald Regan, suggested that the bill would create uneasiness, which, "at a time when the province was encouraging investment...might not be in the province's best interest".[5]

The bill as first presented contained the operative registration requirements in the following language:

> 4.(1) Every non-resident who acquires a land holding in the Province shall immediately upon completion or operation of the document of conveyance deliver to the Registrar a disclosure statement.
>
> (2) Every non-resident who owns a land holding in the province on the day on which this act comes into force shall, within one year of the day on which this Act comes into force, deliver to the Registrar a disclosure statement.
>
> (3) Every non-resident who fails to comply with subsection (1) or with subsection (2) shall be guilty of an offence and liable on summary conviction to a penalty not exceeding one thousand dollars.[6]

In the final version, however, an important change resulted from the urgings of Gerald Regan. This amendment inserted the word "wilfully" into subsection (3) so that the sentence as enacted starts: "Every non-resident who *wilfully* fails to comply...."[7] The result of this minor editorial change was crucial. In effect it removed the likelihood of an effective penalty for non-disclosure, since the prosecution would have to prove that failure to comply resulted from a "wilful" intent. Furthermore, the act as adopted offered no indication on to how to deal with offending absentee owners living outside the province.

The fear of doing anything that would appear to infringe on property rights undoubtedly was the reason for the large loophole in the act with respect to

---

5   Nova Scotia, House of Assembly, *Proceedings*, 27 February 1969.

6   N.S., *Proceedings*, 27 February 1969.

7   N.S., *Proceedings*, 27 February 1969.

corporations. Section 5 forcefully proclaims that "every corporation that acquires a land holding in the Province shall immediately...have delivered to the Registrar a disclosure statement", and further that "every corporation that owns a land holding in the Province on the day on which this Act comes into force shall within one year...have delivered to the Registrar a disclosure statement". But exemptions are made in the case of a corporation —

> (a) that is incorporated by or under any Act of the Legislature of Nova Scotia;
> (b) that holds a certificate of registration issued under the Corporations Registration Act; or
> (c) that actually carries on its business and has erected an office, plant, factory or other structure on the land holding.

Thus, to put it mildly, the 1969 LHDA lacked teeth. If an owner was not inclined to make disclosure, it was easy to see that out-of-province prosecution was impractical, or that failure to comply would have to be proven to be a wilful deed. In any case, complete protection for privacy of ownership could easily be ensured by the simple device of retaining title through a private holding company with provincial incorporation.

When the act came into force on 1 January 1970, its administration was assigned to a registrar within the Department of Lands and Forests. This involved preparation of regulations, the collecting of names of out-of-province owners, distribution of the reporting questionnaire, and finally, tabulation of the results from the replies. The names and addresses of non-resident owners were obtained from lists compiled by the 14 regional municipal assessment offices throughout the province. Owners received a copy of the regulations together with the questionnaire form. Responses initially arrived at a moderately brisk rate, but at the end of the first year the overall response had barely reached 50 per cent of those surveyed.

Apart from this modest numerical response, the first crop of replies revealed serious flaws in the questionnaire. These weaknesses were described in a report delivered to the provincial government in 1972:

> The present disclosure statement form requires information from the owner about (a) names (b) place of residence (c) mailing address (d) location of the N.S. land holdings (e) method and date of acquisition (f) registration date and place (g) a description of the land holding (h) purpose for which the land holding was acquired (i) the names of previous owner if a non-resident (j) details of other owners or nominee relationships.[8]

---

8   Kell Antoft, Paul Brown, Jane Henson, Gerry Mendleson, Michel Tadros, Gordon Zive and Susan Antoft, *Matters Related to Non-resident Land Ownership in Nova Scotia* (Halifax, 1971).

The suggestions for addressing these problem areas included the following:

> In order to provide data significant for research purposes...the Land Holdings Disclosure Act should be amended to require the following additional information:
> (a) disclosure of the name of the former owner, whether resident or non-resident
> (b) the price paid for the property
> (c) the acreage and dimensions of the property
> (d) the amount of water frontage, if any
> (e) the size and approximate age of any buildings erected on the land
> (f) details of any liens, encumbrances, easements or any other restrictions on title
> (g) details of leases and options affecting the property
>
> * * *
>
> Disclosure statements have not been obtained from a large percentage of non-residents. This weakness stems partly from the failure of the Act to provide enforceable penalties, and partly from the overwhelming clerical task of maintaining lists of non-residents, processing statements, and following up those who fail to respond to the initial request.[9]

This report urged that the registrar be provided with sufficient staff to deal effectively with the information collected, and further that a deed transfer tax be made mandatory throughout the province. Such a tax and its accompanying declaration would serve to provide timely data on non-resident acquisitions of real property for the purposes of the Land Holdings Disclosure Act.

These suggestions were received with considerable interest by officials of the Department of Lands and Forests, and some of the recommendations were incorporated in revised regulations. There were also preliminary discussions aimed at drafting amendments to the act itself to simplify enforcement, but these did not result in legislative changes. The proposal to make the deed transfer tax universal throughout the province, thereby forcing disclosure of all future real estate transactions, likewise did not at that time attract support from the political leaders.[10]

---

9   Antoft et al., *Non-resident Land Ownership in N.S.*

10 The N.S. Deed Transfer Tax Act permits, but does not require, municipal units to collect a deed transfer tax calculated as a percentage of the sale price of real property. The affidavit required in jurisdictions where the tax is collected is a valuable source of information for a variety of purposes, including property valuation assessment. In 1972 only about a third of the 65 municipal units in the province had adopted this municipal tax option. By 1989 about half of the municipal units had instituted the tax. In 1990 the province introduced its own deed transfer tax, and presumably the resulting information will provide a means of tracking future land transactions involving out-of-province purchasers.

Thus, beyond discussions and some changes in the formulating questions contained in the disclosure form, little happened to alter the substance or the administration of the legislation. In the face of multiple pleas for better information, why did the government not act to put real teeth into the LHDA? A clue may be found in the statement made by a senior official of the Department of Lands and Forests to a conference on shorelands the following spring:

> It has been argued that a fundamental right to privacy has been violated by the Act.
>
> * * *
>
> While the enforcement of this Act by legal action, even of penalties, might be upheld, the obtaining of political agreement at provincial and municipal levels might be more difficult. The fact that only a few municipalities have adopted the Deed Transfer Tax is evidence of political sensitivity in the area.[11]

Was this concern for privacy a reflection of public attitudes? During the early 1970s, there was widespread debate on the issue of non-resident land acquisition. In 1973 a select committee of the legislative assembly, set up to examine the question, held a series of public meetings throughout the province. It is noteworthy that of all the diverse views offered, not a single brief took issue with the LHDA. Indeed, many of the submissions argued for a concerted drive to assemble more reliable information on how extensive these absentee owner holdings had become. Amendments to the LHDA to strengthen its provisions were urged by organizations as diverse as the Nova Scotia Federation of Labour, the VP and the Union of Nova Scotia Municipalities. In a detailed review of all the submissions made to the legislators, as well as in a careful reading of newspaper reports during the debate, the following conclusion was drawn:

> information gathering, whether under the Land Holdings Disclosure Act or by some form of compulsory deed registry system, is not really an issue that arouses deep political emotions, and that rationalization of the process should cause no major confrontations.[12]

While administrative problems in 1970 and 1971 prevented the Department of Lands and Forests from responding adequately to requests for information on the

---

11 E.E. Atkins, " The Land Holdings Disclosure Act of Nova Scotia", in Canada, Lands Directorate, *Shoreland: Its Use, Ownership, Access and Management* (Halifax, 1972), p. 41.

12 Kell Antoft, "Interventionist Pressures in a Pragmatic Society: A Policy Study of the Non-resident Land Ownership Issue in Nova Scotia 1969-1977", M.A. thesis, Dalhousie University, 1977, p. 102.

extent and nature of absentee ownership, public concern was reflected in an increasing flow of stories in the media. Some headline examples will illustrate the tenor of this discussion:

"Depressed Land Values Skyrocketing in N.S. - MacGlashen" (10 February 1970)

"Americans Becoming Interested in Purchasing Land" (11 April 1970)

"N.S. Acts to Halt Land Sales Trend" (18 April 1970)

"N.S. Land Being Bought Up by Americans" (15 May 1970)

"Colchester County Sale of Lands to Non-Residents" (15 May 1970)

"Non-Residents Own 10,000 Properties" (10 August 1970)

"Must Non-Residents Own our Land, Water?" (28 February 1971)

"Birthright and Beaches" (3 May 1971)

"Puzzled by Reluctance in Providing Details of Land Ownership" (14 May 1971)

"Percentage of N.S. Land Owned by Non-Residents Alarming" (28 June 1971)[13]

Nor was the debate limited to comment from within Nova Scotia. Absentee ownership was becoming a public issue in most of the other Canadian provinces. But national magazines and broadcast networks seized particularly on the buying pressures being experienced in Nova Scotia and Prince Edward Island. This combined national and provincial media interest created an increasing demand for data which could give more factual substance to the debate. From this evolved a number of studies by academics and their students. In several instances, citizens groups sought to collect statistical data within their own communities to help develop their understanding and formulate position papers.[14] But only the provincial government commanded the resources and access to information required to undertake a survey on a province-wide basis. After several false starts, the Department of Lands and Forests appointed Mr. Bruce Wilmhurst to direct the programme, providing him with staff necessary for the systematic analysis of the information collected from the initial LHDA returns. In August 1973 the first of a series of reports on the results of this work appeared.

Although Wilmhurst's first report acknowledged a number of important gaps in the data, it provided a significant starting point. Particularly useful was its profile of

---

13 These headlines, with the exception of the last item, all appeared in the Halifax *Chronicle Herald* on the dates shown. The 28 June 1971 headline appeared in the New Glasgow *Evening News*.

14 For a brief discussion of the scope of those that resulted in public reports, see Antoft, "Interventionist Pressures", p. 106.

the rate at which property had been acquired by the non-resident respondents. This indicated a steep upward trend in the pattern of purchases (see Figure 1). The initial questionnaires revealed some of the shortcomings in the type of information provided, and the previously mentioned revision of the regulations took place. As a result, additional information became available that was more specific and therefore of more value for analysis. The new questionnaire required a plan or sketch of the land holding showing its relationship to abutting properties, as well as a statement of total acreage. Information on water frontage and the name of the previous owner also helped to improve the information collection. From these replies, the department undertook to plot the location of properties on a series of county maps. In this way, the act gradually came to be more useful in its intended purpose, although effective and universal compliance was not achieved. The difficulties encountered are detailed in a subsequent report prepared by Wilmhurst:

> Serious difficulties were encountered in attempting to assemble data on non-resident ownerships. While the [Land Holdings Disclosure Act] requires full disclosure to the province, it is apparent that the requirement is not being fulfilled in many instances. It is estimated that disclosures do not exceed 65% even after follow-up attempts in 1970 and 1972. In addition, of those disclosure statements filed only a small percentage could be accurately plotted on maps.[15]

By 1975 the data collection of the Department of Lands and Forests had become better organized, but the questionnaire returns continued to lag. The previous procedure of relying on figures compiled in the regional assessment offices was replaced by a process of microfilming individual assessment cards from each county, with sorting carried out directly under Wilmhurst's supervision. The result of this careful treatment of the available data resulted in a county-by-county tabulation (see Table I). This shows the situation in 1975, and even today effectively remains the latest available data for sensing the degree of non-resident land ownership in the province as a whole!

What is reasonably well established from Wilmhurst's work is that at least 800,000 acres (324,000 ha) of Nova Scotia land were owned in 1975 by individual non-residents, not including corporate holdings. Of approximately 12,000 absentee owners in that year, about two-thirds were American, with the remainder from other Canadian provinces, Ontario in particular. A considerable portion of these holdings involved water frontage, but the exact distribution between inland and coastal holdings is uncertain. The average size of holdings per owner in 1973 was about 65 acres (26 ha). The rate of acquisition shows that prior to 1967, new additions to absentee ownership had been at about 20,000 to 25,000 acres (8,100 to 10,125 ha) per

---

15   Bruce Wilmhurst and Lee MacNeill, *Nova Scotia Salt Water Frontage: Ownership and Classification* (Halifax, 1974), p. iii.

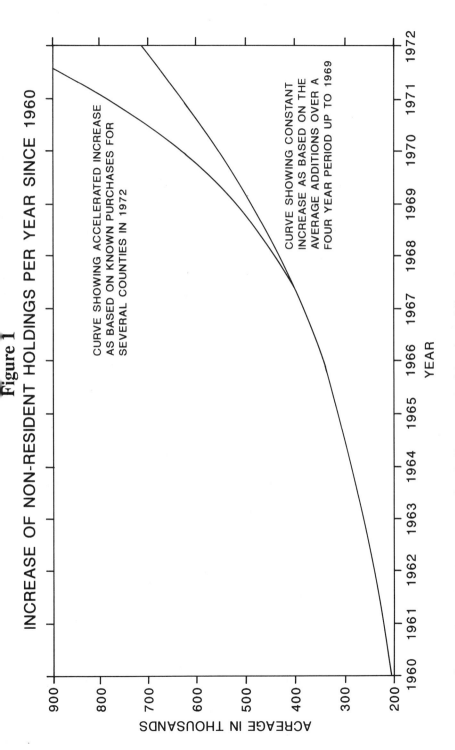

Figure 1

INCREASE OF NON-RESIDENT HOLDINGS PER YEAR SINCE 1960

CURVE SHOWING ACCELERATED INCREASE AS BASED ON KNOWN PURCHASES FOR SEVERAL COUNTIES IN 1972

CURVE SHOWING CONSTANT INCREASE AS BASED ON THE AVERAGE ADDITIONS OVER A FOUR YEAR PERIOD UP TO 1969

YEAR

ACREAGE IN THOUSANDS

Source: Bruce Wilmhurst, Nova Scotia Department of Lands and Forests.

year. Following that year, the annual rate rose at an accelerated pace, and had reached at least 100,000 acres (40,500 ha) by the year 1973.

The 1976 Annual Report of the Department of Lands and Forests contains a table showing the department's estimate of land holdings for 1975 (see Table II). The non-resident land holdings estimate is based on LHDA data. This estimate represents the final year for which questionnaires were circulated and replies actively solicited under the act. Without an alternative method of tracking transactions, there is no current overview of how much of Nova Scotia is in non-resident ownership.

The rate of acquisition has slowed since the mid-1970s, partly due to the subsequent economic downturn, partly due to the "catch-up" of Nova Scotia land prices in comparison to prices in northeastern New England, and partly arising from some degree of resale of land by non-residents. On the other hand, there is considerable indirect evidence that acquisitions continue, but in a much different form. Reports of Nova Scotia land purchases for "investment" purposes by West Europeans, Asians and South Americans are widely circulated.[16] More and more holdings appear on municipal assessment rolls as being held by private companies incorporated in Nova Scotia, but with indeterminate parentage. But much of this is speculation. Political events of the mid-1970s placed the issue of absentee ownership on the "back-burner", and suspended further effective enforcement of the LHDA.

The wave of land buying by non-residents in the decade up to the energy crisis of the mid-1970s left a substantial proportion of Nova Scotia's economically important land surface in the hands of absentee owners. Much of this land was acquired for "recreational" purposes, but the effect was often to put former farm lands and woodlots out of current economic use. A secondary consequence was to drive up land values to levels more closely approaching those of rural property in the New England states. While rising prices for land provided greater prospective security for existing farmers through capital appreciation, the higher costs made farming and woodlot operation a less attractive business venture. The cost of land often rose above the level at which it was reasonable to acquire it for farming or forestry purposes, thereby discouraging young Nova Scotians from entering or continuing in these rural occupations.

It was not only farmers and foresters who felt the competition for the land resource in this way. Native Nova Scotians from the cities and towns have found that the ownership of a cottage lot in rural Nova Scotia has become an impossible dream. A more recent consequence of the competition is the spill-over of buying into the development industry. Prices of town and city lots are undoubtedly deterring thousands of young people from becoming owners rather than renters. The

---

16 For a summary of some of the anecdotal evidence, see Land Research Group, "Whither Our Land? Who Owns Nova Scotia? And What Are They Doing With It?" *New Maritimes* VIII, 6 (July/August 1990), pp. 14-25.

influence of investments from abroad on this part of the market is a subject that calls for further research.[17]

Substantial value increments in Nova Scotia land are accruing to individuals and companies who may eventually remove these profits from Nova Scotia, with negative economic implications for the province. Additional capital costs will have to be added to future land-based economic activities. Such costs will become a further burden on the ability of Nova Scotians to carry on viable activities in agriculture, forestry and tourism.

Prince Edward Island has seen a debate in the past years on whether a differential property tax rate on land owned by non-residents is fair. The argument in favour of taxing absentee owners more heavily than residents centres on the fact that property taxes are only a small proportion of the tax revenues needed to sustain the provincial infrastructure. Non-residents do not contribute to the province's revenues from income tax, sales tax, gasoline and motor vehicle registration taxes. On the other hand, they may not consume some of the services financed by these taxes, such as education, health and social services. Whether the property tax is a sufficient part of the cost of the amenities that go with ownership remains largely a matter of opinion.

In Nova Scotia, this part of the debate has hardly surfaced. In this province, an additional factor is the total exemption from property tax that is enjoyed by farmland, and the reduced taxation of forest land. It is clear that these provisions of the Assessment Act make the owning of resource land in Nova Scotia a much less expensive proposition than is the case elsewhere. But without effective means of tracking ownership and of reporting statistics, both the policy makers and the public remain unaware of the relative importance of such questions, and whether indeed the situation is a cause for concern. The enactment of the Land Holdings Disclosure Act in 1969 was a symptom of public apprehension in that era, but the deeply rooted commitment of the Nova Scotia governmental establishment to the protection of property rights has frustrated most efforts to narrow the information gap.

---

17 A recent study of land ownership in Annapolis County, Nova Scotia, has provided more recent information on non-resident real estate purchases in that part of the province. The author again underscores the difficulty of obtaining information and notes the inadequacy of the Land Holdings Disclosure Act in addressing the problem. See Daniel P. Bulger, *Annapolis County Land Ownership Study* (Lawrencetown, N.S., 1991).

Table I

Projections Based on Information From Land Holdings Disclosure Act Reports, 1973-1975

County	Total Non-Resident Acres		1973		1975*	
	1973	1975	Owners	Lots	Owners	Lots
Annapolis	15,798	61,855	375	519	968	1,245
Antigonish	21,760	22,400	314	445	368	398
Cape Breton	46,748	n.a.**	821	1,001	n.a.	n.a.
Colchester	22,659	31,122	n.a.	587	494	593
Cumberland	75,653	75,746	1,291	1,845	n.a.	1,176
Digby	60,147	51,350	882	1,569	1,373	1,765
Guysborough	61,372	53,165	578	953	686	860
Halifax	55,156	n.a.	1,065	1,490	n.a.	n.a.
Hants	14,528	14,325	194	274	n.a.	444
Inverness	82,548	131,450	824	1,154	1,323	1,528
Kings	12,883	13,497	320	470	355	546
Lunenburg	25,957	36,200	761	1,210	936	1,134
Queens	22,799	26,846	374	606	708	1,071
Pictou	28,118	33,500	509	689	644	908
Richmond	45,940	42,592	486	671	n.a.	605
Shelburne	53,313	46,100	875	1,435	n.a.	1,086
Victoria	55,556	61,947	565	784	660	739
Yarmouth	25,719	35,164	734	1,174	n.a.	1,115
Total Province	726,923	839,163*	11,348	16,976	n.a.	17,703*

* assuming Halifax and Cape Breton to have remained constant from 1973-1975
** n.a. = not available

Source: Bruce Wilmhurst, *Land Holdings Disclosure Act Reports,* 1973-1975.

Table II

1975 Land Holdings Distribution in Nova Scotia

Holdings	Acres
Non-resident holdings, reportable under the Land Holdings Disclosure Act (does not include corporations registered in Nova Scotia)	800,000
Crown lands - provincial	3,282,477
- federal	464,000
Bowater Mersey, Scott Maritimes and others	1,864,400
Total area	13,711,789
excluding lakes and rivers	13,056,422

Source: *Annual Report, 1976*, Department of Lands and Forests, Province of Nova Scotia.

Conclusion:
Maritime Forest Sector Development:
A Question of Hard Choices

Peter Clancy and L. Anders Sandberg

This volume outlines some of the routes by which the pulp and paper sector has established economic and political dominance in New Brunswick and Nova Scotia. The preceding papers advance a number of analytical themes in discussing industry development and state policy formation over the past century. In this concluding section, we seek to project certain of these themes into the contemporary period, offering some speculative comments on the present and future state of forest politics and social conflict in the two provinces.*

Several of the papers have described the forest industry in historical terms, delineating the dominant class interests of the day. Maritime merchants and independent sawmillers dominated the era of square timber and rough lumber exports in the 19th and early 20th centuries, but the pulp and paper sector achieved industrial status after the First World War and sectoral dominance after the Second World War. While the postwar generation saw impressive expansion in industry investment and output, considerable evidence now suggests that this prosperous interlude has come to a close. As is usual during a period of industrial restructuring, the socio-political order struggles to perpetuate itself, creating both opportunities and challenges for its constituent class interests.

What will come next in the pulp and paper industry? At the manufacturing level, the Maritime industry shares the predicament of the Canadian forest sector as a whole. The industry is now constrained by the same factors that brought it strength in past decades: its product mix, scale of production and international competitive position. As Woodbridge Reed has pointed out, the success of the 1950s, 1960s and 1970s was based on the low-cost production of several standard commodities, in particular market pulp and newsprint.[1] Over the past decade, there has been dramatic global change in these segments: fast-growing tropical hardwoods provide low-cost fibre inputs; hardwood pulp now rivals northern bleached softwood kraft as the premium grade; new pulp and paper plant capacity far exceeds the Canadian

*   We are currently exploring many of these issues in a broader study of Nova Scotia entitled "From the Woodlot to the Mill: Forest Capitalism in Twentieth Century Nova Scotia". We gratefully acknowledge the financial support of the Social Sciences and Humanities Research Council under Grant No. 410-91-0460.

1   Woodbridge Reed and Associates, *Canada's Forest Industry: The Next Twenty Years* (Ottawa, 1988).

and Maritime norm; and the standard commodities are no longer high-profit products.[2]

Even as these structural forces unfolded, the Maritime industry remained broadly profitable. Companies rode the forest product cycle, with new entrants and capacity expansions during the growth phases of the 1960s and 1980s, and retrenchment during the slumps of the mid-1970s and late 1980s. New pulping processes such as thermo-mechanical and chemi-thermo-mechanical were installed in some mills, while others adhered to the more conventional sulphate (kraft) and sulphite processes.[3] In the case of paper-making, the technology changes have been more modest, focusing on higher machine speeds and improved finishing. Over the period 1979-84, a federal pulp and paper modernization programme disbursed over half a billion dollars nationally, to accelerate capital investment within the sector in the face of declining exports. This was a belated acknowledgement that Canada's aging plants were ill-equipped for long-run competitive production.[4]

Canadian plants were fully exposed to the new international competition during the 1989 downturn in the pulp and paper markets. As the reference price for market pulp slipped from $860 U.S. per tonne (June 1989) to $500 U.S. (October 1991), Canadian companies were forced to curtail and in some cases cease production in their higher-cost plants. The newsprint sector was also hit, and total shipments declined by 5.5 per cent in 1990 and 3.5 per cent in 1991. The predicament of Canadian producers was exacerbated by a rising Canadian dollar, which imposed an additional burden in the drive to defend export market shares. Total industry capacity in 1991 stood at 85 per cent. In aggregate, Canadian firms lost a record $1.5 billion that year, which was five times more severe than the worst year of the previous recession.[5] At the time of writing, the Eastern Canadian firms are seeking across-the-board wage freezes from their unionized workers.[6]

As most Maritime companies are headquartered beyond the region, they also operate plants in other provinces and countries. Their rationalization strategies are determined largely by the product mixes and comparative cost structures of various plants. Older mills may house dated equipment, new facilities may denote high-

---

2   M. Patricia Marchak, "For Whom the Tree Falls: Restructuring of the Global Forest Industry", Paper presented to the Canadian Political Science/Anthropology and Sociology Meetings, Victoria, 1990.

3   For a discussion of pulp and paper processes, see William F. Sinclair, *Controlling Pollution from Canadian Pulp and Paper Manufacturers: A Federal Perspective* (Ottawa, 1990), ch. 2.

4   K.E.A. de Silva, *Pulp and Paper Modernization Grants Program — An Assessment,* Economic Council of Canada, Discussion Paper 350 (Ottawa, 1988).

5   *Globe and Mail* (Toronto), 24 January 1992.

6   *Globe and Mail,* 23 January 1992.

debt leverage, and the wage costs and delivered cost of raw wood may vary significantly.

In times of recession, conditions in the processing industry tend to attract exceptional attention. Here plant closures and job losses are easily measured, in contrast with the smaller scale and seasonally fluctuating state of the primary market. New Brunswick, like Ontario and Quebec, has been hit particularly hard by mill closures. One industry executive forecasts that, by the end of this business cycle, the province's 11 plants could be reduced to six or seven.[7] Already there has been one permanent closure, while two others were only averted through major financial bail-outs by the provincial government.[8] For the rest, permanent job cuts and more frequent temporary shutdowns are the order of the day (Table I).

The severity of the downturn in New Brunswick has had a cathartic effect on the provincial government of Frank McKenna, which in January 1992 announced an "industry survival package" in hopes of stabilizing the situation.[9] Significantly, the programme was formulated to stabilize the processing segment of the forest sector, by means of "[reduced] power rates, deferred payments of stumpage rates, and changes in regulations governing wood supply". These policy concessions are contingent upon corporations reaching new wage agreements with their unionized employees. In effect, the severity of this recession has managed to open the entire forest policy regime for renegotiation, on company terms. While the initiative is being resisted by the woodlot owner organizations, paper worker unions and opposition politicians, it nonetheless marks a decisive turning point in provincial forest policy.[10] There is a strong likelihood that Nova Scotia's "cheap fibre" strategy will be emulated in New Brunswick.

This in itself marks a major role reversal, since for the past decade it has been New Brunswick that offered the model to which small primary producers in Nova Scotia could aspire. The McKenna forest initiative assumes even greater significance in light of the Maritime premiers' recent joint initiative on a regional economic union. Since 1990 the three provinces have sponsored studies, negotiated

---

7   Adam Zimmerman in CBC Television interview, Saint John, New Brunswick, 7 October 1991.

8   "N.B. Bails out Repap", *Telegraph Journal* (Saint John), 13 June 1991; "Stone Consolidated, Union, Reach Deal to Save Mill", *Globe and Mail*, 23 March 1992.

9   See "Forestry Survival Plan in Works: Graham", *Telegraph Journal* (Saint John), 10 January 1992; and "N.B. Ties Strings to Forestry Aid", *Telegraph Journal*, 24 January 1992.

10 See "Forest Survival Plan Protested" and "Woodlot Owners Denounce Policy", *Telegraph Journal*, 24 January 1992; "Don't Single Out One Group as Scapegoat: Woodlot Owners", *Miramichi Leader Weekend*, 31 January 1992; "Mills Like Survival Plan but Unions Have Reservations", *Telegraph Journal*, 25 January 1992.

accords and begun harmonizing economic policies.[11] Through this they seek to achieve advantages of scale economies in both private production and public-service provision. Marketing regimes for primary commodities in agriculture, fishing and forestry will obviously form a major part of the plan. In the recessionary forest climate of 1992 and beyond, there is a strong possibility that policy harmonization will converge around the lowest common denominator.[12] The recent New Brunswick initiatives mark the beginning of this process.

For Nova Scotia, the present slump has been less volatile for the processors. The larger mills have been riding out the business cycle with temporary shutdowns and layoffs. While there has been no pressure to date for exceptional bail-outs, the Nova Scotia government under premier Don Cameron has shown its concern for wood fibre costs. Since September 1991 it has vigorously reaffirmed the status quo by discharging the chairman of the Pulpwood Marketing Board, and rejecting the reform process initiated by the board to realize higher prices and a larger market share for small private wood suppliers.[13]

Despite these recent developments, the tenuous position of the pulp and paper companies in the Maritimes should not be exaggerated. Forest companies came to the region on very favourable terms. When the industry calls on the state to "assist" it in weathering hard times, it is reading from a well-worn script. As the preceding papers have shown, most companies jealously guard their operating environment in the Maritimes. They enjoy unparalleled access to raw fibre. Wood from Crown leases is obtained on generous if not concessionary terms, and purchased wood is the cheapest in Canada. While some plant closures may be inevitable in the present slump, the overall impact on Maritime industry should be gauged not in absolute terms, but relative to the pulp and paper industry as a whole.

The closure of plants is never welcome, and the economic and social dislocations cannot be minimized. Such events can, however, hold opportunities as well as costs. Where the underlying assets are sound, facilities may be reopened or strengthened under new ownership, as Quebec's Tembec mill has demonstrated. Where no corporate buyer shows interest, employee ownership can be considered with state support, as in the case of the Spruce Falls Pulp and Paper Co. in Ontario. In cases where the business cannot be revived, its forest land rights (Crown and private) may be redirected to entirely new enterprises, in order to diversify the processing sector in higher-value directions.

---

11 An intellectual foundation for this initiative can be found in Charles J. McMillan, *Standing Up to the Future,* Council of Maritime Premiers (Halifax, 1990). The policy agenda was outlined in Council of Maritime Premiers, *Challenge and Opportunity* (Halifax, 1991).

12 For a discussion of the forest sector impact see Peter Clancy, "The Political Significance of Maritime Economic Union: A Case Study from the Forest Industry", mimeo, 1992.

13 "Pulpwood Marketing Plan Scrapped", *Chronicle Herald* (Halifax), 6 May 1992; "Resources Minister Being Taken to Court", *Mail-Star* (Halifax), 5 June 1992.

It is important to remember that the new era involves much more than a global crisis in the secondary processing sector. In the Maritimes, some of the most important pressures for restructuring come from within, and many of these emerge from the primary forest (logging) sector.

Some of the contributions to this volume have shown that private woodlot owners faced sustained obstacles in their efforts to organize collective representation, and to elicit provincial state support for private wood marketing. In New Brunswick, the woodlot owners have achieved much greater organizational success, combining a series of seven regional marketing bodies within a provincial federation to act as a common voice. In Nova Scotia, two regional supply groups and one sectoral group (of large sawmillers) were formed in the early 1980s, after which the process stalled. Significantly, the average roadside price of private pulpwood in New Brunswick has led Nova Scotia for the past 20 years by as much as $25 per cord.

It is tempting to hypothesize that private woodlot interests enjoy policy leverage when wood supplies are tight, and that raised prices are viewed as an incentive to increase both the volumes produced and the numbers of producers. To the extent that mills can meet their needs from private corporate holdings and long-term Crown leases, the small private woodlot segment lacks market leverage and risks being marginalized and treated as a stored wood supply for future needs. Since 1980, the New Brunswick policy of designating private woodlots the primary source of supply, and making access to Crown leases contingent on signing contracts with the regional supply groups, has had some influence in protecting the woodlot share of the market and the roadside price levels.

While the woodlot owner groups continue to champion the cause of organized marketing, the structure of the woodlot owning segment has changed over the last generation. Rather than selling continually on the market, many of the small owners choose to sell occasionally, as their cash needs, or prevailing prices, dictate. Secondly, far fewer of the small and medium-sized woodlot owners — those owning fewer than 990 acres (401 ha) — choose to cut and haul their own logs to roadside. It is increasingly common to find small owners selling stumpage rights to logging contractors, who acquire the trees on the stump and market the logs that they harvest. As this occurs, the woodlot owner ceases to be an active market participant, and confines his or her involvement to the pre-harvesting stage. This can have a corrosive effect on the political mobilization of the woodlot owner constituency, seen most clearly to date in Nova Scotia.

As for the logging segment, where wood fibre is produced, marketed and regenerated, the story is also one of increasing differentiation among producers. The woods of Atlantic Canada were among the last in the nation to be mechanized. The small-scale independent logging contractor, utilizing mechanical skidders, truck transport, and power-saw cutters, came to the fore in the 1960s, as most pulp and paper mills opted to reduce or eliminate their direct woods labour force. In this way, much of the uncertainty, slack time and overhead costs associated with logging were shifted to a competitive, low-margin, small-business segment. This enabled the processors to fill their woodyard inventories while minimizing fibre supply costs.

As with any commercial small-producer category, logging contractors were squeezed between their costs of production and their returns on sale. While the wages paid to pulp cutters were notoriously low, the costs of financing capital equipment were substantial. Over time, logging operations either grew in size, with the acquisition of more harvesting equipment and the absorption of mounting debt loads, or remained small scale, seasonal and labour intensive. The processing mills often played a facilitating role in this process, by guaranteeing equipment loans or high-volume, long-term contracts (on the mills' Crown leases or corporate land). Since these underwriting decisions were highly discretionary, the pulp and paper mills not only shaped the logger's prospects for business growth, but also forged networks of closely aligned but formally independent contracting enterprises.

It is likely that these practices were confirmed and even accelerated by the state policies for private pulpwood marketing that came to fruition in the 1970s. Despite their manifest aim of increasing the price and market share for privately sold pulpwood, the mixed impact of the new marketing regimes allowed the processors to solidify supply networks beyond the reach of the marketing regime, through the agency of tied contractors. While this process went further in Nova Scotia than in New Brunswick, the political impact was similar by the late 1980s.

In Nova Scotia, another chapter in the politics of pulpwood marketing began in 1986, when the provincial government released its new forest policy statement.[14] For the next five years, the Primary Forest Products Marketing Board led an initiative to strengthen the Marketing Act, and devise a new procedure for organizing additional bargaining groups. While the detailed story cannot concern us here, these efforts were sharply resisted by the pulp and paper firms.[15] A key aspect of their strategy entailed mobilizing the contractors, whose vocal and visible representations were a decisive factor in staying the government's hand on the new procedure.

The situation in New Brunswick is equally revealing. For the past decade it was far more supportive of private woodlot interests. As described above, New Brunswick showed that with the political will, small-producer marketing could work effectively.[16] Over the past few years, however, the province has undertaken a

---

14 See Department of Lands and Forests, *Forest Policy* (Halifax, 1986).

15 For an analysis of Nova Scotia pulpwood marketing policy since 1986, see Peter Clancy, "Probing the Limits of Progressive Bureaucracy", Paper presented at the Annual Meeting of the Atlantic Provinces Political Science Association, October 1990, St. John's.

16 See Peter deMarsh, "Pulpwood Producer Marketing Organizations in New Brunswick", in Bryant Fairley, Colin Leys and James Sacouman, eds., *Restructuring and Resistance: Perspectives from Atlantic Canada* (Toronto, 1990), pp. 227-33.

review of the private marketing system.[17] This has culminated in the recently announced "survival strategy", which, by abandoning key features of the marketing
regime, accedes to the corporate agenda.

All of these controversies have revealed a basic cleavage in the logging segment,
with the larger, more mechanized contractors opting to consolidate their position in
an "open" market, while the smaller loggers and occasional operators join with the
woodlot owner groups in defending a group supply system. Increasingly, the latter
groups find themselves on the defensive. In the new, official forest policy discourse,
the primary forest industry is perceived as antiquated and inefficient, and the logic
of fully integrated mechanical harvesting is presented as the only way forward.
Corporate woodland managers, government foresters and aggressive contractors
seem to converge around the Swedish slogan "from the stump to the mill, no hand
upon the log". Whether by accident or design, federal policy has significantly reinforced this trend. In 1989, Ottawa's regional development arm, the Atlantic Canada
Opportunities Agency, began to dispense grants and loan guarantees for machinery
acquisition in the logging sector. Over the following two and a half years it assisted
many of the leading contractors to augment their stocks of harvesters, feller-
bunchers, forwarders and skidders, and in the process increased the financial
exposure of these contractors just as the pulp and paper cycle was beginning a
downturn. This sort of state incentive reinforced significantly the segmentation of
the contractor class.

Given the flux of the international forest industry, and the favoured position of
the Maritime pulp and paper segment within it, the time is long overdue to push for
wider benefits from the industry, and to plan strategies for their attainment. Such alternatives have been advanced in the past but, as shown in this volume, they have
been effectively squashed. Even today, the forces that might advance alternative
strategies remain divided, defensive and repressed. How are these forces to mobilize and formulate a shared alternative development agenda in the forest sector,
which is at once more socially equitable and more environmentally sound? They
can start by identifying some of the obstacles to genuine change in the forest sector.

Paradoxically, a first obstacle stems from the environmental concerns and
dialogues that have emerged among forest sector interests. None of these has yet
addressed the stark inequalities that persist within the sector, and their implications
for policy. In Nova Scotia, a Commissioner of Forest Enhancement was appointed
in 1987. Unfortunately, this watchdog has had very little bite, since he reported not
to the legislature but to the cabinet, which has declined to release any reports to the

---

17 This process began with the "Report to the Minister of Natural Resources and Energy
on Changes in Legislation Regarding the Authority and Administration of the New
Brunswick Forest Products Commission and Forest Products Marketing Board"
(Fredericton, 1989). This was followed by Minister of Natural Resources, *Private
Woodlots: Considerations for Future Action* (Fredericton, 1990).

public. This experiment in policy auditing was recently terminated with the abolition of the commissioner's post.[18]

Another experiment in consensus-building is the "Envirofor" symposium, in which a broad spectrum of forest-sector representatives discuss environmental problems, issues and responses. The National Envirofor Symposium of 1990 was recently replicated in Nova Scotia.[19] In such cases, there is a danger that environmental issues will be defined superficially and descriptively, in an effort to avoid policy debate and to deny power relationships. The underlying premises are that direct interpersonal contact among stakeholders promotes reasonable dialogue, and that the missing link is communication and education. In such settings professional foresters are prepared to recognize deficiencies in forest management, but contend that progress is being made, and that a properly educated public would accept the legitimacy of industrial forestry. For their part, industry representatives are certainly more environmentally sensitive than in former years. They stress corporate innovations such as "special place" recognition (the setting aside of forest lands with special ecological significance) and the opening of wilderness trails to public access. At the very least these are advanced as proof of responsible corporate citizenship. While such actions are unlikely to trigger an alliance with environmental activists (who tend to be suspicious of such exercises), they are aggressively promoted in corporate public relations, and they also divert attention from the political and economic inequalities in the forest sector.[20]

A second obstacle is the lack of collective representation and empowerment of the many interest groups that are integral to the forest sector. There are many reasons for this. Environmentalists, wildlife and recreation enthusiasts, and Native people are relatively independent of the commercial forest processors for their livelihood. They often view the industry's forest and mill practices as unacceptable. Small woodlot owners, forest workers, logging contractors and pulpmill workers are more or less dependent on the industry for their livelihood. This serves to fragment and isolate the various groups.

Environmentalists and wildlife enthusiasts are often seen as outsiders — urban-based, middle-class activists who are out of touch with the economic realities of

---

18 *Chronicle Herald*, 23 March 1991.

19 See *Proceedings ENVIROFOR: A Provincial Dialogue on Nova Scotia's Forests*, Canadian Institute of Forestry (N.S.)/ Canadian Forestry Association (August 1991).

20 See, for example, "Bowater Lauded for Saving Forest", *Chronicle Herald*, 18 May 1991. In Nova Scotia, the pulp and paper companies are also working closely with provincial forest authorities in establishing a "model forest" management zone in Guysborough County, under the sponsorship of the federal government's "Green Plan". See *The Casket*, 22 May 1991, and *Chronicle Herald*, 30 August 1991. For the neo-conservative promotion of environmentalism, see Robert Paehlke, *Environmentalism and the Future of Progressive Politics* (New Haven, 1989).

rural life. Pulp mills located in cities such as Saint John can be the target of resident protests for their airborne effluents, while mill workers and small town merchants commonly describe the same sulphur dioxide as "the sweet smell of prosperity".[21] A similar cleavage emerges from the business of marketing cottage and wilderness land to affluent city dwellers as a recreational commodity.[22] Directly or indirectly, such cottage developments often threaten the livelihoods of local rural producers.[23] Native people likewise are viewed as unreasonable when their land claims appear to threaten the forest access of loggers, the tenure of private owners, or traditional use rights.[24] All of these issues can serve to set local communities against broader political interest groups. The interests of all parties need to be identified and discussed in more detail. There may well be many shared interests and common concerns.

A third obstacle stems from the divisions between the primary (harvesting) and secondary (processing) sectors of the forest industry. Many logging contractors are staunch individualists and free enterprisers who are willing to take significant risks to control their own businesses. Integral to their operations are the woodcutters — wage-earning employees who lack any voice at all. By contrast, pulpmill workers are relatively well paid, and are organized into national and international unions. The differences between the two sectors are crystallized politically during strike actions at the mill. Here the contractors, and even forest workers, commonly participate in community protests against the strikers, and join in calls to government to impose back-to-work orders.[25] We have also seen loud protests from contractors against the Nova Scotia Primary Forest Products Marketing Board, opposing the board's efforts to improve the procedures for organizing and certifying

---

21 P. Chisholm, "Confronting the Irvings: New Brunswick Threatens to Shut Down a Mill", *Maclean's* 102, 42 (16 October 1989), p. 50.

22 The chairman of a recent Nova Scotia environmental panel held out his own Outdoor Land Company as a good way to "integrate economic, social and environmental goals", *Chronicle Herald*, 28 September 1991.

23 Land Research group, "Whither Our Land? Who Owns Nova Scotia? And What are They Doing With It?", *New Maritimes*, VIII, 6 (July/August 1990), pp. 14-25.

24 See, for example, Ron Arnold, "Loggerheads over Land Use" in Aaron Schneider, ed., *Deforestation and Development in Canada and the Tropics* (Sydney, 1989), pp. 130-2. For the tensions between wildlife groups and natives see "Micmac Plan Angers Wildlife Group", *Chronicle Herald*, 24 September 1991; "Native Lobster Fishing Making Waves", *Chronicle Herald*, 4 October 1991; and "Wildlife Group Demands Accurate Count of Moose Killed by Native Hunters", *Chronicle Herald*, 4 November 1991.

25 See, for example, Sheri King, "The Scott Paper Strike, 1982", in C.H.J. Gilson, ed., *Strikes in Nova Scotia, 1970-1985* (Hantsport, 1986), pp. 114-28.

private woodlot supply groups.[26] As noted earlier, the private pulpwood marketing structure in New Brunswick has recently come under attack as well.

A final obstacle, we suggest, is the federal government's involvement in Maritime forest policy. Over the past 15 years, Ottawa has provided substantial funds through the federal-provincial forest development agreements in aid of forest management practices. Despite the importance of this goal, and the need for innovative departures, these programmes have served to placate and redirect, rather than to empower, the weaker elements and their potential leaders in the forest sector. By offering incentive funds to small woodlot owners (and large industrial landholders) to draw up management plans, while ignoring the issues of improved prices and expanded market shares, Ottawa has channelled the political processes, and helped define the primary issues of Maritime forestry.

At the same time, the federal government shapes the prospects for logging contractors and forest workers through the impact of other agencies. Contractors are eligible for capital grants and loan guarantees to support the purchase of expensive machinery such as skidders, feller-bunchers and harvesters.[27] For those who acquire such equipment, there is pressure to operate at extremely high volumes in order to maximize their revenues and cover their loan obligations. This syndrome drives the contractors into tight dependence and even collusion with the mills, which apportion wood contracts. At the same time, such highly mechanized operations, with their debt and payment cycles and the risk of business failures, distract political attention from the issue of fair market prices that preoccupies small producers and woodlot owners.

Forest workers are provided with federal funds for training programmes, which are aimed at lessening the risk to, and improving the productivity of, contract employees.[28] However, the advantage of unionizing woods workers, or regulating the working conditions in private woods camps, is systematically ignored. At the same time, people in business criticize the impact of unemployment insurance benefits in distorting the seasonal supply of woods workers by overly generous payments.

In spite of some victories on the part of the environmental movement, small woodlot owners and pulpmill workers, the pulp and paper industry is still politically dominant in the forest sector. The end result of such dominance, a Maine economist suggests, will be an industrial system of forest *mining*, using massive machines for

---

26 Peter Clancy, "Crossroad in the Forest: Change is in the Air for Nova Scotia Woodlot Owners", *New Maritimes*, IX, 5 (May/June 1991), pp. 5-8. For the pulp and paper companies' critique of the same proposal, see "Bowater Chief Blasts Marketing Board", *Chronicle Herald,* 27 September 1990.

27 See Atlantic Canada Opportunities Agency, "List of Approved Projects, Nova Scotia, Forest Sector, 1988-1991" (Halifax, 1991).

28 Richard Corey, *An Atlantic Forestry Vocational Training Program. Final Report* (Maritime Ranger School, 1989), and *Forest RITC Annual Report* (Halifax, 1990).

clearcutting, followed by the reforestation of mono-culture, even-aged, softwood pulp stands to be treated by herbicide and pesticide applications.[29] In this situation, forest harvesting contractors are forced to invest heavily in expensive machinery, in conditions of absolute dependence to the banks and pulp companies. Forest workers are exploited and eventually replaced by machines. Small woodlot owners are bought out or marginalized as passive owners, whose lands are managed by contractors under the federal-provincial agreements. Such a system aims to ameliorate future wood shortages for the pulp industry and, in the minds of many woodlot owners, constitutes a systematic subsidy to the pulp and paper mills.

The future of the New Brunswick and Nova Scotia forest sectors does not have to look this way. The provincial governments own 47 and 25 per cent of forest lands in New Brunswick and Nova Scotia, respectively. Much of this is presently under lease to the pulp and paper companies. Another 33 per cent of all forest lands in New Brunswick, and 52 per cent in Nova Scotia, are owned by woodlot owners. This ownership pattern is diverse, and it offers a potential way to achieve new and innovative management regimes. Growing softwood forests for pulping should not be abandoned altogether. However, we also need to plan for more diversity of species, and end uses, which will leave the forest sector better positioned for future employment, income and markets. Within this initiative, there must be room for the weaker sectoral interests to play a stronger role.

The Scandinavian countries illustrate some of these possibilities. In Sweden and Finland the forest ownership pattern resembles that of the Maritimes. In both countries, the forest is intensively managed for high volumes of production. Yet the goal of maximum production has not precluded the involvement of other organized interest groups, which possess real political power. In Sweden the forest is *domesticated*, and small woodlot owner and labour relations are characterized by *co-determination*. What does this mean? Small woodlot owners are well organized and are guaranteed a fair share of the wood market at a fair price. This is achieved through contract bargaining and through the existence of co-operatively owned and operated sawmills and pulp and paper mills. Real estate development is subordinated to stringent land-use plans which, among other conditions, restrict the pulp and paper companies in acquiring more than their present 25 per cent of forest land. Forest workers are assured wages equal to other industries as well as input, through their unions, into setting working conditions. Clearcuts are kept small, and the use of chemical biocides is restricted. State, industry, labour and small woodlot owners promote research on, and use of, environmentally "soft" logging equipment (with,

---

29 David Vail, "The Meanings of Mechanization: Technological Transformation of Logging Systems in Sweden and Maine", in S. Marglin and F. Apffel-Marglin, eds., *Decolonizing Knowledge: From Development to Dialogue* (Oxford, forthcoming).

for example, high flotation suspension to minimize root damage, and high manoeuvrability to minimize the damage to residual trees during thinning).[30]

In New Brunswick and Nova Scotia, the government has proved unwilling to confront the skewed and biased relations of power in the forest sector. If we work under the assumption that some empowerment is desirable to counter these trends and challenge the industry agenda, coalitions must be built between the various stakeholders who are looking for alternatives. This may even help the pulp and paper companies to be viable in the long run. While they have built their operations on a combination of cheap resources, cheap labour, government aid and an intensively manipulated forest environment, this complex will be less viable in the new era. Instead of corporate complacency, and the desperate defence of past practices, the industry will need to adopt new innovative approaches to woods operations, production processes and product mixes in the global market.[31]

In closing with a call for renewed political action, we might be guided by the words of geographer Peter Kropotkin:

> In history we see that precisely those epochs when the small parts of humanity broke down the power of their rulers and reassumed their freedom were epochs of the greatest progress, economic and intellectual...[32]

In the Maritime forest, the small parts of humanity face an immense challenge: to voice their interests, explore their differences and build common ground. This must be done in a politically charged and highly contested environment. But transitional moments such as the present can offer exceptional opportunities to transcend the status quo in favour of progressive alternatives.

---

30 Many of these comments are inspired by Vail, "The Meanings of Mechanization:".

31 Nicholas Sidor, *Forest Industry Development Policies: Industrial Strategy or Corporate Welfare* (Ottawa, 1981).

32 Quoted in Jim MacLaughlin, "State Centred Social Science and the Anarchist Critique: Ideology in Political Geography", *Antipode,* 18, 1 (1986), p. 33.

Table I

Lay-offs and Shut-downs,
Maritime Pulp and Paper Mills, 1991-1992

Company	Layoffs		Shutdowns		Present Status
	1991	1992	1991	1992	
Fraser Inc. - Edmundston	—	—	—	1 week	—
Fraser Inc. - Atholville	271	—	—	—	Closed
NBIP Forest Products Inc. - Dalhousie	—	400	—	—	Paper capacity cut in half
Stone Consolidated - Bathurst	—	125 24 temp	1 mo.	—	Closure reversed by bail-out
Miramichi Pulp and Paper	133	—	—	—	—
Ste. Anne - Nackawic Pulp Co.	125	—	—	—	—
Irving Pulp and Paper	29	—	—	—	—
Norbord (OSB sheet manuf.)	—	186	—	—	Closed
Bowater Mersey	—	—	3 wks	Cut working days from 7-5 per week	—
Scott Maritimes Ltd.	—	35	—	—	—
Stora Forest Industries	—	90 temp	3 wks	2 wks	—

Sources: *Telegraph Journal* (Saint John) and *Chronicle Herald* (Halifax), various issues.

ABSTRACTS/RÉSUMÉS

RAYMOND LÉGER

Land, Labour, and the Forest Industry on the Acadian Peninsula, New Brunswick, 1875-1900

In the last quarter of the 19th century, the sawmilling industry on the Acadian Peninsula, Gloucester County, New Brunswick, was quickly centralized in the hands of a few large, politically well-connected foreign corporations. The pines all but gone, spruce lumber was the main commodity produced and exported, primarily to the United Kingdom. Production varied widely from year to year, depending on the state of the sawmills and the market. This paper describes the importance of resource control in the emergence of the sawmilling concerns on the Acadian Peninsula. Here, in the northern half of the province, where the provincial government retained control of most forest lands, the sawmillers were generously accommodated. One absentee capitalist was granted large areas of virgin forest lands. Other sawmillers received generous cutting rights on the best and most accessible Crown lands. The granted lands covered from 8.27 to 18.7 per cent per year of the total land area of the Acadian Peninsula — large areas considering the scant forest resources of the coastal region. By 1893 the sawmillers and their financial backers were sole recipients of such rights, lasting 25 years, at a cost of $8 per square mile for the first year and $4 for each subsequent year. Stumpage payments increased, then decreased, when the sawmillers claimed to be disadvantaged by high freight rates. They were still not, however, paid in full since the sawmillers employed various measures to conceal the amount of wood harvested. Government scalers, appointed on a patronage basis, could do very little given the collusion between the industry and government. Even conscientious scalers were hampered by overwork and cheating by the leaseholders.

Settlers were distinctly disadvantaged in the lumber trade. Census records and directories fail to record their importance and numbers. Other data show that at least 12.4 per cent of the male labour force over 16 years of age was involved in the lumber trade in 1881. Anecdotal evidence suggests much higher figures. Yet, the province did not facilitate wood production among settlers. In some settlements, wood cutting rights on granted lands were retained by the Crown and assigned to the sawmillers. In many instances, the sawmillers cut wood illegally on granted land before or even after the settlers arrived. This forced settlers into dependence on the forest industry, and they were often forced to sell their labour and wood on terms that were less than favourable. Some large farmers and sub-contractors profited from this system, but the resource control and dominance of the sawmilling industry on the Acadian Peninsula also contributed to underdevelopment and general poverty.

SERGE CÔTÉ

The Birth of the Pulp and Paper Industry and Forest Management in New Brunswick: A Case Study of Bathurst

The emergence of the pulp and paper industry in New Brunswick, as illustrated by Bathurst Lumber, is documented. The emergence of the New Brunswick pulp and paper industry was preceded by the accumulation of vast areas of forest lands by sawmillers. By the turn of the century, New Brunswick forest companies (holding more than 1,000 acres or 405 ha) possessed 20 per cent of all freehold forest lands. Two hundred companies leased most of the Crown forests, which constituted 50 per cent of all forest lands. Twelve of these controlled cutting rights on 55 per cent of all Crown lands. By 1913, such leases, invariably purchased for the minimum fee of $8 per square mile, extended for 50 years for pulp and paper industry operators and 30 years for sawmillers.

Such favourable terms were allegedly granted to protect the heavy investment in the pulp and paper industry and to promote forest management. In reality, the leases were robbed of raw wood, used for speculation and stock-watering. The large leaseholders treated them as private property and lobbied the government to institute perpetual leases. One such large leaseholder was Bathurst Lumber, which managed to consolidate several sawmills and extensive forest holdings over a period of 10 years. By 1915, just before Bathurst Lumber built the first large and long-standing pulp and paper mill in New Brunswick, the company possessed 2,600 square miles (673,920 ha) of Crown leases in New Brunswick and on the Gaspé Peninsula in Quebec and 15 square miles (3,888 ha) of freehold lands. The promoters were Americans and Upper Canadians with good political and economic connections who were part of a continental network of financiers and industrial promoters.

Yet, the rise to hegemony of companies such as Bathurst Lumber was not inevitable. Considerable resistance was launched by the smaller leaseholders, who protested the size of leases given to their larger counterparts. Settlers, given the restrictions of access to the resource, often reproduced the behaviour of the large leaseholders by merely posing as settlers and then harvesting the wood on their grants and moving on. Settlers were thus forced to pursue immediate profits without concern for the long-term conservation of the forest.

The lease system of Crown lands in New Brunswick, in short, constituted the most powerful means of the large forest companies to prevent other users access to, and a just return from, the forest.

/

L. ANDERS SANDBERG

Politique forestière en Nouvelle-Écosse : La "Big Lease" [la Grande Concession], Île du Cap-Breton, 1899-1960

Cette étude porte sur l'histoire de ce qu'on appelle la "Big Lease" de l'Île du Cap-Breton — seule grande parcelle de terres contiguës de la Couronne restant en Nouvelle-Écosse — depuis son début, en 1899, jusqu'à son rachat par le gouvernement provincial, en 1957, et sa cession à la compagnie suédoise de pâtes et papiers, Stora Kopparberg, en 1960.

Initialement, les termes de la "Big Lease" stipulaient que devaient être construites deux usines à pâte et payé un loyer annuel de 6000$, sans aucun droit de coupe, en échange de l'exploitation des 620 000 acres (251 100 ha) de terres boisées pendant 33 ans. Ces termes furent rapidement révisés, étendant la durée de l'exploitation à 99 ans et permettant l'exportation de bois à pâte, à condition qu'il fût écorcé.

La "Big Lease" fut avant tout une entreprise spéculative, lancée par un entrepreneur de l'"Âge d'or" et soutenue par le gouvernement provincial. La "Lease" connut toutes sortes de tractations — cessions répétées, inventaires forestiers gonflés, opérations truquées — jusqu'à ce qu'elle fût vendue, avec un joli profit, à l'Oxford Paper Company de Rumford (Maine). L'Oxford Paper Company exploita une partie seulement de la concession et, durant une période d'essor pour l'industrie des pâtes et papiers, exporta le bois à pâte dans son usine du Maine. La compagnie fit tout en son pouvoir pour réduire les coûts et tirer de la "Lease" un profit substantiel. Elle ne faisait alors que se conformer aux pratiques des années 20 — époque où des compagnies américaines absentéistes achetaient, pour se livrer à la spéculation, des terres à bois bon marché en Nouvelle-Écosse, les exploitaient au minimum, luttaient contre les impôts fonciers et les taxes municipales et, par là, augmentaient considérablement la valeur de leurs concessions et de leurs propriétés franches, à l'intention de nouveaux actionnaires et d'acheteurs potentiels. La compagnie réalisa des profits spéculatifs en deux occasions, les deux fois aux dépens de son bénéficiaire initial, la province de Nouvelle-Écosse. En 1936 l'administration Libérale d'Angus L. MacDonald reprit les parties les plus pauvres de la "Big Lease" pour en faire, avec le patronnage du fédéral, le Parc national des hautes-terres du Cap-Breton. En 1957, l'administration Conservatrice de Robert Stanfield racheta les parties restantes pour attirer dans la province la compagnie suédoise de pâtes et papiers, Stora Kopparberg.

Les termes de la "Big Lease" n'étaient pas uniques, mais ils correspondaient à la politique provinciale de développement industriel — qui cherchait à alléger le fardeau des mises de fonds. Comme il le fit pour le développement des charbonnages et des aciéries sur l'Île du Cap-Breton, le gouvernement se tourna d'abord vers les gros promoteurs industriels pour les encourager à investir. La recherche d'investissements provenant de l'industrie des pâtes et papiers fut élargie plus tard, et la "Big Lease" devint alors une partie intégrante du programme provincial de rachat des terres de la Couronne en vue d'attirer dans la province des industriels des pâtes et papiers étrangers.

NANCY COLPITTS

De l'industrie du sciage au parc national : Alma, Nouveau-Brunswick, 1921-1947

Cette étude décrit la croissance et le déclin de l'industrie du sciage à Alma, comté d'Albert, au Nouveau-Brunswick, entre 1921 et 1947. En 1921 le principal employeur et propriétaire terrien d'Alma, le scieur C.T. White, fit faillite. White, qui représentait la tradition du sciage au Nouveau-Brunswick, était un patron qui dominait politiquement et économiquement sa communauté. Mais, il succomba au déclin que connut, après la guerre, le commerce du bois. White, comme beaucoup d'autres de la corporation, fut forcé de vendre ses terres à une compagnie de pâtes et papiers.

Ceux qui s'efforcèrent de reconstruire l'industrie du sciage à Alma, après la débâcle de 1921, durent oeuvrer dans un climat d'adversité politique et économique. La plupart des terres boisées étaient aux mains d'un propriétaire absentéiste, la compagnie papetière Hollingsworth and Whitney de Boston, qui faisait de ses terres une réserve de bois à pâte — ce qui était une source de spéculation et une sécurité financière — et qui, de ce fait, contrôlait l'accès des scieurs aux billes de sciage. Les grandes banques centrales canadiennes désavantageaient les scieries au profit de l'industrie des pâtes et papiers. Et une structure de commercialisation inefficace, dominée par les intermédiaires, constituait finalement un sérieux obstacle pour de bons revenus et de bons investissements dans l'industrie.

Les scieurs d'Alma, dont les usines fonctionnèrent de 1921 à 1947, ne pouvaient prospérer que sous la domination de l'industrie des pâtes et papiers. Ces hommes venaient d'importantes familles de colons de la première génération — les Cleveland, Colpitts, Keirstead, Strayhorne et Hickey — dont certains avaient déjà travaillé pour White. Dans les années 20, ils possèdaient des usines mobiles ; puis, dans les années 30, ils en firent construire de fixes. Comme la dépendance politico-économique était toujours de mise, les scieurs locaux en profitèrent pour soutirer des droits de coupe au propriétaire absentéiste, et ils obtinrent ainsi des capitaux des succursales locales des banques et trouvèrent des débouchés commerciaux et, parfois aussi, des capitaux auprès de grandes firmes d'exportation. La remontée était faible et dépendait assez souvent des relations politiques qu'on possèdait à Fredericton. Dans ce contexte, il ne fut pas étrange de voir les scieurs locaux montrer peu de résistance à la promotion d'une industrie touristique locale et à l'établissement du parc national fédéral de Fundy, en 1947.

BILL PARENTEAU

"En toute bonne foi": Le développement de la commercialisation du bois à pâte pour les producteurs indépendants du Nouveau-Brunswick, 1960-1975

Cette étude relate la naissance des associations de propriétaires de boisés et leurs revendications pour la création de structures commerciales en vue de lutter contre le déclin de l'économie rurale et les bas prix du bois à pâte au Nouveau-Brunswick. Au début des années 60, le marché du bois brut, naguère diversifié, s'était réduit à un marché du bois à pâte (à la fin des années 50, 80 pour cent de tout le bois de ferme était destiné aux usines à pâte), et les fermiers dépendaient plus que jamais des ventes de bois à pâte pour leurs revenus, spécialement dans les régions éloignées du nord de la province. À la même époque, les quantités de bois à pâte vendues par les propriétés agricoles étaient inférieures à celles provenant d'autres propriétés. Dans les deux cas, les propriétaires de boisés souffraient des bas prix imposés par les compagnies de pâtes et papiers. Cette situation résultait des monopoles régionaux, ainsi que des généreuses concessions de la Couronne et des propriétés franches exploitées par l'industrie.

Les propriétaires de boisés s'adressèrent d'abord au gouvernement provincial pour obtenir des primes pour l'exploitation forestière et une législation avec arbitrage obligatoire pour la commercialisation. Ils réclamaient aussi que les compagnies de pâtes et papiers achètent leur bois d'abord aux propriétaires privés avant d'exploiter elles-mêmes des terres de la Couronne — cela pour encourager ces compagnies à négocier "en toute bonne foi".

Le gouvernement accorda peu d'attention aux aspirations des propriétaires de boisés et, vers la fin des années 60, les divisions régionales et la montée des prix du bois à pâte touchèrent durement les jeunes organisations. Mais, après une nouvelle récession, qui frappa l'industrie des pâtes et papiers au début des années 70, à laquelle vinrent malencontreusement s'ajouter la négligence technologique des usines de pâtes et papiers de la province et le désir du gouvernement d'utiliser les commissions de commercialisation pour la promotion de l'aménagement forestier dans les petits boisés, une législation faible fut alors timidement introduite pour la commercialisation. Les protestations des producteurs indépendants n'eurent qu'une faible influence sur le gouvernement. Comme par le passé, l'industrie des pâtes et papiers put faire prévaloir sa position privilégiée, d'une part, en arguant que "les entraves [à la commercialisation] finiraient par rendre économiquement impossible la survie" des usines de pâtes et papiers et, d'autre part, grâce au soutien de certains arguments gouvernementaux avançant que cette industrie était créatrice d'emplois et de revenus et que, comme le déclara un porte-parole du gouvernement, "elle [était] prête à négocier en toute bonne foi", sans qu'aucune réglementation ne fût nécessaire.

PETER CLANCY

La politique de commercialisation du bois à pâte en Nouvelle-Écosse, 1960-1985

Cette étude a pour objet la législation de commercialisation du bois à pâte et la croissance des organisations des propriétaires de petits boisés en Nouvelle-Écosse. Ces petits propriétaires, qui possédaient moins de 1000 acres (405 ha), représentaient plus de 50 pour cent des forêts de la Nouvelle-Écosse, dans les années 50 — répartition qui est restée stable depuis cette temps. Le pouvoir des petits propriétaires demeurait faible, cependant, et les prix du bois étaient toujours sous le contrôle d'un réseaux de "courtiers", qui servaient d'intermédiaires entre les usines et les propriétaires de boisés.

Les années 60 mirent un nouveau fardeau sur les épaules des propriétaires de petits boisés de la Nouvelle-Écosse. Deux compagnies de pâtes et papiers transnationales furent attirées dans la province et se virent généreusement offrir des concessions de la Couronne qui leur promettaient du bois en abondance et à bon marché. Les propriétaires de boisés comprirent alors que ces concessions de la Couronne pouvaient servir à les leurrer dans la fixation des prix du bois à pâte provenant des propriétés privées. Inquiets, ils se mobilisèrent, mais leurs revendications en faveur de la création d'une commission de commercialisation dans le cadre du Natural Products Maketing Act [loi sur la commercialisation des produits naturels] ne furent pas entendues. Les propriétaires de boisés entreprirent alors de s'organiser en une association à l'échelle provinciale, pour laquelle ils obtinrent une aide financière dans le cadre de la loi fédérale-provinciale sur le développement rural et agricole.

Toutefois, les liens directs et indirects entre le secteur des pâtes et papiers et la province, ainsi que la restructuration du secteur des boisés dressèrent des obstacles à l'organisation des petits propriétaires de boisés, dans les années 70. La Commission de commercialisation du bois à pâte, instaurée par le gouvernement en 1972, représentait à coup sûr une victoire importante pour les petits propriétaires. Mais, elle était de création trop tardive et fut combattue par le Ministère provincial des Terres et Forêts et, juridiquement fragile, fut constamment traînée en cour, le plus souvent avec succès, par le secteur corporatif. Tandis que ces batailles faisaient rage, le secteur des petits boisés se transformait. Au début, il était dominé par les petits propriétaires, qui étaient souvent des fermiers exploitant eux-mêmes leurs propres boisés. Puis, avec le déclin des exploitations agricoles et la croissance de l'industrie des pâtes et papiers, le fermier-exploitant céda la place à l'exploitant à plein temps, équipé d'un matériel coûteux et travaillant sous contrat pour les usines à pâte. Comme dans le Nouveau-Brunswick, ce fut ce nouveau type d'exploitation qui divisa l'association des exploitants et des propriétaires de boisés et qui, au début des années 80, entraîna des divisions parmi les producteurs fournissant Stora Forest Industries et Scott Maritimes, dans le nord et l'est de la Nouvelle-Écosse. Les propriétaires de petits boisés qui alimentent l'usine Bowater Mersey, dans le sud de la province, n'ont toujours pas d'association.

Durant cette période, la politique provinciale a toujours clairement favorisé un approvisionnement en bois bon marché pour les usines à pâte, au détriment des efforts d'organisation et du bien-être économique des propriétaires de boisés de la Nouvelle-Écosse.

GLYN BISSIX et L. ANDERS SANDBERG

L'économie politique du Nova Scotia Forest Improvement Act [loi sur le développement forestier], 1962-1986

Cette étude présente l'historique du Forest Improvement Act (FIA) en Nouvelle-Écosse, entre 1962 et 1986. Le FIA s'inspirait de la législation forestière suédoise rendant obligatoire l'aménagement forestier et opérait, sur le modèle suédois, à l'aide de commissions chargées du développement des pratiques forestières. Des commissions de district furent créées vers la fin des années 60 et au début des années 80, mais elles n'eurent qu'une existence éphémère. Une commission provinciale fut créée en 1973. Les commissions étaient le siège d'intérêts multiples: y étaient représentés l'industrie forestière avec ses secteurs des pâtes et papiers et des scieries, les défenseurs de la faune, les propriétaires de petits boisés, les forestiers, ainsi que les gouvernements municipaux et le Ministère des Terres et Forêts. Conçue et défendue par l'industrie papetière et par les forestiers de la province, la loi fut promulguée en 1965. À cette époque, la plus grande partie du bois à pâte provenait des petits propriétaires, et la loi avait pour but d'augmenter la production dans ce secteur. La loi avait aussi pour but de remplacer le Small Tree Act [loi sur les arbres de petite taille], qui promouvait l'aménagement forestier en imposant des restrictions sur le diamètre des arbres. Le FIA fut alors promulgué en dépit du mécontentement causé par certaines infractions faites aux droits de propriété de petits propriétaires et de corporations.

Les commissions du FIA chargées du développement des pratiques forestières en vinrent rapidement à défier l'industrie des pâtes et papiers. Les propriétaires de scieries, les propriétaires de petits boisés, les défenseurs de l'environnement et de la faune, déroutés par les dispositions prises par la Couronne en matière de concessions et par les pratiques forestières des compagnies de pâtes et papiers, parvinrent à contrôler les commissions. C'est alors que l'industrie papetière, le Ministère des Terres et des Forêts, les organisations provinciales du commerce et du travail forestier s'unirent contre le FIA et, finalement, le menèrent à sa ruine.

Le premier accord fédéral-provincial aboutit à la proclamation intégrale du FIA, en 1976. Mais aucun budget ne fut prévu pour son application. À la place, les fonds de l'accord fédéral-provincial furent consacrés à l'installation, sous l'égide du Ministère des Terres et des Forêts, d'un conseil d'administration des propriétés privées, dont les membres étaient des forestiers et des techniciens de la forêt. Cette nouvelle unité administrative, qui disposait de fonds substantiels pour l'aménagement forestier, était une arme puissante contre les commissions chargées du développement des pratiques forestières et contre le FIA. Les arguments en faveur du professionnalisme, l'ignorance du grand public en matière forestière et l'"inviolabilité" des droits de la propriété privée se combinèrent pour abattre le FIA.

KELL ANTOFT

Symptôme ou solution?
Le Nova Scotia Land Holdings Disclosure Act
[loi sur la divulgation des propriétés foncières] de 1969

Vers la fin des années 60, "le droit de propriété des non-résidents" pour les propriétés foncières littorales, agricoles et forestières de la Nouvelle-Écosse fit l'objet de débats souvent passionnés. Pour répondre à l'agitation régnante, le lieutenant-gouverneur de la Nouvelle-Écosse accepta, le 25 avril 1969, une loi autorisant la divulgation des propriétés appartenant à des non-résidents et à certaines corporations. La présente étude examine les dispositions de cette loi, la manière dont elle fut promulguée, les efforts qui furent déployés pour encourager son application, ses points forts, ses points faibles et, finalement, le renoncement effectif à son exécution.

La première version du Land Holdings Disclosure Act demandait aux non-résidents de produire par écrit une déclaration décrivant leurs propriétés et précisant comment elles avaient été acquises et à quels usages elles étaient destinées. Toutefois, la version finale de la loi permettait facilement d'éviter de telles déclarations. Le chef de l'opposition avait manigancé un amendement stipulant que seuls les non-résidents qui négligeraient "intentionnellement" de produire leur déclaration tomberaient sous le coup de la loi. En outre, une lacune exemptait de cette formalité les corporations enregistrées en Nouvelle-Écosse mais appartenant à des non-résidents. Cela eut pour résultat que seulement 65 pour cent environ des non-résidents répondirent aux questionnaires envoyés conformément à la loi.

Si la loi manquait de mordant, ce n'était pas à cause de l'opposition publique. En 1973 le gouvernement provincial chargea une commission spéciale de l'Assemblée législative d'étudier, par une série d'auditions publiques, la question du droit de propriété des non-résidents en Nouvelle-Écosse. Pas un seul dossier ne s'attaqua vraiment aux termes de la loi, laissant clairement entendre que la collecte des renseignements requise par elle n'était pas un problème qui tracassait beaucoup les milieux politiques.

Depuis le milieu des années 70, le taux d'acquisition de terres de la Nouvelle-Écosse par des non-résidents a diminué, mais les ventes aux non-résidents continuent. Le Land Holdings Disclosure Act n'est donc toujours pas observé. L'échec de la loi s'explique, semble-t-il, par le souci du gouvernement provincial de ne pas empiéter sur les droits de la propriété privée et de ne pas fausser l'image de la province perçue comme un lieu d'investissements avantageux pour les corporations étrangères.

CONTRIBUTORS/ COLLABORATEURS

Kell Antoft holds a post-retirement appointment as Senior Associate at Henson College at Dalhousie University.

Glyn Bissix is a member of the Recreation Management Programme at Acadia University.

Peter Clancy is a member of the Political Science Department at St. Francis Xavier University.

Nancy Colpitts holds Masters degrees in History and in Library and Information Science from Dalhousie University.

Serge Côté est professeur au Département des Sciences humaines de l'Université du Québec à Rimouski.

Raymond Léger travaille pour le Syndicat de gros, de détail et magasins à rayons [Retail, Wholesale and Department Store Union], Local 1065, à Chatham, Nouveau-Brunswick.

Bill Parenteau is a Ph.D. student in History at the University of New Brunswick.

L. Anders Sandberg is a Canada Research Fellow in the Geography Department at York University.